DARKEST HOUR

A Testimony of the
Delivering Power of God's Love

JAMES GILBERT

ISBN 978-1-63874-373-6 (paperback)
ISBN 978-1-63961-568-1 (hardcover)
ISBN 978-1-63874-374-3 (digital)

Christian Faith Publishing, Inc.
832 Park Avenue
Meadville, PA 16335
www.christianfaithpublishing.com

Printed in the United States of America

Priscilla Logan and Theresa Ilene

Dedicated to God the Father, Jesus the Son, and the Holy Spirit, along with His promises: my wife, Fawn Marie Gilbert and our son, Aaron Isaiah Gilbert, a constant source of encouragement.

ACKNOWLEDGEMENTS

I want to thank the people in my life, who gave of their time to consult with me during the writing of this testimony. Thank you, Fawn Marie Gilbert, Pastor Roger Ball, Rachael Gilliver, Lacee Moretti, Shannon Flores, Joel Smith, Johnny Ginex, Shawn Rencoret, Theresa Illene and Priscilla Logan for providing helpful advice or direct consultation.

I want to also thank the friends who encouraged me throughout this endeavor. Thank you, Michael Blythe, William "Billy" Mann, Johnny Ginex, April Roberts, David, and Kristin Bransky, Ranee Harris, Rowena Crabtree Anderson, Gail Anderson, Professor Sharpe, James Sammons, Diana Romanowski, James Sanders, and my parents who never stopped helping me, Jim and Janet Gilbert. God richly bless you all!

CONTENTS

An Introduction to Evil

October 28, 1977, started out like any normal day, but it did not end that way. On that day, something went wrong, terribly wrong. An unbelievable sequence of dramatic life events would, over the course of thirteen years, lead this young man into a life surrounded by death. The events that took place in my life, after that day, would have led to my destruction if it were not for Jesus's intervention of His grace and His love. It would be revealed many years later October 28 was nothing more than a scheme of Satan, a trap of sorts. So deep did a seduction for darkness and death become a part of who I was that bizarre experiences would be accepted as being normal. Satanic lies occupied and were entrenched deeply in my mind. Demonic messengers hid themselves behind the symbols of an ancient, pagan holiday. Compelling lies, which I believed, would come within twenty-four hours of killing me and possibly five other souls. The bloodlust I received grew to be so intense that if it were possible, I wanted to kill forever.

Why?

The only thing that I understood, near the end, was a "force" was driving me to want to avenge myself. A violent rage inhabited my heart. I no longer could control my emotions. By the age of twenty-one, I was practically stuck on rage. I had no hope to help me want to live. I wanted to be set free from the fear and torment that so plagued my useless existence. It seemed, however, that I was given a mission sent from Hell. Before I could leave this world, on my terms,

I had to avenge myself. I would make myself available to Satan on the night he gave to me. I would put the terror back into Halloween. This is my testimony.

In one form or another, many people are in bondage to Satan. Whether it is drug abuse, alcoholism, pornography, rape, false religions, or murder, without turning their sin to Jesus, they are already condemned, doomed. When I was under the influence of a spirit of murder, I did not believe in the God of the Bible. My parents would practically have to drag my only older brother Scott (not his real name) and me to church every Sunday. I never felt the presence of God, and all that I believed I saw was hypocrisy. I heard a lot of gossip. I saw backbiting church members. Something was missing. To my young eyes, love was missing.

I admit, I did not believe in Jesus Christ or the overwhelming truth that He is the Son of God. Yet, near the end, I railed against Him. As a man would fight against a tangible enemy, I resisted God. I had raised my tightly clenched fist into the sky and growled, "You better kill me quickly before I kill someone!" That incident happened around March 1990.

On March 15, 1991, I received Jesus as my Lord and Savior. The path took me past seeing a psychotherapist in Tampa, Florida. He was a self-described atheist. That psychotherapist, Morris Gus, was not perceived to be a threat. However, my parents arranged for me to see a Christian counselor, whose office was in Vero Beach, Florida, where my parents lived in nearby Sebastian. I am telling you—I was on guard! I would not allow myself to be brainwashed, like every Christian, I believed then.

After the Lord saved me from my living death, all hell seemed to break loose! I quickly began to see the patterns of Satan's incredibly effective lies that influenced me for thirteen years! I write this to help expose many of the tactics that were used against me and countless other souls from the past, present, and future. I write to say, "There is no other name under Heaven given to men by which we must be saved" (Acts 4:12). Jesus!

2

ONCE INNOCENT

I was born on July 9, 1969, in Portsmouth, VA. I was raised in a middle-class home. Even to this day, my family always had a good reputation among neighbors and friends. All spoke well of my family. To the outside world, they earned their honored name. My parents became churchgoing people. They were religious, but it is not clear that they were born-again Christians.

After I was born, my father was honorably discharged from the United States Navy in October 1969. (I am fortunate to have even been born, because my father was nearly washed off the deck of his ship, somewhere in the Mediterranean Sea.) A month later, my family moved to Oberlin, Kansas, for about four months. We—my parents, six-year-old half brother, and I—stayed with my dad's parents, on their wheat and cattle farm. My mother told me that I slept in a dresser drawer. Mom and Dad took a hotel management class, which was made available by the VA. They left my brother and me with some adult cousins and drove to Denver, Colorado, searching for opportunities. They loved Colorado, and we moved to Aurora in April 1970. Dad found a good job at Western Electric, and we moved into a beautiful two-story home in Arvada in September 1971.

Here, I spent some formative years of my life. I was given the nickname "Scaredy Cat." By the age of three, I remember being afraid of the wind's dull whistle, blowing through slightly opened windows. I remember being afraid of the dark, always thinking I was being watched by some presence. Whenever I had to turn the light off in my room, I would anxiously dash out of the room before the "presence" got me. Once, my brother and I collided on the stairway after I ran out of the room. This may sound crazy, but it is true. One of my first memories was of it snowing on Halloween. I have the memory of seeing snow drift past a streetlight, and in my peripheral vision, I saw a glowing jack-o'-lantern sitting on the porch. It startled me. I was probably three. I was just a fear-filled, little kid.

My mom's parents, Nana and Papa, had been living on the east coast of Florida, Vero Beach. My family flew down for a visit. They were quickly growing tired of the snow and what they have described as Colorado's "freaky weather." They explained that you could have the air-conditioning on, and a severe cold front could roll down the Rocky Mountains, and a short time later, "You're freezing with the furnace blasting!" My parents decided to move to Florida, the Sunshine State.

My father moved first. He found a job at Piper Aircraft immediately. While he was working and overseeing the construction of our new home, I forgot him. Maybe I tried to forget about him. I tended to be close to my mother, and some of my earliest memories (which they have confirmed began around the age of two) is my parents arguing, loudly. This stirred up not only more fear but also a kind of protective nature toward my mother. When we were all reunited in Vero Beach, my dad was like a stranger to me. Whatever kind of relationship we had was broken. It was awkward to say the least. Psychologists would probably come to believe that there could have been a parental relationship problem. In time, I believe Satan turned me against him. We moved into the home in nearby Sebastian in September 1973. My mom nearly wept when she first viewed the house. It was quite a bit smaller than the last house, and it only had one story. I had just turned four. Everything looked big to me.

Basically, I was a good and conscientious boy. My strong, cautious nature prevented me from being radically rebellious. I was an all-American boy. I even joined the Cub Scouts. Although I repeated the God and country oath, I had no idea who God was. I remember worrying about my next good deed. I had been a normal kid. I had friends. Depending on who I hung out with could determine how impulsive and reckless I could be. I could be a follower. I got into a rock fight with my friend, Patrick, and one stone split my forehead, while we were playing. Hanging around with some of the neighborhood friends, I learned to curse. Words, I did not understand, would erupt from my mouth.

I was popular, yet shy. While most of the boys in the first grade thought girls were icky and contaminated with cooties, I found early that I liked them. I had my first crush in the first grade. This made me willing to play house with them on the playground. I played daddy, and my crush played the mother. The boys would also want

4

me to play *Starsky and Hutch*[1], a 1970s cop show. I was normal, until that one autumn afternoon.

OCTOBER 28, 1977

I stepped off the bus, looking forward to another relaxing afternoon with my friends "Bugs Bunny" and "Scooby Doo." It was a clear, sunny day, typical for the Atlantic side of Florida. The road I walked was old, with tar mixed with rocks. It was not easy on bare feet. Sometimes I would find a loose rock and kick it on the way home. I parted company with the kids who lived on the other side of County Road 512. The other side had some dirty, run-down homes. The kids on the other side were different, rough in their speech and behavior. I was wary of those kids. I walked the other way in silence.

A small forest of pine trees was swaying in an unusually cool afternoon. A soft whispering noise was being emitted by the pine needles rubbing against one another in the breeze. As I rounded the corner of Wimbrow Road and Futch Way, I became aware. Aware of what? The eight-year-old me could not articulate thoughts that seemed to run through my mind.

It would be almost three years after I received salvation and deliverance through Jesus Christ that I would come close to understanding what happened to me. How I changed so drastically and quickly! One minute, I am an innocent kid. The next minute, I perceived dark thoughts going into my mind. A demonic oppression was beginning. The once innocent, well-meaning Jeff would become increasingly antisocial over several years. Evil ideas, concepts, images, and perceptions became the foundation of a stronghold. Thoughts that had no optical or verbal comparison were embedded into my mind. How could one teach a child about death, murder, and suicide when the child has never seen these real-world realities? Try describing the color green to a person blind from birth. He would never understand you! The thoughts made no sense, but they would *stay*. I am sure I could not have articulated the violent feelings and ideas to

---

[1] https://en.wikipedia.org/wiki/Starsky_&_Hutch.

anyone. I was eight years old. I did not understand! Possibly because of violent entertainment media, the depraved thoughts would be defined. Video images would match up to thoughts and feelings. I would learn, in time, that I was the definition. I was instantaneously corrupted. Because I had been a low-maintenance child, my family did not notice the changes that would subtly take place. A pagan holiday that was celebrated with people who dressed up in alternative, oftentimes, evil personalities was a partial depiction of the thoughts planted in me—death, suicide, and murder. This paradigm shift is what Halloween would soon mean to me in an ever-increasing way.

Thoughts were planted in me, and like someone invading a farm and spreading strange seeds, the farmer would have to wait to see what kind of crop grew. Time would tell what was planted in me, because I can say that no one was teaching me about violence as a child.

There were some immediate effects. I was always on the quiet and shy side. Anyone who knew me knew this to be accurate. An intense feeling of inadequacy came over me and stayed. I had a stronger sense of self-consciousness, and I began to not like who I was. This disdain for myself would encourage me to search for a new identity. In my eyes, I was suddenly less than others. I began to recoil and withdraw from life. I drifted from my classmates. I began to be alienated from my friends. I developed a fierce temper. My rage, however, was balanced by a cautious nature. I always had a fear of evil, but the fear intensified! In what could sound like a contradiction, I also began to develop an intrigue with evil, dark things. In time, intrigue turned to fascination to love for darkness! I grew to not be able to tolerate anything good or pure the year before I gave my hopeless life to Jesus.

Seeds of distrust were planted, as well. I barely trusted anyone near the end. Imagine the fear inhabiting the heart that distrusts everyone! Now, imagine that person being desperate enough to accept the feelings of murder, because he hated fear! A large amount of rage eliminates almost all fears.

In the many years since receiving Christ, I have marveled and, honestly, been a little annoyed how some have taken my faith in God, lightly. I count it a miracle that I put my faith in Jesus before I trusted anyone. He taught me how to trust people, again. Please, do not take my faith in God lightly.

> I know in whom I have believed and am
> convinced that He is able to guard what I have
> entrusted to Him for that day. (2 Timothy 1:12)

This book is not "church" in the sense that some outside or inside of church may view it. This will get intense, but I made sure to add a biblical perspective when I have felt led to do so. This book is about the God, who loved us all as though there were only one of us here. He died an agonizing death to set me and all of us free!

Back to that day in the Fall, the evil ideas had apparently been planted, now they had to be explained and defined. The process took years to complete. An emotional, internal struggle ensued. I remained what many, many people would describe as nice. I realize that that sounds like a contradiction. Only through several unusual events, and instances of being abused by a teenager, could Satan place me on his chosen path. I was quiet, living with a family who was not very intimate. No one would learn my private thoughts.

"How was school?"

"Fine."

"What did you learn?"

"Not much."

I never came out and asked, "Does anyone else feel this way?" I truly lived in my own little world. My world was introduced to violence by outside forces. An example would be when I lost a T-ball game for half of my class. It seemed as though they were all over me with insults and harsh critiques. I thought I could not handle life anymore, and I wanted to leave it. No one had taught me about suicide as far I could remember. Yet there it was, in my mind, waiting to be released. Was it unusual to have suicidal tendencies before the age of nine in the mid-1970s? Yes, but I had them. The problem for me was I did not know how to do it. I had accidentally stabbed my left hand with a steak knife when I was six years old. (I was trying to separate seashells that were glued together and made a little character sculpture.) I remember bleeding, a lot! I suspected that a knife could do the job, but I was not sure where to stick the knife to receive the fatal wound that I desired. I did not know how to kill myself. Television was not filled with violence during the hours that I could watch. When I returned to school that Monday, nobody mentioned the T-ball game, again. I did not learn the lesson—people can be cruel, but they often do not mean to be. This would be one of many examples of unusual things happening, how negative situations would come to logically call for someone's death. It could be theirs or mine or both. I stayed quiet. The thoughts departed for a season.

FAIR WARNING

I cannot tell you, specifically, all the thoughts that were introduced to me during that cool autumn day. I can tell you that solutions to life's problems would trigger a strong temptation toward solving it with violence. I stress, again, that no one in my family taught me these values.

There are many mysteries embedded in this world and God's Kingdom. After I accidentally received Christ (and that will be fully explained later), Satan totally confirmed God's Word. I saw him for who he is. He is brilliant. He has existed among people for thousands of years, and he has spent that time learning about what motivates us and how he might keep us from God. He is not all-knowing. Unlike God, he can be at only one place at a time. He has been allowed power, but he is not all-powerful. Honestly, I think he is insane. He is the inventor of the lie (John 8:44). He is a murderer and prompted the first human murderer Cain to kill his brother over jealousy of God's favor. He wishes he is God (Isaiah 14:12–14). I wish to reveal Satan and his kingdom of darkness to you. When Jesus entered my life, my prayer is that you will see God for who He is. Have courage to believe the truth. Jesus is the way, the truth, and the life (John 14:6). Join me in this sixteen-year depicted journey.

Satan's bombardment of temptations on my mind only lasted for about a minute. It did not take long for him to build a foundation of deceit. I remember looking up into the whispering pine trees when

I sensed, at least a little, "new" reality. The thoughts were dormant, existing in a temporarily inactive and hidden form. I looked up into the lofty, evergreen trees, towering above me. Being different, but not realizing how, I continued my walk home. I would come home to learn that our Shetland Sheepdog, or Sheltie, had given birth to four puppies! My joy and concern at seeing them, and desperately hoping we could keep at least one of them, grabbed my attention, wholeheartedly! That a magical time could be so spoiled!

In the book of Deuteronomy, Moses, servant and friend of God, encouraged the Hebrews to keep God's commands.

> Only be careful and watch yourselves closely
> so that you do not forget the things your eyes
> have seen or let them slip from your heart as long
> as you live. Teach them to your children and to
> their children after them. (Deuteronomy 4:9)

I have a warning to proclaim. Christian parents, make sure you teach your children about who God is—the Father, the Son, and the Holy Spirit. You must do your best to live exemplary lives. The cliché is true—our actions speak louder than our words. Do not be afraid to pray out loud in front of your children. Enjoy God's presence in the presence of your family. Honor and respect God, but have fun with Him also. He made us for His good pleasure, and He wants to spend time with us. Deeply love and cherish your wife, as Christ loves His bride, the Church. When temptations to rebel come, your children may know they will be walking away not only from God but also from a friend of the family. The emotional attachments will be difficult to not miss. Is God a friend of yours, of your family?

To any who have not experienced the great salvation that God has revealed through the death and resurrection of His Son, His nail-scarred hand is still held out to you. He wants you to make peace.

> For he himself is our peace...and has
> destroyed the barrier, the dividing wall of hostil-
> ity. (Ephesians 2:14)

THROUGH THE DARKEST HOUR

My heartfelt advice is make your peace with God and then live your new life in front of your family and friends. God will bless you and stir your family to envy the victory He has given. I believe He wills to do this for you, because members of my own immediate family were drawn to God, after they witnessed my radical, positive change. The evidence was nearly impossible to ignore, and I am their evidence!

If you choose to ignore God's offer of salvation, I have another warning.

> Be self-controlled and alert. Your enemy the
> devil prowls around like a roaring lion looking
> for someone to devour. (1 Peter 5:8)

You and your children, especially, are being hunted. Have you ever watched lions hunt? First, the lions usually have the lionesses do the hunting. In a similar way, evil, demonic spirits are sent by Satan to "steal, kill, and destroy" (John 10:10). To continue this visual presentation, I will let you know that I used to watch nature shows. When I was nine years old, I studied animals. It kept me occupied. I have watched lionesses hunt on some of the shows. They would usually hide and camouflage themselves in tall grass. Quietly the determined cat would move closer to her prey. A zebra ignorantly would walk closer to the lioness, eating and drinking and frolicking in the African sun. Suddenly, the lioness would lunge at her prey— razor-sharp claws extended and powerful jaws ready to take down the zebra. The herd of the zebra, once unaware, but now understanding, would stampede in panic! You'd gasp when the lioness narrowly would miss a large zebra. Undaunted, the lioness would veer to the left. Her claws would rake away the flesh of the unsteady leg of a young zebra. He would stumble, head over hoofs, from pain never experienced. The other lionesses would pounce on the young zebra before he could stand. The zebra would inhale one last time, before he was eaten.

The young—Satan hunts for all humanity, and he starts when we are young. Look at the kids today. Tell me you do not see the "fang marks" all over them. They are dying—emotionally, sexually, and some physically. Abused, many lives are destroyed. Many women dancing in nude bars were molested by a relative. Babies come into this world experiencing the painful withdraws from cocaine, meth, or other drugs. Children have been born HIV-positive, because their mothers were being "devoured" by drugs and promiscuous sex.

> But God is not willing that anyone to perish, but everyone come to repentance. (2 Peter 3:9)

Only One can defeat the lion. He is the Lion of the Tribe of Judah, Jesus Christ (Revelation 5:5).

Do you know that? Does everyone in your family know that, or are you eating and drinking and frolicking in the African sun?

In 1977, my life was severely wounded by the "false lion." His plan for me had been initiated.

A NIGHT UNLIKE ANY OTHER

*Demonic messengers hide themselves behind the
symbols of an ancient pagan holiday.*

REALLY

For some, I have spoken about subjects many people have not encountered, even in their nightmares! Satan, demons, Jesus, God—many have never encountered these biblical beings. I would stress that you have, but you may not know it. If anyone chooses to search for God, he should make a full investigation of the Bible. Christians hold that the Bible is the inerrant Word of God. We do not believe it is a book of mythology and history. We believe in a revealed God, revealing Himself through Israel's history. Unfortunately, a growing number of people do not have a correct concept of God.

Who is God, really? Do you care? Is there any curiosity in you concerning the existence of God? Before I press on with my testimony, I want to help you understand a world that is invisible to our eyes. If you will weigh the evidence contained in this book, you may understand that I speak the truth. Our sole purpose is to know God and give Him glory. Then He will glorify us. He is worth knowing. I never thought He was worth knowing when I was younger, but He *really* is. I ask you to look at the world around you. Investigate the Bible. Open your eyes.

I would hope all would heed the encouragement from the late author, Finis Jennings Dake, who wrote in his book, *God's Plan for Man*, the following:

> There is no excuse for anyone to misunderstand God's Word if he will, like a child, accept the Bible for what it says, and be honest enough to consecrate himself to obey it. He must accept the Bible as God's Word. He must believe that God could not be honest if He sought to hide from man the very things, He will judge him by in the end. He must accept the Bible as the final Court of Appeal on its own subjects and forget man's interpretations and distortion of the Word. He must believe that God knows what He is talking about; that He knows how to express Himself in human language; that He did say what He meant, and meant what He said; and that what He says on a subject is more important than what any man may say about it.[2]

One of Jesus' first disciples, Peter, would later write these words, "We did not follow cleverly invented stories when we told you about the power and coming of our Lord Jesus Christ, but we were eyewitnesses of his majesty" (2 Peter 1:16).

OCTOBER 31, 1977

Before 1977, Halloween did not mean much to me. It was just an ordinary night, except I would dress up in a costume and get candy from neighbors. My mom had told me that she had always enjoyed Halloween when she was a young girl. My dad had lived on a secluded farm, ten miles from any generous, candy-giving neighbors.

---

[2]   Finis Jennings Dake, *God's Plan for Man* (Lawrenceville, GA: Dake Bible Sales, Inc., 1949).

My mom expressed that it was a fun time of the year. As a young boy, I loved this holiday. It was second to Christmas. It did not, however, have much meaning to me. In fact, there was a vacuum concerning its meaning. Until 1977, I was content for its meaning to include dressing up and getting candy—nothing more.

Compared to our neighbors, my family would eventually go "all out" in displaying Halloween decorations. On our porch sat a scarecrow. He had a plastic jack-o'-lantern head, sitting with an old, button-down shirt filled with rags, towels, and some hay. His pants were strapped to the shirt and also stuffed. My mom had taken a hobby in ceramics. Some of her projects were displayed, as well. Another ceramic jack-o'-lantern sat on a windowsill, giving off an eerie glow. On our Zenith System 3 television set sat a ceramic witch, with outstretched arms, casting a spell over a bubbling cauldron. A rubber vampire bat, wings in slight fold, hung from the ceiling, near the front door. These were simply spooky little symbols that appeared near the night I received candy. They meant little to me. I was ignorant of their meanings. I was ignorant of this night that happened one time, every, year. I needed definitions. That night, my new identity would start to be defined.

I was a hobo. I had the old man's mask on, with his bushy black mustache and eyebrows. I wore an old gray fedora hat. An old tan trench coat, with a tin whisky bottle, completed my garb. My family had kept a large black plastic bag that was filled with Halloween costumes and props in my brother's closet. I do not exactly remember wanting to dress up as a bum. The other masks in the bag included a witch with a crunched-in nose, a skull with a hunter's blade slammed in its temple and piercing out of its jaw, a lion with a bushy brown mane, and a pirate mask. I may have picked the hobo because I had already been the lion, and the other masks scared me. The other masks looked evil, and I, at this point, was still afraid of evil. Later that night, however, an intrigue with evil would begin to overcome me. All other Halloweens, I had worn harmless costumes. I had been Casper the Friendly Ghost, Scooby Doo, Batman, and the lion. All those costumes did not have an evil appearance. After 1977, however, this would change. The costumes following were increasingly evil-looking. This Halloween night, I was a hobo.

The crimson ball fell just beneath the tops of the towering pine trees. The crooked limbs were a silhouette against the brilliant orange-red sunset. It had been a dreary gray day. It seemed every Halloween in Florida, we were having our night threatened by all-day rains or thunderstorms. The rain had finally ended. I was afraid I would have to miss trick-or-treating. I looked to the south and saw the storm drifting away. A tiny bright star pierced the darkening sky as the sun was being swallowed by the earth. It was time for me to become a hobo.

My brother was fourteen years old, and he was old enough to take me out alone that year. My parents were entertaining my grand-parents (Dad's parents), and the three-day old puppies needed to be watched.

"Hey, Scott. Let's go!"

I think my pacing back and forth gave him the clue that I was ready. He finally came out of his room. He wore regular clothes. Mom gave the safety lecture to us, "Look both ways before cross-ing the street." "Keep your flashlight on." "If you get too hot, take your mask off." "Be careful. There are lots of nuts out tonight. Have fun! Don't go too far!" She called out to us, as we walked down our driveway.

Splash. Slosh. Sitting rain puddles scattered as I stomped them.

"Jeff! Cut it out!" My brother commanded after some dirty water spattered his pantleg.

I stopped. We headed toward the lake near our home. The night sky was almost completely clear. Only the edge of the storm remained to the south. My brother and I hit the neighbors' homes first. I clutched the flashlight in my hand. It was a plastic skull that lit up and flashed. There were only six houses on our block, so we went farther. My brother and I strolled down Columbus Street when we came up to a double-wide trailer. A boy peered out the front door. He had a doleful expression on his face. It was one of my classmates, Brad. A sign near his door grabbed my attention.

It read, "Due to religious beliefs, we do not believe in Halloween. We have no candy. Thank you."

I did not understand, and I remember some of the thoughts that went through my head. *I don't understand. How can you not believe in Halloween?* I thought to myself. It was Halloween, after all. How could they not believe in something that existed? You see, to me back then, if someone could experience something, then that "something" was real. I was experiencing the pagan holiday, so everyone should have experienced the holiday, my mind reasoned. I was confused. I noticed that religion played a part in the family's beliefs. They did not believe in something I believed in, and they believed in something that I was not sure I believed. I had never seen God. I had never felt God. I, however, had seen Halloween, or at least its participants. I had also heard its participants, and later that night, I would feel Halloween. The encounter with the religious people made a negative impact on me.

My shoes sloshed through more puddles as my brother and I walked away from Brad's house. I now had a slightly distorted view of God. I do not believe that Satan or a demon was involved in the encounter with Brad, but it strengthened his case. We headed back to our own home.

My breath was a high-pitched hiss behind my mask. The skull light continued to blink in my grasp. I was getting tired of walking. My brother and I turned the corner of a road that led to our street. There were a few houses, and only one had the porch light burning. My brother stood near the driveway, while I walked to the door. There were no streetlights on this street. The light breeze was becoming stronger. A cold front was sweeping through. The home appeared neglected with patches of grass and an older, run-down appearance. A thick oak tree was a shadowy giant. The wind whispered through its leaves. I felt anxious, and I was ready to go home. The intensity of the hiss behind my mask increased. I felt fear. I pressed the doorbell. An old man answered.

"Trick or treat!" I chimed.

He looked down at me. Then he reached behind him and pulled out an apple. It dropped into my bag with a loud thud. I thanked him and walked back to my brother. My brother heard the thud.

"What did he give you?"

"Mmm, just an apple," I answered.

"Momma will probably make you throw it out."

"Why?" I asked.

"Because you can't trust him. Some nuts stick razors in apples, so when kids bite into them, they'll get hurt," he answered.

I do not understand what happened, but it happened. I saw a razor sticking out of someone's neck with a steady line of blood streaming down. I believe that it was a vision. It would not be the last violent vision I would experience. It was my first.

The temperature that night was chilly. It was still a little humid. It is difficult to describe, but the moment that I saw the vision, the night felt like it descended on me. It felt like the night, its coolness and humidity, wrapped around me. It felt like it touched me. It felt like it was in me. To my highly impressionable mind, I probably thought it was Halloween inside of me.

The stars continued to twinkle above me as I peered into the windy night. The hiss of my breath resumed. I felt what can only be described as intrigue. My interest was aroused. I felt a tangible evil surrounding me, yet I was not scared. I was intrigued. This night was different from all other nights. This night meant more than I ever considered. Somehow, in time, I would come to believe that the pagan holiday had a part in my life. A decade later, I would be made to believe that I had a major role in Halloween's destiny. Next Halloween, I would feel the night again, and the next one, and the next one. The feeling would increase.

After I was delivered from evil and Satan confirmed his existence in the form of demonic attacks, I searched my past to try to understand what went wrong—"When did it start? When did I change? How did I lose my popularity and lose the ability to relate well with others?" I have been blessed with an awesome long-term memory. In 1994, I searched my memory and stopped on October 28, 1977. This is when my whole perspective of life began to change.

I went forward in my memory search. I stopped at the night I just described. This seems to be when I combined my new violent-prone perspective with the identity of the pagan holiday.

Was it a setup of Satan, or was it a coincidence? This side of eternity, I may never truly know. Evidence of Satan playing some part in all of this would rush in, like a tsunami, the night that I received Christ. I ask that you weigh the evidence in this book. You be the judge.

Unsafe World

The events that took place in my life, after that day, would have led to my destruction.

Greatest Is Love

In the last chapter, I began to present the case that Christians love and serve God, who revealed Himself through the Bible. This God could not have been invented. This God blasted away evil influences and desires in my life after a prayer. I present to you that humankind is too selfish to make up such a God. Man cannot produce righteousness from an exclusively unrighteous experience. Evil people cannot invent perfect goodness.

Listen to what the Heavenly Father said about Himself.

> For my thoughts are not your thoughts, neither are your ways my ways… As the Heavens are higher than the earth, so are my ways higher than your ways and my thoughts than your thoughts. (Isaiah 55:8, 9)

Some may say, "Those are just words. Mythological lies!" I would ask, "Have you ever loved someone? A parent? Relative? Husband or wife? How about a son or daughter? As a person's name you have loved comes to your memory, how have you loved this special person?"

Remember the good times and bad. Have you loved this person like this?

> Love is patient, love is kind. It does not envy, it does not boast, it is not proud. It is not rude, it is not self-seeking, it is not easily angered, it keeps no record of wrongs. Love does not delight in evil but rejoices with the truth. It always protects, always trusts, always hopes, always perseveres. (1 Corinthians 13:4–8)

> God is love. (1 John 4:16)

Have you ever loved someone like this? Have you been patient and kind? Have you been filled with pride? Do you boast? Have you kept a record of your loved one's failures? Do you protect and trust your loved one? Has your loved one ever needed protection from you? This passage from 1 Corinthians about love is revealing God's level of love for you. Have you fallen short? I know I have. Let's face it—everyone but Jesus has! Would you like to love the special person in your life like God does?

> Whoever lives in love lives in God, and God in him. In this way, love is made complete among us so that we will have confidence on the day of judgment, because in this world we are like him. There is no fear in love. But perfect love drives out fear because fear has to do with punishment. The one who fears is not made perfect in love. We love because he first loved us. (1 John 4:17–18)

Jesus gave the church a command, which was a radical request, "Love one another. As I have loved you so you must love one another.

By this all men will know that you are my disciples if you love one another."

The world at Jesus's time was dark. Mercy and compassion were not exactly the order of the day. The Jews had been under Roman Empire rule for generations, and the Romans were exceedingly cruel to the peoples of their conquered territories. Criminals or suspected insurrectionists would be hung on crosses and left as a lesson to others. Even today, the modern Saudi Arabia has a set day for public executions, where their citizens are beheaded by large swords, or they may have their hands or arms cut off for stealing someone's property. The "eye for an eye" regions of the world of today are like how life was in Jesus's time, till around AD 33. Jesus promised His followers that after He ascended to Heaven, the Holy Spirit, the Third Person of the Trinity, would come and bring a God kind of love to all who received the gospel. Through the ages since, the church has not consistently lived up to our God-empowered potential and has behaved as badly or worse.

To anyone who has been offended by a possibly careless act or act of omission by any Christian, please do not write off God! I have been on the redeemed side for almost thirty years, and I have learned that I always must resist becoming complacent. When I have, my life has felt like an earthquake, until I turn back for guidance from God. Please forgive us! Please understand we are human. I have witnessed many well-meaning Christians appearing to fear the increase of evil that the world is exhibiting. The church's love is not perfected. You could read 1 Corinthians 13 again and see that it is true. The church's love is not perfected, because it fears the world. That is exactly how Satan wants it. Jesus said, "I have given you authority to trample on snakes and scorpions and to overcome all the power of the enemy; nothing will harm you" (Luke 10:19). The snakes, scorpions, and enemies are demonic foes—literally, the angels that fell with their leader Lucifer. Any of my skeptic readers, stay with me, and do not forget I was an agnostic that leaned toward the beliefs of the ancient Druids because they worshipped a lord of the dead, Samhain, thousands of years ago, on the very night that was empowering the eight-year-old to twenty-one-year-old me.

I WILL

Who is Satan? I would say my first exposures to the concept of a devil came from cartoons. Is he some red guy with a goatee, horns sticking out of his head, and holding a pitchfork? Most Evangelical Christians, Catholics, and even some liberal theologians agree that Satan is a living being, on earth, who is greatly responsible for the evil in the world today. The Bible no more sets out to prove his existence than it does with God. The Bible progressively reveals God. If you read every page, you would witness a supreme being whose holy character is consistent throughout. The Bible also reveals the much lesser but once exalted cherub called Lucifer. After his fall from his position, when he attempted to overthrow the Creator God, he is ascribed no glory or honor. He is a created being. God reveals His inferior, evil, and outmatched foe in Ezekiel 28:11–16. Satan was the model of "perfection, full of wisdom and perfect in beauty." The following verses go on to describe his beauty. A word to any satanists—he does not resemble a goat.

> You were anointed as a guardian cherub, for so I ordained you… You were blameless in your ways from the day you were created till wickedness was found in you. Through your widespread trade you were filled with violence and you sinned. So, I drove you in disgrace from the mount of God, and I expelled you, O guardian cherub… Your heart became proud on account of your beauty, and you corrupted your wisdom because of your splendor. So, I threw you to the earth. (Ezekiel 28:14–17)

> Jesus said to his disciples, "I saw Satan fall like lightening from heaven." (Luke 10:18)

There was a holy war.

> And there was war in heaven. Michael and his angels fought against the dragon and his angels fought back. But he was not strong enough, and they lost their place in heaven. The great dragon was hurled down—that ancient serpent called the devil, or Satan, *who leads the world astray* [emphasis added]. He was hurled to the earth, and his angels with him... But woe to the earth and the sea, because the devil has gone down to you! He is filled with fury because he knows that his time is short. (Revelation 12:7–9, 12)

Satan really did choose to oppose God. In Isaiah 14:12–17, the account of Lucifer's fall is described in detail.

> How you have fallen from heaven, O morning star, son of the dawn! You have been cast down to earth you who once laid low the nations! You said in your heart.
>
> "I will ascend to heaven; I will raise my throne above the stars of God; I will sit enthroned on the mount of assembly, on the uttermost heights of the sacred mountain. I will ascend above the tops of the clouds; I will make myself like the Most High."
>
> But you are brought down to the grave, to the depths of the pit... Is this the man who shook the earth and made kingdoms tremble, the man who made the world a desert, who overthrew its cities and *would not let his captives go home* [emphasis added].

HIS WORKS

Paul, an apostle of God, wrote to a church in Ephesus, a city that had been influenced by pagan religions, including worship of demons,

> For our struggle is not against flesh and blood, but against the rulers, against the powers, against the world-forces of this darkness, against the spiritual forces of wickedness in the heavenly places. (Ephesians 6:12)

Satan is not God. He is not omnipresent, everywhere at once. He is not omniscient, all-knowing. He is not omnipotent, all-powerful. God is the Father, the Son, and the Holy Spirit. Satan cannot be everywhere in the world tempting and deceiving millions of people at the same time. Satan tempts the world through demons, or evil spirits, or fallen angels. Christians are literally involved in a satanic war. Just like the military, Satan's army consists of ranks. Rulers, in Paul's passage, would be the royal court. Powers refer to host-level demons. World forces are legion-level demons. Spiritual forces are like the buck private demons in a person's life.

The Bible uses several different titles when it refers to Satan. The list of his names reveals his nature and his self-appointed job to "kill, steal, and destroy" (John 10:10). The following are a few of his descriptive titles:

- "Accuser of the Brothers" (Revelation 12:10)
- "Adversary" (1 Peter 5:8)
- "Beelzebub" "Prince of Demons" (Ezekiel 28:14)
- "Enemy" (Matthew 13:39)
- "god of this world" (2 Corinthians 4:4)
- "Murderer" (John 8:44)

Satan's minions, or demons if you will, appear to be *perfectly loyal* to their cause. They rebelled against God, but their fate is sealed now. They are devoted to Satan. Luke 11:24–26 sheds much light about the mannerisms of an evil spirit.

When an evil spirit comes out of a man, it goes through dry places seeking rest and does not find it. Then it says, "I will return to the house [man] I left." When it arrives, it finds the house swept clean and put in order, and then it goes and takes seven other spirits more wicked than itself, and they go in and live there. And the final condition of that man is worse than the first.

These verses will be explained, but I would want for you to think about people who have appeared to come out of an addiction and "get their lives together" only to fall even deeper into their vices.

From the above verses, we can learn how these spirits work. First, demons can exist outside or inside a person, as found in the verse "when an evil spirit comes out of a man."

They can travel. "It goes through dry places." They can communicate. "I will return." Each spirit has a separate identity. "I will." They can remember and make plans. "I will return to the home I left." They can think and make decisions. It found its human target, "swept and in order." (He found that the man's mental state had made a recovery in its absence.) Demons can collect reinforcements. "It goes and takes seven other spirits." They vary in degrees of evil. "Seven other spirits more wicked than itself" (Luke 11:24–26).

PEOPLE ARE BASICALLY GOOD?

In my experience, the characteristics mentioned above are all true, first and foremost, because it is revealed in God's Word and because after receiving Jesus, I endured multiple, spiritual attacks. I understand there are many skeptics in this world. You must understand that I had been a skeptic, as well.

I remember in April 1990 my mother exclaiming, in a growing exasperated tone, "If you kill someone, you will go to Hell!"

I very coldly and foolishly answered, "Is that the best you have? I don't believe in Hell!"

I have presented the enemy of humankind's soul in this chapter. As difficult as it may be for some to accept, "our struggle is not against flesh and blood" (Ephesians 6:12). Evil inhabits the earth because of Satan and his kingdom and because people have chosen his evil ways.

Think of the millions of Jews and mentally disabled that were lined up and shot, gassed in chambers that they thought were showers, and burned in ovens in Nazi concentration camps. Throughout the ages, people have been tied to logs and set on fire. People have had their arms and legs bound and tied to four horses, which gallop in four different directions, tearing the victim apart. In prisons around the world, eyes are plucked, fingernails are ripped off, and men and women are repeatedly raped.[3] In recent years, Islamic extremists have thrown accused homosexuals off tall buildings, set people on fire in cages, drowned men who were trapped in cages, and beheaded hundreds, perhaps thousands, of men, women, and even children![4]

These horrible acts have all come about through the influence of Satan. I have discussed this to reveal the striking contrasts between the Lord, Jesus Christ, and Satan. Just as the world needs a revelation of God's goodness, mercy, justice, and loving-kindness, so we must also have a revelation of Satan's evil, destructive nature, so we blame the evil one. Never forget, Satan's sole purpose and goal is to destroy you, physically and spiritually! I thank God for His protection!

Psalm 34:7 says, "Angels encamp those that fear [respect] the Lord."

After

Once we have formed an incorrect idea into our reality, we have more difficulty perceiving the truth. This could be a case of "seeing is believing" or, in my case, to experience is to believe. Halloween 1977 came and left. The evil atmosphere that seemed to descend on me lifted, or my memory of the night gradually faded. Afterward, I may have experienced what some psychologists may call perceptual set or

[3] https://listverse.com/2017/04/04/10-barbaric-forms.
[4] https://www.thefiscaltimes.com/2015/03/22/ISIS-s-10-Most-Extreme-Acts-Terror.

a mental predisposition. Some could call it a mindset or paradigm shift. Basically, a concept of violence was planted on Halloween. As that strange night drifted into the past, I did not dwell on what happened. I was too busy with school and my life to sit and think about that night and its implications. My life at that time was filled with too many good things. My family, up to this point, was basically good. I still went to church. (I would frequently try to help my mother in the nursery, when she volunteered, to avoid church.) I helped raise the four sheltie puppies. They melted my heart daily. Television was not permeated with violence as it is today.

Hindsight is always 20/20. My troubles began after the pagan holiday. I cannot say that the very next day, November 1, 1977, I consciously detected specific thoughts going through my mind. I would not even be aware of the thoughts, which ran like a subconscious tape recorder. The thoughts were, *You aren't normal. No one can understand you. You can't understand anyone. You aren't normal. No one can understand you. You can't...*

I had an incredible sense of self-consciousness. I became *too* aware of myself. I did not know how to react or respond to others in a nice, fluid communicative way. I did not know how to act! I would constantly think, *Now, what should I do? What should I say? What do I think of this? What should I do?* My ability to easily relate to people was damaged. I felt different. People would become "entities" to me—entities that caused me pain and became a source of annoyance. My withdrawal from my peers and elders began. The violent thoughts were dormant, but not for long.

INCIDENTS

I had been moderately popular, up until this time. Suddenly, I felt like an open target. I had been friends with a new student, a boy from New Jersey. "Rogan" seemed to be awkward and open to a friendship with me. I vividly remember getting along with him during a recess in the third grade. I learned that he lived only a few blocks from me. I visited him at his house several times, learning that his parents were divorced and that he and his older sister lived with their grandparents. His grandmother was a genuinely nice person. His grandfather must have been so busy working that I cannot remember him. Rogan was one of those kids who likes to tinker with things and take things apart and put it back together. I remember being in awe that he built a flashlight. He was the one who taught me that you could get a mild shock from putting your tongue on a nine-volt battery. Rogan seemed quiet and unassuming, but his awkward stage was short-lived. It is obvious to me now that my new withdrawn and awkward behaviors were not working well with Rogan's boastful, outgoing, and inquisitive personality. Since I did not share much of anything about my life with my parents, I did not give them the opportunity to give me guidance and perspective. That was a major problem that would compound itself—I did not give anyone the chance to bring me proper perspective. I, now, lived in a deception I accepted.

Rogan, because of his thick, New Jersey accent, had been a bit of an outcast with me. Then, after some of my other classmates accepted him, he changed. Unfortunately, a bully of mine accepted Rogan too. Rogan turned against me after befriending the bully.

Looking back, I see that too many people had a wrong idea about me. I was a very skinny kid, who did not speak much, so I was thought of as a wimp. I became an easy target for bullies. Now, before I point fingers, let me tell you, as a younger kid, I had spirit. In kindergarten, I remember a boy putting his hands on me, messing with me while we were in line to go into the classroom from lunchtime. I lashed out, hit him, and gave him a bloody nose. Somehow, I was not sent to the principal's office. I do not even remember getting in any trouble. (Maybe my classmates were witnesses of the boy's disruptive behavior.)

Another time, another classmate tried to steal my best friend's Andy's bike. I stopped him from making off with the bike, but we fought. My memory tells me I was holding my own, until this classmate knocked a scab on my left elbow, and it bled all over, again. I panicked when I saw the blood, and that is how I remember losing that fight. He ended up not stealing the bike, though. So that was good.

Coming back to the Rogan incidents, one day I experienced a near confrontation with him and a boy named Donald. Donald befriended my New Jersey friend, and soon Rogan became a bully to me. (As I mentioned, after the oppression began, it became difficult to relate to my peers. My new awkwardness was like a bully magnet.) One Sunday, around Easter 1978, I set off for a short trip to a lake about two blocks from my house. My brother and our neighbor's adult daughter were walking there as well. (She visited around Easter, every year.) I rode my bike, beating them by at least five minutes. Donald and my New Jersey friend came up to me and blocked my path. I can honestly say, to this day, I have never felt so much fear and felt so helpless. I remember thinking, *Come on Sue, Scott. Where are you? I need you!* While I waited and hoped they would come before I got pummeled by these two, I endured what people call trash talk. It served to make me feel weaker. Finally, my neighbor's daughter and Scott were in sight. My two tormenters left me, but I knew I would see them at school the next day.

My third-grade teacher, Mrs. Lorton, broke off a commotion between Rogan and me. The class grew silent as Rogan and I were scolded. I hated being scolded, another opportunity to feel small and inadequate. Mrs. Lorton leaned on me, lightly. "Jeff would never…" Yes, I could be nice. My good reputation was already set. Honestly, I would have liked to have stayed nice, but after that Halloween, the world seemed meaner, and I felt I needed to open up to aggression too.

The argument resumed during recess, and I was supposed to meet Rogan at school, after school on a certain day, to finally fight. Now, I wanted to get rid of him! *Make the trouble go away. Destroy the troublemaker!* That seemed to be what was running through my mind. I accepted the fight. After I told my brother about the impending fight, he took me to his friend's Tony's house. Tony practiced boxing with a heavy bag in his backyard. My brother and Tony tried to instruct me about how to fight. I beat the heck out of my knuckles! It did give me some self-confidence.

The day before the big fight, I did something unusual. I drew and colored a picture of Rogan's face. (Even at that age of eight, I was an aspiring artist and would in ten years enroll in a commercial art school and earn an associate's degree.) His face, in the drawing, was bloody. I'm not talking about scribbled red blotches, but blood was realistically flowing from that face. I wrote, "This is what you will look like when I'm done with you!" I went to the school to fight, but Rogan never showed. Maybe the drawing startled him. Maybe his grandmother kept him home that day. He and Donald did not bother me, too much, again. Whether I took this to heart back then, I do not remember. It seemed that I had more evidence that fear can be a great weapon and ally. The first time I learned this is when I came after my brother with a steak knife but did not know if I really wanted to stab him when I found him in our parent's shower. He did not bother me for a while.

I want to point out something crucial—I had yet to see a murder on television. I authentically drew that bloody picture without knowing what a murder victim looked like. The point is—I kind of threatened a kid's life at the age of eight.

We live in a darker era now. It is becoming more common to have reports of children killing other children. The suicide rates for children and adolescents have steadily increased, and shows like Netflix's *Thirteen Reasons Why*[5] and videos of how to kill yourself have been found on the popular YouTube Web site. This book is an overdue alarm for the church and the world. Our children have the mark of fangs on them.

> He lies in wait like a lion in cover; he lies in
> wait to catch the helpless and drags them off in
> his net. (Psalm 10:9)

One sunny, hot afternoon in the summer of 1978, my brother and I went to the lake. The lake was not large enough to hold motorboats. (It could, but they would be making a lot of turns.) It could hold plenty of people, though. It was a neighborhood draw for children and teens. There were about ten teenaged girls gathered in a

---

[5]   https://www.netflix.com/title/80117470.

clique near a cement grill. It was the kind that looked like a chimney without a home surrounding it. Rogan's sister was among them, along with Donald's older sister. I do not remember why it happened—it just did. For some reason, I became a target of ridicule for the sisters. Suddenly they zeroed in on me. My brother must have been with his friends, and his usual aloof self, because he was not near me anymore. The girls were about sixteen years old. I was eight, going on nine. They towered over me. I must have smarted off to them because the sisters rushed aggressively toward me.

"Let's throw him in!" one connived.

"Yeah!" some of the other teens agreed.

No! I screamed in my head.

I felt some fingernails dig into my arm, and my feet were no longer planted on the ground. Some of the other girls grabbed my feet to help them carry my uncooperative, thrashing body.

"Let me go!" I shouted.

Once I was firmly in their grip, they quickly carried me to the end of the pier. I was facedown, and I remember seeing the old paint-chipped wooden planks moving swiftly beneath me. With each plank passing beneath me, I knew my time was growing short. My, apparently, smart mouth was earning me a trip into the lake. I was scared. Who does this? As they approached the end of the pier, the girls slowed down. I saw the last planks come to a halt below me. I do not remember if I was thrashing anymore.

"Let go!" I violently shrieked.

"Ready to take a swim?" one of the girls mocked.

No, I was not ready to swim. I only wanted to be free.

"Ready?"

"Yeah!" the others said in near unison.

"One," she counted.

I felt my arm being tugged, hard. Fingernails pierced deeper into my skin. The others caught on to what she was doing. They were going to swing me first. I saw the wooden planks fly past me and coming back again.

"Two!" they cheered, as the planks flew past my bound body again.

31

"Three!"

Some of the girls must have thought they were joking because they did not let go. The remaining girls holding me lost their grip. Instead of being tossed away from the pier, they dropped me. My head missed the pier (thank God). Starting at my chest and ending with my shins and feet, I slid, scraping my whole body. It felt like needles poking and scratching my body. I hit the warm water and landed on the sandy floor, screaming. I stood up in the three feet or so of water, making my way back to shore. I was in disbelief. Who does this? I calmly walked toward the beach not knowing if I should be crying, afraid they would attack me again or be angry from the embarrassment. The water dripped off my stinging body. I walked back over to the picknick tables, almost in shock. I heard some, "Are you okays?" from some of the younger kids. I did not answer.

I looked down at my chest. It was a bad brush burn. That eight-year-old boy lost it! My eyes scanned for the girls. The pier shot in my view. They were not there anymore. My head quickly cranked to my right. They were not at the shore or in the water either. Then I turned to the left. They were congregated near the concrete grills.

"You—! I screamed beyond the top of my lungs. "I'll kill you! I'll Kill you!" My face burned in humiliated rage. I barely understood what I was screaming. I threatened the girls without knowing how to do the deed. I still had not seen a murder.

The difference between me in 1978 and the children of the new millennium is access to information. Children see tens of thousands of acts of violence by the time they are teenagers. Children are killing today. Simply because they have seen murder, they know how to murder. When I was nine, I did not even know where to stick a steak knife in me to kill myself. My heart came to mind, but I was not sure. Today, children know how to commit suicide and murder.

Today, I am a mental health counselor for children, and some have been hospitalized for suicide attempts or ideations, and bullying can be a catalyst to self-harm behaviors. Those aforementioned incidents were not my only examples of being harassed. I encountered others. I lived in a family that had rules and penalties were paid for breaking them. I just wanted to avoid trouble. After the age of ten, I knew there would be consequences for threatening other kids' lives, so I repressed most of my anger. I would just seethe in quiet fury. My parents recently confirmed that I never told them what happened at the lake.

ILLUMINATION FROM
THE DARKNESS

*So deep did a seduction for darkness and
death become a part of who I was.*

HIGHLY IMPRESSIONABLE

Looking back, I would describe myself during those mid to late
1970s years as being highly impressionable. I was, like many children
I am sure, easily influenced and easily led. I can remember pestering
my mom until she took us to a Burger Chef[6], thirty-five miles away
in Melbourne, Florida, over a commercial touting a special toy eagle.
I am glad that director/writer George Lucas placed his space fantasy, *Star Wars*, in a setting that clearly was not on Earth—lest I had
believed in those fantastical aliens, ships, and Jedi.[7] I had watched
that movie with my childhood best friend, Alex (not his real name).
The movie did influence me to want almost every *Star Wars* toy that
was available. After seeing an ad for a contest to win a robot, I wanted
to build my own. My brother and his friend encouraged me to build
one out of a Charles Chips[8] can. I remember being profoundly serious, but not having the faintest idea of how to build my own droid,

---

[6] https://en.wikipedia.org/wiki/Burger_Chef.

[7] https://starwars.fandom.com/wiki/Star_Wars:_Episode_IV_A_New_Hope.

[8] https://charleschips.com.

like Artoo-Detoo[9]. Those were frustrating few months. I had wanted a Pontiac Trans Am since I saw Burt Reynolds outrun sheriff deputies in his movie *Smokey and the Bandit*[10]. (I confess, I still would love to own one, one day.)

I saw a movie that changed what I thought about, for a time. It was called *Close Encounters of the Third Kind*[11]. It was a movie directed by respected Oscar-winning director Steven Spielberg. It was released in November 1977. For you who may not have seen the movie, it was about friendly aliens exploring our world and abducting some people and bringing them back. The special effects were spectacular for those days. I cannot say for how long, but I remember looking intently into the sky to see if I could find a UFO. The Sebastian Municipal Airport[12] was less than a mile from our home. If I saw some unusual lighted aircraft at night, and I thought it was moving too fast or slow, I would wonder, *Was that one?* Then it would draw closer, and I would be disappointed when I heard the prop engine. I wanted to be taken away, like the kid that was temporarily abducted in the movie. (At times, I wanted to run away, but I kept sleeping through the night.) I became convinced that we are not alone. Again, I kept this to myself.

One way or another, we are beings that are led. We are influenced by the Kingdom of God or the kingdom of darkness. We make choices of who we believe every moment of every day. One of my arguments about the Bible is it explains everything. It has an answer to all our questions, but the vast majority rejects it. Let me give you a few examples of questions that the Bible has answers to.

Why is it difficult to genuinely appreciate and get along with others? Why do I focus on my own needs and wants even if it hurts others? Why are there diseases? Why do people die, and why do we fear it so much? Why is there depression and anxiety? Why do some become addicts?

---

[9]   https://starwars.fandom.com/wiki/R2-D2.
[10] https://www.imdb.com/title/tt0076729.
[11] https://www.imdb.com/title/tt0075860.
[12] https://en.wikipedia.org/wiki/Sebastian_Municipal_Airport.

The Bible answers every question, presenting a Savior who overcomes all those difficult questions. Jesus told His followers, "I have told you these things, so that in me you may have peace. In this world you will have trouble. But take heart! I have overcome the world" (John 16:33).

Does the Bible explain why and how we first became alienated from God and from each other? Yes, it does. In Genesis, the first book in the Bible, it explains how all of humanity's problems started. Satan tempted Eve and Adam, the first parents, to question God's words. God placed two special trees in the Garden of Eden, the tree of life and the tree of the knowledge of good and evil. The Lord told Adam to not eat from the tree in the middle of the garden. Satan asked Eve, "Did God really say, 'You must not eat from any tree in the garden'?" Satan purposely misquoted God and presented Him as being harsh and unreasonable. A pastor and friend pointed out that Satan wanted to cause Eve to doubt God's instructions and His warning. Eve gave a flawed answer. She was accurate about eating the fruit of the knowledge of good and evil would lead to death, but God said nothing about touching it. Satan lied again, saying she would "not certainly die" (Genesis 3:4). He continued lying, saying that by eating, it would lead to her eyes opening and that she would *be like God*.

The impressionable Eve took a second look at the fruit and "saw that the fruit of the tree was good for food and pleasing to the eye, and desirable for gaining wisdom, she took some and ate it. She also gave some to her husband, who was with her, and he ate it" (Genesis 3:6). Remember all those negative and depressing questions I asked earlier? Here is the answer to all those questions. When the first parents disobeyed God, negative consequences were the result. An immediate separation from that special relationship with God happened. An alienation, estrangement between the first two humans and every human after happened. Earth itself was cursed. Now useless weeds flourish, while we must work to clean them out and take great care to grow useful grass, plants, and trees. (Why can't hibiscus plants pop up in my flower garden instead of weeds?)

Can you imagine how the first parents reacted as they witnessed each negative consequence happen? They had been living in an area more alive and lusher, teeming with animals, than any place on modern Earth. There had been no death up until they rebelled. Their unmarred concept of God was wiped away, eventually leading to their offspring worshipping false gods, demons. Genesis 3:7 says, "Then the eyes of both of them were opened, and they realized they were naked; so, they sewed fig leaves together and made coverings for themselves." Then they heard God, and they *hid* from Him. God had to initiate contact and called out to Adam. Adam explained himself by blaming the wife God gave him. This would be the first time Eve likely felt emotionally hurt by betrayal. Eve would blame the serpent for tricking her. Their disobedience brought down a curse, and God cursed the serpent, predicting that a man, specially born from a woman, would crush his head after the serpent struck his heel (v. 15). God would cause women to face severe pain during childbirth (v.16). The very land that Adam had been in charge with was cursed, and he and every person after him would sweat and toil to make a living. Adam was told he would die and return to the ground. I encourage you to read chapter 3 of Genesis to witness all the negative consequences that came about from Adam's disobedience.

Can you imagine living the life and suddenly your body and environment are subject to the destruction and death you helped bring? They would have children, and the sin nature they brought on themselves would be passed to their first child and everyone after. After Cain murdered Abel, what were Adam and Eve thinking? Their son's body would move no more and return and become the dust God told them about. They were the first to experience grief and great loss. I wonder if God helped them through it. Adam and Eve had been driven away from that pristine land. The perfect, lush leaves would slowly brown and die, but new leaves would grow back! Earth became a sermon from God. Death would come, but new life was possible. All that misery we witness today had been contributed by a highly impressionable person.

WHAT ARE YOU OPEN TO?

While watching the horror movie *Hellraiser*[13], I heard a line that really did not impact me at all, until years after I had received Jesus. The line was, "What's your pleasure, sir?" The line provided a theme for a story about a man who opens a portal to Hell and torment after he opens Pandora's box. It was written and directed by British author Clive Barker. I learned that Satan wants to know specifically, "What are you open to? What's your pleasure?" You see, since the first parents' fall, this world has so much to offer us and lead us away from God. I, personally, see media and vices as tools of enticement for Satan. If he cannot lure someone toward pornography because that person's heart is not open to that, his minions will watch and learn what that person is open to. For instance, a boy many years ago may have been excellent at playing Pokémon cards[14]—or, in older times, marbles—betraying a possible tendency to enjoy gambling. Several years later, that boy could be on the verge of losing his wife, family, job, and home, because he became enslaved to the thrill of winning a bet, a hand of cards.

Perhaps some of his demons had been watching me for years. If this is true (and I believe it is), this is how it may have played out for me. They knew I was a fearful kid that had a fighting spirit. They would see I was loyal to my friends, but some friends could turn me against others also. They had influenced a strained relationship between my dad and me. They may have prompted my mother to speak negatively about my father in times of frustration and marital discord, which caused hate to grow in me.

"What else are you open to, Jeff? You're constantly fearful, but you watch those silly black-and-white horror movies. You like those a lot, don't you? Are you open to violence, to death, Jeff?" The demons could have conferred with each other and moved against me when they saw an opportunity.

---

[13] https://en.wikipedia.org/wiki/Hellraiser.
[14] https://www.pokemon.com/us.

Yes, I watched many of those 1950s–1960s black-and-white B horror movies. I watched from the mid-1970s until Sebastian no longer received a signal from a station in St. Petersburg, Florida. The double-movie feature was called *Creature Feature*[15], and it was hosted by a macabre character called Dr. Paul Bearer[16]. For me, Saturdays were about watching the *Bugs Bunny* show and later *Creature Feature*. I preferred the Toho giant monster movies, like *Godzilla*[17]. (To this day, I am a Godzilla fan, and my wife is beginning to be.) There were some movies that did scare me. I do not remember most of the titles. I remember being afraid when I visited my cousin, Wendy, and she had a canopy over her bed, like one that I saw in a haunted house movie and the canopy had come down on the person lying in the bed, smothering him. I spent some of my early years getting acquainted to horror movies. I was also terrified when I heard my parents and brother watching a more modern (for that day), horror movie. A draw toward this kind of entertainment kept growing, but there was a nagging fear mixed with *intrigue*.

JUST A MOVIE?

The late 1970s were truly an eccentric season in America's relatively short history. It was a time that was increasingly influenced and swayed by pop culture. It had been known as the "Me" generation. Many people, who were promiscuous, were a few years from being rudely awakened to a deadly sexually transmitted disease. Acquired Immune Deficiency Syndrome (AIDS) would devastate certain communities that had thrown caution to the wind and disregarded God's warnings.[18] Disco music was soaring high on the charts. A British brother group, the Bee Gees,[19] were "it." It was a time when men and women wore clothes that most people would deny they ever wore or mock them outright. Hundreds of millions had seen the Star Wars

---

[15] en.wikipedia.org/wiki/Creature_Feature_(WTOG).
[16] drpaulbearer.com.
[17] https://godzilla.com.
[18] https://www.mayoclinic.org/diseases-conditions/hiv-aids.
[19] https://www.allmusic.com/artist/bee-gees-mn0000043714/biography.

event (bigger than just a movie, to me). Technology was advancing faster than you could say, "Amana Radar Range[20]!" Microwave ovens, digital watches, electronic clock radios, video cassette recorders, and cassette tapes were taking over the eight-track tapes. (Millennials, you can look these late twentieth-century technological advancements on the Internet.) America's hottest stand-up comic was Steve Martin[21]— definitely 1970s! Robin Williams, however, would soon overcome his popularity. Tragically, Robin would take his own life, partially due to experiencing major depressed moods[22]. Who, from those times, could forget the television shows from that odd decade? There were classics, such as *M*A*S*H*[23], *All in the Family*[24], *the Waltons*[25], and *Little House on the Prairie*[26], and I personally liked *Happy Days*[27].

It was a time when Hollywood exerted tremendous influence through certain movies. A young director scared millions, on October 25, 1978. The movie would spawn sequels and inspire similar types of movies. It was inspiring, all right. Not counting Alfred Hitchcock's *Psycho*[28], *Halloween*[29] was Hollywood's first popular slasher film. No one who saw it would look at a boy in a clown mask the same again. No one would look at a man with a bone-white face mask (a model of William Shatner's head) the same again. Nor would I when I would see it on a regular broadcast station at the age of twelve. The movie was subtitled, "The night he came home."

Before I describe how the movie would gradually influence my views of who I was and what the holiday meant to me, I want to talk about who I was at this stage of the testimony. I was twelve years old in 1981, the year the movie was shown on network televi-

[20] https://www.thehenryford.org/collections-and…
[21] https://www.britannica.com/biography/Steve-Martin.
[22] https://www.britannica.com/biography/Robin-Williams.
[23] https://en.wikipedia.org/wiki/M*A*S*H_(TV_series).
[24] https://en.wikipedia.org/wiki/All_in_the_Family.
[25] https://en.wikipedia.org/wiki/List_of_The_Waltons_episodes.
[26] https://www.imdb.com/title/tt0071007.
[27] https://en.wikipedia.org/wiki/Happy_Days.
[28] https://www.imdb.com/title/tt0054215.
[29] https://en.wikipedia.org/wiki/Halloween_(1978_film).

sion, in October 30. A pioneer in psychological development studies, Jean Piaget, had a theory that children's minds develop in stages. For children in the seven to eleven age group, Piaget called the stage of cognitive growth "concrete operational." The stage is characterized by the development of logical thoughts. From Piaget's point of view, I should have been thinking logically. I was, to a point. It had been made clear by my parents that disobedience and outright rebellion would not be tolerated. The fact is fear of consequences held my slowly growing violent tendencies in check. I was afraid of punishment and my dad. (After being diagnosed with multiple sclerosis, my father's volatile temper was potentially so much worse.) I made no death threats until I was fourteen. I was, to a degree, thinking logically.

A testimony is challenging for me to write because seemingly little things were shaping me too. Good things and bad events were forming me, and my weakness was my lack of communication to seek guidance from my parents or others. I thought I would share some experiences in hope that it will bring more context of how I nearly went on a rampage at the age of twenty-one.

In the summer of 1974, I met my next-door neighbor's grandson, Alex, and we became instant best friends. Alex seemed to always be more self-confident and daring, and I developed an adventurous spirit with him. We were free-range children, and we explored nearly every mile of our town on our Huffy, BMX-style bikes. There had been times when I felt inadequate around him and his family, though. I was quieter and shier. It caused me to feel like I stuck out when I wanted to blend into the gatherings. Alex's parents were divorced, and he would stay half of a year in Sebastian and return to his mother in the Northeast. I would miss him, terribly. I only cried when I was bored to tears.

I believe Alex and I could have drowned at Wabasso Beach when we were seven years old. His father was watching us but must have become distracted, and an undertow of current gradually pulled us out to where we could not stand anymore, and the father was not aware of how far we were from him. I had, thankfully, just completed swimming lessons and was trying every form of swimming I could think of—the breaststroke, the butterfly, and the dolphin. We were not moving toward shore, but away! We told each other not to panic, and I remember floating on my back when I was too tired to struggle anymore. According to Alex, his father was trying to get to us after he saw us away from him and struggling. We had been pulled far from where waves were breaking, but I felt a stronger tug of current and looked to see a big wave crashing on us, and it pushed us to a point where we could stand again! I did count it as a miracle.

I had a strong friendship with my cousin Wendy, who was only two months younger than me. She was always excited to see our car pull up for visits. She would cry out, "They're here! They're here!" I loved her like a sister and felt bad when her older brother and sister teased her when she was four years old. She would cry, and I felt helpless to console her. When I was eleven, and my personality was becoming more awkward, I may have upset her or caused her to become frustrated with me. She slammed a beach ball into my face, while we swam in my grandparents' neighbor's pool. It hurt my face, but it crushed me on the inside. This friend, who always begged to stay the night at my house when she visited, she was socially out-growing me. She was leaving me behind. Our relationship was never the same. I was not mad; she was the one who appeared to be frustrated with me. We never reconciled, and it honestly still hurts.

In the fourth grade, there was a girl, Ranee (pronounced Renee), who it seemed I would make her mad too. There were at least a couple of times, maybe more, when I upset her, and she would grab my arm and her fingernails would leave superficial slits in my skin. In the fifth grade, I grew to like Ranee more, at around the time I began to suffer sexual abuse. (That will be discussed later). She was the type of girl who would probably talk to anyone, and I became the type of boy who would take any attention as a sign that I was liked. She was moved to a seat in front of me for at least three weeks, because she was in trouble for excessive talking. The teacher moved excessive talkers. We passed some notes, I drew her a picture of an eagle, and her talking to me caused her to be moved, again. I was so upset that winter day that I tried to tear a melaleuca tree apart, literally! I ripped and broke twigs, sticks, and branches, scratching its paperlike bark off while cursing my teacher. Alex happened to be living at his grandparents, and he joined me and tried to console me. In middle school, I would waste time liking her and at least five other girls, including Ranee's best friend.

"Adam" (not his real name), from Long Island, New York, moved a street behind me. He came to my house a couple of Sundays before school started and introduced himself to me. We became friends, and I was no good at juggling more than one friend at a time. I did not mean to, but I think I left Alex out, and he returned to the Northeast. Our friendship would never be the same again. My ten-year-old self seemed to be learning that New Yorkers are overconfident and brash, based on Adam and his family's behavior. His father belittled me often and would call me "Jeffie." I hated that. I am grateful, today, that his was an athletic family that pushed me beyond my limits. I was so skinny and weak (seemingly earning the nickname "Stickman" in the fifth grade) that I struggled to keep up and develop like Adam. He was a good friend, but I would feel inadequate around him, and as we became teenagers, the feeling would increase to an excruciating level. He would get girlfriends, and I would be a third wheel. There was, however, a certain time in the fall when my mind would not focus on my own perceived shortcomings, but on Halloween.

Now I Knew

The intriguing atmosphere that always seemed to accompany my Halloweens and linger a day or two after was back. It caused me to be conscious of the night. I watched the movie *Halloween* with my parents. I had asked to see the movie after I had seen a commercial a week before. My father was not a big fan of horror movies, but we all watched it. The lights were out, and I tossed my pillow on the floor and watched it.

I will not describe the scenes, but this is what I saw. The lead character Michael Myers stabbed his older, teenaged sister when he was six years old. He killed his sister after she slept with a teen boy, while their parents were not home. The young murderer did not speak when his parents found him in their driveway moments after he killed his sister. The headlights caught him holding a bloodstained knife, and the father called his name and pulled the clown mask off his face. The boy looked like me. He had blond hair, like I had at the time, and he had a slight gap in his front teeth, like I have. I seemed to identify with him. The scene fades to black, as eerie piano music started to play. An image appeared on the screen and burned itself into my mind. It was the sinister orange glow coming from triangular eyes, nose, and a devilish tooth-gapped grin of a jack-o'-lantern.

The antagonist in the movie escaped from a mental asylum at the age of twenty-one, fifteen years after he was institutionalized. The antagonist scared me, but I thought he was cool too. The movie may have had a very subtle effect on me. I became even more conscious of that "night." As years passed by, I began to ponder these things—the intriguing atmosphere, the night, the death threats, the movie, and its character and me.

The character's psychiatrist said that his patient escaped as though there was some "silent alarm" that went off in the young man. By the age of nineteen or twenty, I wondered if the same alarm was counting down in me. I came to understand that it was not the character who did the killing. His psychiatrist, in the movie, kept referring to an evil inside of the boy. I felt that an evil was growing inside of me—slowly, but steadily. I had not surrendered to it yet.

As a result of seeing the movie, more thoughts were planted in my mind. I believe these thoughts also remained dormant, existing in a temporarily inactive and hidden form.

A CRUSHED ROSE WILL
NOT BLOOM

An unbelievable sequence of dramatic life events.

ATMOSPHERE OF DESIRE

Five years after I received Christ, I attended a Bible college that held great significance before and after I received Jesus. While attending, I learned that sometime during the spring months, the college held what they called a Spirit Week. The administrators would choose and invite a dynamic speaker, usually a pastor or missionary, to speak to the students during special chapel and nighttime assemblies. Around March 1996, Pastor Garcia, who led a congregation in Brooksville, Florida[30], led Spirit Week. During his first message, he spoke about sexual immorality. He could be a very dynamic, hard-hitting speaker. He brought up the topic of sexual abuse and asked all the students who had been molested to stand. I began to see young men and women stand, and I slowly rose up to my 6'5" frame. I scanned the crowd, partially because Pastor Garcia asked us to, and was shocked to see a dozen or more of my schoolmates standing and scanning the crowd as well. I felt sadness and anger, as I thought about everyone's innocence being taken through child sexual abuse. *This is a Bible college. These are Christians. How is this happening in their families?* I

---

[30] https://en.wikipedia.org/wiki/Brooksville,_Florida.

thought. My eyes were opened to how widespread this form of abuse really is.

The following paragraphs give an accurate account of the first time I was sexually abused and alludes to how the abuse continued for four years. I do not share this to be salacious, to receive some self-gratification, or to subject any of you to any emotional or mental health harm. It is my hope that you would see this section's account as another avenue of attack that Satan's kingdom used against me and so many others so you may be able to help people who have been abused or seek godly counsel, as well. If you would prefer to not be exposed to the rest of this section, I encourage you to skip the following few paragraphs and begin reading again at the section "Damaged." For any who want to continue to read, I want to pray for you before you do.

> Father, I pray for any who continue to read this account that You would protect their hearts and minds. I pray that this would be instructive, in a spiritually enlightening way, and that all would find deliverance and healing through You. In Jesus' name, I pray. Amen.

Everyone seems to remember their first time, especially when it happens in the context of abuse. I am no different. I remember the circumstances that led to my first time being abused. My parents were out to dinner, probably at the Officer's Club in Patrick Air Force Base, Florida. They were infrequent guests of our neighbor's son, who happened to be a captain in the US Air Force. The base was about an hour's drive away from Sebastian. My brother was not watching me, like he normally would have been. Another teenaged boy of seventeen, who my parents thought they knew, watched me. My friend, Alex, was there as well.

The incident happened in mid-January 1981. I remember a premium channel had been playing family-friendly Disney movies as a promotion. *Mary Poppins* was playing that month, I believe. The teenager offered for us to play poker with him. Sitting at my dining room table, he convinced us to play the strip version of the card game. It was not too many games later that I was completely naked, and Alex was as well. I felt shame and excitement at the same time.

My memory, I admit, becomes topsy-turvy for a good chunk of time during that night. I do not remember how we went from the dining room to my parents' bedroom, but we did. The teenager began to ask me in a repetitive pleading way to perform oral sex on him. He was voluntarily naked at this point, and I remember being in awe of his manhood. He looked so different from us two eleven-year-olds.

I said no, but not as forcefully as I could or should have. That half-hearted no has haunted me for many years.

The teenager responded with, "Come on. Please!"

His "Come on, pleases" slowly wore down my weak no's.

Somehow, I began negotiating with him. He agreed to let me put a sandwich baggie on his erect penis. I remember it and feeling uncomfortable and wrong. I remember it vividly and do not want to share details. I do not remember how long it went on for. I remember standing near him when he masturbated and ejaculated into the toilet in my bathroom. I remember thinking, *What is that?*

The teenager told me not to tell, but he did not threaten me with anything. The teen seemed to go back from where he lived. When Scott, my brother, was attending college in Macon, Georgia, the teen would come around when my brother returned from his school on summer and Christmas breaks. When the teenager came over, unbeknownst to my parents, he would call me to my brother's room and ask me, "Have you grown any?" The teenager, now about nineteen years old, gave me an inferiority complex over his concern about my size! After a few years, I was fourteen years old, and apparently, he was satisfied enough with my "size" that he reciprocated on me. By this time, we both were not using bags. I was going through puberty solidly knowing I liked girls, but my psychotherapist offered in 1990 that my "body disobeyed me." The abuse or what I used to call "misuse" happened from January 1981 till fall 1985. The young man stopped abusing me when he learned that I had told it to another friend. In a twisted way, I thought he did not like me anymore. Alex was never present for any other episodes of abuse, and we both kept it to ourselves.

DAMAGE

I am not clear on the extent of the damage that the four years of abuse had wreaked on me. In some ways, I think it could have turned out much worse for me. Statistically, males who are sexually abused as children become abusers themselves. Satan's minions learned that they could distort my sexuality only so far. I had known that I liked girls since I was six. So Satan tried to lure me toward homosexuality, and I did have three encounters with a male friend I have not mentioned yet, and whose name is never mentioned. The attraction toward women was too strong, and my heart was opened more toward violence—violence toward those society would likely agree are strong.

The psychotherapist from Tampa had said that my body had disobeyed me. My body, embarrassingly, disobeyed me when I had to take showers in middle school. I had a few times of feeling that excitement, and I decided I would skip showers. In high school, I was in the marching band, so I did not have to take physical education. I would say that it felt like I did go through puberty with a question mark over my head. After receiving Christ, it felt like I, mentally and emotionally, went through puberty all over again. I came out the other side with a strong desire to prepare myself for my future wife.

In September 1990, I had known I was abused, but I did not think of it or dwell on it. The atheist psychotherapist began asking questions during a session. It felt like he was crawling around in the dark, haunted attic of my mind. Then he said it, "You were sexually abused." That afternoon, I resolved to kill the family friend who abused me, but he lived out of state. I figured I would be caught by law enforcement because I already had thoughts and plans to kill a family of three from Tampa, Florida. They were to be my first stop on Halloween 1990.

The effects on a child who has been sexually abused can be described as a train wreck of natural and sexual development. The derailed train can do extensive damage to its surrounding environment. The "train," short of a miracle, or years of extensive therapy, will remain in a "twisted, mangled state." It takes experienced help and a long time to clean up the carnage. While the train remains in its derailed state, it could cause other good trains to follow its fate. Satan knows this.

Normally girls reach the age of puberty around the age of twelve. Boys usually reach puberty a year or so later. It is normal for young teens, who are experiencing the changes involved in puberty, to develop a heightened awareness of their sexuality. Those icky girls suddenly do not seem so creepy. Those weird, dumb boys suddenly seem pretty cool. It does not take long for the boy meets girl stories to happen. It is God's way. From the beginning, He told humans to "be fruitful and multiply…replenish the earth" (Genesis 1:28).

When an adult, however, forcibly or through verbal persuasion, threats, or actual violence has sex with a child, then that child's mind, emotions, and sexuality has been *activated* before his or her time. What is worse is the child's very first exposure to sex is perverted. The effects of this evil act are astounding! The child may become preoccupied with sex, especially if the abuse persists. The child will almost certainly exhibit confusion and concerns about sexuality and his or her sexual orientation. The child will usually experience changes in sleep patterns, recurring dreams, and nightmares. The child may withdraw into fantasy. The child may exhibit regressive behaviors, such as wetting their bed or staying in a safe room, refusing to leave. The child may have trouble concentrating on tasks, having a short attention span. The reason may be, for many, that their minds are being assaulted with graphic sexual visions and memories. They literally see the abuse in their minds. They exhibit symptoms of post-traumatic stress disorder (PTSD), including nightmares, intrusive thoughts, hypervigilance, and avoiding similar situations/ environments. I confess that approximately fourteen years after I received Christ, I experienced an anger outburst. I punched a wall at work, and I was sent for a psychological evaluation. It was then that I was tagged with PTSD and recommended, eventually, to not work outside of an office setting. I know I have had recurrent nightmares about the abuse, maybe once or twice a year, but other than that, I have no other symptoms to match that anxiety disorder. So I disagree with that diagnosis.

If the sexual abuse continues, the child will likely experience a depressive state. The effects of the damage to the child—emotionally, mentally, sexually, and socially—can be clearly seen as the victim grows to adulthood. The sexual and emotional destruction reaches out from the abused to society at large. As the child grows older, he or she may exhibit antisocial behavior. Usually, female victims will take their anger out on themselves. The shame and guilt she may feel may transform into self-blame and self-rage. Tragically, she may become suicidal or engage in self-harm behaviors if she continues to hold the feelings in herself. Both males and females may manifest extreme forms of antisocial behavior. The victims of sexual abuse may develop a lack of trust for all members of society who share the sex of the offender. They can become hostile and be aggressive, physically or sexually. Their behaviors can range from outbursts and tantrums to delinquency, stealing, and substance abuse. They have poor self-esteem, see themselves as inadequate, and may feel they forever deserve to be abused. In short, they may feel dead already, betrayed by themselves and the world.

They may become promiscuous. If not detected, reported, or stopped, the male victims are likely to become sexual abusers. This behavior is not uncommon for females; however they usually become promiscuous. Some female and male victims become prostitutes, never really escaping their abuse, which is tragic.

SHAME

The most common response of a sexually abused child is an intense feeling of shame. Shame is "a painful emotion excited by a consciousness of guilt, shortcoming, or impropriety." It brings feelings of disgrace and dishonor. Until I investigated this subject, I never realized how destructive this emotion can be. Everyone has experienced it, in one form or another. Some students have felt shame when they have been caught cheating on an exam. How about the man who tripped on an uneven sidewalk? (Uneven, that is what they all say.) The man was embarrassed, and that was a form of shame. What does a nine-year-old girl feel as her uncle sexually assaults her? Shame. I have learned that shame, even undeserved shame, can kill.

Not all shame is necessarily bad. Shame is an emotion that allows us to be human. It is like a reminder and tells us we all have limits. As mentioned above, it can come in the form of embarrassment. Shame can manifest as shyness. Shame keeps us in our human boundaries, letting us know that we can and will make mistakes. It is the emotion that tries to tell us, "You need God's help."

Toxic shame is torturous and almost always demands a cover-up, a *false* self. Victims of sexual abuse typically acquire this type of shame. Deviant behaviors can arise from this type of shame. This shame divides the victim from himself or herself and from others. They may become antisocial and disown themselves. Bradshaw writes, "Once one becomes a false self, one ceases to exist psychologically...the process of false self-formation is what Alice Miller calls, 'soul murder.'"[31] The false self tries to be more than human or less than human. The abused child comes to believe, as they get older, that they are damaged goods, not worthy of the effort or love. An utter sense of hopelessness may set into them. The victim resigns, and he or she quits the struggle for normalcy and *becomes* the sin that has him or her in its tightest grip. Often, they themselves become sexually perverted. The cycle may continue.

GIFT

Sex is a gift from God, and Satan has tempted people to the point that the gift has been twisted and mangled, barely recognizable. I have had it explained this way. If you were to draw a small circle within a huge circle, you may begin to understand God's plan for us. Place an "M" for marriage in the small circle. The small circle represents sex within marriage to one spouse of the opposite sex.

---

[31] *Healing the Shame that Binds You*, Deerfield Beach, FL Health Communications, Inc. 1988.

For this plan to work perfectly, each spouse must never have had sex before they were married. Now, write these words in the large circle, premarital sex, extramarital sex, homosexuality, bisexuality, bestiality, rape, molestation, and necrophilia. If the married couple remains in the small circle, they are safe. They will truly know their spouse. They will experience the satisfaction of knowing that they have been kept for each other's sole enjoyment. However, people are constantly being tempted to ignore or leave the lifestyle represented by the small circle. What happens if the wife or husband just steps out of the small circle and steps into the large circle? Look at the large circle literally or in your mind. Think of the wounded emotions, the perverted minds, and the diseases that exist in the large circle. That is what a spouse could be walking into when he or she is enticed to be unfaithful.

If you do not know God through the saving knowledge and relationship with Jesus Christ, then you have not experienced true love. The Bible says, "We love because he first loved us. If anyone says, 'I love God,' yet hates his brother, he is a liar. For anyone who does not love his brother, whom he has seen, cannot love God, whom he has not seen" (1 John 4:19, 20).

I am not just saying that God's way is the only right way for sexual relations, but it is the best way! His plan is beautiful! The world's love is based on taking a continual "what's in it for me?" God's love, however, is based on giving. I know this to be true. I had three semiserious girlfriends. One was before I became a Christian and two after. The one before, my attitude was always centered on me. I was more attentive to the ones after I became a Christian. Now, I have been married to the last girlfriend, at this writing, for twenty-three years. I always want to please her, as God empowers me to love this way.

This is how we know what love is: Jesus
Christ laid down his life for us. (1 John 3:16)

I would not begin to understand this type of love until I was around twenty-five years old. As mentioned before, the sexual abuse victim may seek out a new identity. I did, but I do not think it was a conscious decision. The identity that I would choose, to me, should have been asexual, like Michael Myers. It bothered me, and I believe it encroached on my beliefs of my ideal identity that there remained a yearning for normalcy, a yearning for a meaningful relationship threatened my plans.

NIGHTMARES FOR A PURPOSE

Bizarre experiences would be accepted as being normal.

When I think my bed will comfort me
and my couch will ease my complaint,
even then you frighten me with dreams
and terrify me with visions.
                                    —Job 7:13–14

INFLUENCES

As I progressed from late elementary school age to early middle school years, I felt a growing, insistent pressure that I needed to act more mature. The messages from peers, adults, and society at large were unmistakable. I had to grow up. I had to be a man, to "man up," and "don't cry." I almost never cried. Another set of messages I received was that girls don't like wimps and "you need to be strong." "No pain, no gain" was the motto during my teen years in the 1980s. You can't have weird interests. Put away the *Star Wars*[32] toys and buy some sport cars magazines. "Keep up with us or we'll leave you behind."

I did want to mature. I watched my older brother and envied his level of freedom. *Do I have to stop liking everything that I enjoy?* I felt some hope toward my future, and I have learned that hope is

---

[32] https://starwars.fandom.com/wiki/Star_Wars:_Episode_IV_A_New_Hope.

a great motivating force. Reality would get in the way. Great times were being interrupted by pressures, an inconsistent presence of inadequacy, and I started having some nightmares.

On a particularly boring Saturday afternoon, I pulled out my brother's old Howdy Doody ventriloquist puppet and played a record that came with it. The *Howdy Doody*[33] show was before my time, but I had watched clips of the show and maybe some reruns. I placed the record on my phonograph and heard the ventriloquist, the one who speaks for Howdy Doody, "Say, kids, what time is it?" The kids said in unison, "It's Howdy Doody time!"

Side A of the record was a recording of one of the shows. Side B was an instructional on how to learn the skills of a ventriloquist. There are many things about my testimony that part of me is very embarrassed about and somehow enormously proud at the same time. My bored self-played that Side B, and I taught myself how to speak with mouth nearly closed and barely moving my lips. I learned that ventriloquists substitute certain letters that would cause a person to have to move their lips. For instance, the letter b cannot be said without moving your lips. What the record taught me is that ventriloquists say a subdued d in place of a b. You can say d without moving your lips. I also learned to throw my voice. I remembered seeing comic book ads about learning to throw your voice, "Amaze your friends!" I was disappointed to learn that it was basically controlling the pitch of your voice and volume. In a matter of a few hours of practice, I had a new obsession. Doing the art of ventriloquism was like playing Simon Says in your head. You had to know when to be able to move your mouth and when you could not. I was proud at the time. Now, I am proud but embarrassed too.

I believe I taught myself the art during the summer of 1978, and I was influenced by the broadcast of the *Muppet Show*[34]. I also preferred puppets over dolls from as long as I can remember. *Sesame Street*[35] debuted the year I was born, and I was a fan of the character

---

[33] https://www.tvguide.com/tvshows/the-howdy-doody-show/cast/202132.
[34] https://en.wikipedia.org/wiki/The_Muppet_Show.
[35] https://www.sesamestreet.org.

"Ernie." He seemed to have a grouchy, impatient roommate named "Burt." I was more like Ernie, so I had his puppet when I was three years old. My mother sewed denim fabric legs onto my puppet and gave it an appearance of a full-bodied puppet. I also had a Big Bird puppet, but it was about eighteen inches tall. In the summer of 1978, I had been using an Oscar the Grouch as a puppet and my primary ventriloquist puppet. I also had a fascination with lizards, and my mother sewed a full-bodied lizard using Oscar's measurements. Now, when friends like Alex or Adam were not around, I would practice ventriloquism. To this day, I kind of wonder if I was having conversations with myself or something spiritual.

While puppets and ventriloquist dummies seemed to captivate my fascination, a popular spoof about soap operas called *Soap*[36] ran on ABC from September 13, 1977, to April 20, 1981. The show infrequently (for my tastes) showcased a talented ventriloquist named Jay Johnson. His character on the show was named "Chuck," and his dummy/alter ego was called "Bob." *Soap*, I believe, was the first nonfamily-friendly show I had watched with my family. I watched it for Chuck and Bob. I remember being disappointed if a show ended without seeing the comedy team. While doing research for this part of this chapter, I learned through an interview with Jay Johnson how the characters of Chuck and Bob were to develop. Jay stated that Chuck was supposed to be mentally disturbed and that Bob was originally written to be like a horror novel character. The novel was called *Magic*[37], and in the novel, the ventriloquist had schizophrenic-type symptoms, and he used his dummy to kill some hapless souls who got in his way. Fortunately, Chuck and Bob's characters were slightly rewritten so that Bob basically said the things the self-repressed Chuck would not say. This made the characters more kid-friendly, and *this* kid was greatly influenced by the comic duo.

Before the Christmas of 1979, a Sears *Wish Book* was brought home by my mother. As I flipped through the pages of the toy section, I came across a page devoted to several ventriloquist dummies.

---

[36] https://en.wikipedia.org/wiki/Soap_(TV_series).
[37] https://en.wikipedia.org/wiki/Magic_(novel).

I saw Charlie McCarthy[38], the dummy that the legendary Edgar Bergen used in his radio and TV shows. Next to him was Lester, a hip African American dummy who was brought to life through the ventriloquist/comedian Willie Tyler. I just want to say, I loved Willie and Lester. [39] Howdy Doody was there as well. There was also a puppet I had never seen before—a puppet that looked remarkably like me, in fact. It was called Simon Sez. I decided right there that I would ask for that puppet. I must share this. As presents were beginning to be placed around the tree, I measured each one that I was going to receive. The *Wish Book* noted the dummy's measurements, including length. I had no present that measured thirty-two inches. I was surprised and felt a little stupid that Simon Sez was folded in his boxed packaging. I loved that gift! I did not think anything could come between Simon and me, except he would be in later nightmares.

NIGHTMARES

My dreams, especially nightmares, lacked detail and I almost never remembered them. The worst "normal" nightmare I had happened the night that I had seen a preview for Mel Brook's *Young Frankenstein*[40]. My family had seen the trailer before watching an *Airport*[41] disaster movie. All the dream was, was me seeing the top of the Frankenstein's monster's head poking out of the shower of my bathroom. Apparently, I was sleepwalking at the time, and I startled our sheltie (the future mother of the four puppies). The sheltie barked and woke me up, and I screamed. That was frightening, but there was a clear connection between me seeing the movie trailer and having the nightmare. I was six at the time.

In the spring of 1981, not long after that sexual abuse had started, I stayed the night at my friend's Alex's house. I had a vivid, thematic nightmare that left me shaken after I woke up. My normal

---

[38] https://en.wikipedia.org/wiki/Charlie_McCarthy.
[39] willieandlester.com.
[40] en.wikipedia.org/wiki/Young_Frankenstein.
[41] https://en.wikipedia.org/wiki/Airport_(1970_film).

dreams usually had no plot or theme. This dream at Alex's house was so vivid that it almost seemed real. In this dream, and many nightmares afterward, virtually all senses were used—sight, smell, touch, hearing, and even taste! When I woke up, it felt like I was transported from one reality to another.

This nightmare was presented like a movie. I realize that sounds unusual. There was no title or credits, but I somehow knew that the dark winged creatures in the dream were called blue ants. They were not actually blue, and they stood about five feet with insectlike wings. They looked more like demons, although I have never seen one. Some Christians are said to be able to see them when God permits it. Their "skin" appeared to be a very dark gray to black. The dream did not last long.

I remember, in the dream, being on a school bus. I was that current age of eleven. The bus was headed toward Wabasso Beach, about six miles from my town of Sebastian. The bus was full of children around my age. The bus driver had the radio on, and I heard a report about the "ants." They were said to be dangerous. I heard the report say, "They can hypnotize by the sound of their wings."

The bus stopped on a tall bridge. I found myself walking outside of the bus when one of the dark winged creatures hovered near me. Its buzzing noise drove me crazy. Through the noise, I heard, "Jump off the bridge." At that point, I could perceive myself walking toward the edge of the bridge, and I did not want my "dream self" to obey, but he was. I remember crawling beyond the railings and the feel of my fingers and hands scraping against the concrete.

I was obeying the order, yet fighting it also. I felt strong arms pull me up and save me. The buzzing stopped.

Suddenly I felt like I was in another scene in this dream. I was in a home, an apartment close to a busy road. There were people in the apartment, but I did not recognize any of them. We began to "hear" many creatures flying near the apartment. I remembered an older man saying in a tone of disgust, "I've had it!" He rushed outside. I ran after him. The old man grabbed a pole or stick, and he started trying to swing at them. I screamed at him to come inside before they hypnotized him. The man dropped his weapon and lowered his arms. I ran toward him and he stood there. One of the creatures swooped toward him, and large insectlike mandibles appeared. They closed on the man's neck. The man's head bounced toward my feet. It was realistically graphic, and I woke up sweating in the den of Alex's grandparents' home.

Not long after that nightmare, I had another in which my friend Adam and I were victims trying to escape an abductor. Adam and I, in the dream, were taken forcibly by a huge muscular man. He was stocky in build and wore long-sleeve flannel shirt and stained, faded jeans. The man had very rough features. His hair was black, long, and matted with a putrid, sweaty smell. His eyes were black and wild. It was a Florida-cool, dreary day. Adam and I suspected that he was a murderer. After he abducted us, he had us tied up in his white van. Adam and I knew he was insane, and he was going to kill us if we did not escape.

I want to pause and give you the option to pass through these next few paragraphs if you would rather not read about a very graphic nightmare I had when I was eleven. I do not want anyone to be unaware of Satan's devices. I do want you to be aware that the enemy, Satan, will and can use dreams. If you want to skip this first particular dream, please resume reading at the asterisk. For those who would like to read further, please continue.

He drove us far from our homes (at least it seemed that way in the dream). The kidnapper hardly spoke a word. For some reason, the dream had us stop at a hardware-type store. This nightmare and others following would place weapons or tools that could be used as weapons, and I would find them and use them. If this nightmare had a specific purpose, it was to place a huge fear of being a victim and to, perhaps, encourage me to fight back with extreme violence. The man allowed Adam and I to come into the store, and while he was not looking at me, I snatched a few sticks of dynamite into my pocket. I also grabbed some matches. It became my goal to kill him first. I would blow him up in his sleep. The man grunted for us to follow him out of the store. Suspecting our time was ending, Adam and I nervously walked out with him. I felt we were going to die, and I felt even more intense fear.

The man drove us for what felt like another hour. (I'm quite sure the dream lasted less than ten minutes.) The crazy man drove far into a secluded field and finally stopped. He brought us out of the van, and I looked to see a tent that was shaped like a teepee. My heart pounded. The crazy man tied Adam and I to large poles. I remember he felt the sticks in my pocket, and he pulled them out. He shoved them in my face and asked, "Are these for me?" He sounded developmentally delayed. He turned away his mad stare and looked at Adam. I could see terror in Adam's eyes. He untied Adam and grabbed him by the arm, tugging violently. He pulled him into the tent.

I, up to this point, had never felt so much fear. I was dead, and I knew it. My mind raced. I had to get free! I heard a muffled no come from the tent. It was Adam.

What is he doing to you? I thought.

I heard Adam start screaming. (It really sounded like how he could sound, screaming.)

Krrrack. Krack-krack. Ch-kraack. Kraack.

The screaming stopped. It had sounded like branches being broken on a tree, except there was a wet sound as well, like a liquid surrounding the branches. I knew I had seconds left. The man flung the flap of his tent and dragged me into it. He was dripping with my best friend's blood, the wet sound.

I do not remember fighting him. I may have begun to look forward to an end of the fear. As he dragged me to the far end of the tent, I understood how Adam died. He was ripped to pieces. Blood was everywhere. I remember shooting a stare of hate at the man. I think I wanted to tear him apart. This dream, however, was meant for me to be a *victim*. The man grunted and told me to kneel. As my knees hit the ground, I felt them become wet with Adam's blood. His rough large hands grabbed my face, and his thumbs aimed for my eyes.

Then I saw the dream from a double screen, as if two cameras were filming this—one was from my direct point of view, and the other was from his point of view. From my point of view, I saw his thumbs coming directly for my eyes. It was like I was killing me and being killed at the same time. The first screen goes black as I close my eyes. Then I felt his thumbs rest briefly on my eyelids. I can see his thumbs on my eyes. Suddenly I felt intense pressure and pain. He pressed hard. I heard myself scream. His thumbs penetrated my eye sockets, and the last part I saw was blood streaming down my face. Both screens went black. The dream did not wake me, but when I did wake up, my eyes were sore, as if I had been rubbing them in my sleep. As you can imagine, I went to school traumatized about the dream and that my eyes were sore!

*I died. I am sure my heart kept beating in real life, but I died that night. The dream was so realistic that in the memory file of my mind, this happened. My best friend and I died! I felt it. I heard it. I smelled it. I saw it. I lived it! If it were not for me waking up for school the next morning, I would say that I died that night. I told Adam about it that afternoon. As usual, I did not tell my parents or seek guidance. I may have sworn that I would never be a victim, which would fall in line for what the enemy wanted.

My fifth-grade year was when these nightmares took place. I was eleven, going on twelve. I believe around the end of the school year I experienced a short, disturbing dream. If it were not for its high level of detail, I might think that it was just one of my normal nightmares. There was not any story to it. It lasted for a minute or two. It was very graphic and bloody, and it also shook me, emotionally.

The dream opened in a large barn. There was a large crowd of people there. I sat on a bleacher, and the crowd seemed to be excited. I heard an announcer, a voice over a microphone, drowning out the voices in the crowd. The announcer said something like, "Welcome to the first annual hog-cutting contest." I looked down and saw about a dozen large pigs. They did not move, but I could not see if they were tied. Standing over each similar-sized pig was a man with a chain saw in each one's hands. I heard the announcer say, "Start your saws." The high-pitched squeals of the pigs were louder than the twelve or so chain saws for just a brief time. I saw the horror, and the dream just ended. When I woke up, I was shaken, again.

In the sixth grade, I began to have nightmares about that ventriloquist puppet I had wanted so badly. I had a good run with Simon Sez. After I received him for Christmas in 1979, I practiced with him almost daily. I had used a variation of the voice Jay Johnson had used for Bob in *Soap*. Simon had a hard-plastic torso with a hole in the back large enough to have a grown man's hand in it. There was a pole in the hole that had a trigger that controlled his mouth. At the time, I thought that was a big deal, because all the other dummies had drawn strings to open their mouths. When you pull on the string, your arm moves, and your other arm would have to hold the dummy up straight. With the trigger mechanism, I could hold the puppet and move his mouth and turn his head all at once. I remember the feel of the cloth-fabric legs draping over my left arm, like it was sitting on my arm. It weighed, I believe, around five pounds.

I remember bringing it to Adam's house a few times. His dad belittled me about bringing it to his house. I may have embarrassed Adam, and I stopped bringing it. At my home, I continued to practice, and I worked up the nerve to ask my fourth-grade teacher to do a little show for the class. The show went well. During and after the show, the teacher allowed students to ask me questions. I liked the attention, and I remember feeling comfortable about performing.

When I was around twelve years old, I had what I believe were recurring nightmares about Simon Sez. It felt like I was dropped into a scene where Simon had moved threateningly against me. In this dream that I believe I had maybe three times, I was not a victim. I was a defender of my own life. The dream starts and the puppet moves, arms outstretched, toward me. I do not have to find a weapon in this dream, because a hatchet is already in my right hand. I just start swinging and cutting my ventriloquist doll to pieces. I cut off the head and the arms, legs, and torso until it stops moving. The dream ends. I did not tell anyone, and after some time, I decide to stop playing with Simon and I put him in Scott's closet.

Another talent was being explored when I was in the sixth grade. I had signed up for concert band and was learning percussion. Band helped me stay busy and emotionally grounded, at first. I did not miss Simon. One day, I was looking for something under my bed and was mildly horrified to find Simon under there. I promptly took him back to Scott's closet and hid him. That was the end of my three-year ventriloquism career.

During my middle school and high school years, I had recurring dreams about shadowy threatening figures roaming outside my home. I had at least one similar dream that took place in Adam's home. It seemed like the electricity in both homes did not work, but the sky was a dark gray. There was just enough light to clearly see in the homes. Every dream there was a useful weapon placed near me, either a hatchet or a machete. These dreams were never violent because either they ended before any attacks or I would awaken before it came to violence. They still terrorized me, because I did not know who was lurking outside and if they would attack. I just remember grabbing the available weapon, and not long after, the dream would end. All these dreams haunted me, but none more than one I had when I was around twenty years old.

I am not sure, even today, if it was a dream, a vision, or a kind of "knowing." It haunted me beyond anything I had ever seen or experienced, whether in my reality or in dreams. The vision or dream scared me so much that I would embrace the thought of killing myself, anything to avoid the fate the vision seemed to foretell. It is a deeply personal vision or dream. I have learned, as a licensed counselor, the meanings we attach to things are deeply personal and can profoundly affect us. I did not want the vision to happen.

A small dank motel room was the setting. It was dark, save for a small table lamp. I saw a sad, lonely old man sitting in a worn recliner-type chair. He was sitting near a small table with crackers or cookies (I could not tell which) and a cup next to it. Behind him, I saw the neon motel sign with vacancy written in red. The old man was me if I continued to live. If I did not follow through with Satan's wanting me to lose it, go off, and go on a rampage and kill myself after, I could look forward to dying poor, alone, in a most depressing motel room.

"Never!" was my response as a younger man.

The young man I would become, before receiving Jesus, would gladly avoid that "fate" at nearly any cost, which meant an early death for me whether it was by my own hand or I put myself in a situation where I could be killed by law enforcement or maybe an armed homeowner. I resolved that old man would never be.

In His Presence

Fast-forward thirty years, of course I have a different view about almost everything compared to my exceedingly early adult years. This includes giving up the foolish idea that I should be the one who determines how long I live. At this writing, it has been almost twenty-nine years since I received Christ. I have had plenty of times since then when I was not with friends, family, or coworkers, but not for a second have I been alone. I want to pull some light into this darker chapter by sharing that this year, 2019, I purposely visited that memory of the old man in the motel room. Whether that man represents me or not, I am not afraid to not have loved ones in my life. I cannot be afraid of that dream or vision. I cannot let it control my future decisions. God has been with me since March 15, 1991. I will never be alone again. I have no future to fear, while God is with me.

> Anyone who loves me will obey my teaching. My Father will love them, and we will come to them and make our home with them. (John 14:23)

> And I will ask the Father, and He will give you another advocate to help you and be with you forever—the Spirit of truth. The world cannot accept him because it neither sees him nor knows him. But you know him, for he lives with you and will be in you. (John 14: 16, 17)

As you can imagine, the nightmares stirred a lot of fear in me. As I mentioned at the beginning of this chapter, I was feeling pressure to be brave and to try to be a mature middle school kid. Fear had to be addressed, and the decisions that I describe in the next chapter would set my course straight to Hell.

7

MY PRETEENAGE
SOUNDTRACK (VOL. 1)

I wanted to be set free from the fear and torment.

OPEN FOR A LIMITED TIME

Jesus said, "A farmer went out to sow his seed. As he was scattering the seed, some fell along the path, and the birds came and ate it up… When anyone hears the message about the kingdom and does not understand it, the evil one comes and snatches away what was sown in their heart" (Matthew 13:4, 5, 19).

I stood along with several other children in the main sanctuary of the Sebastian United Methodist Church. In its day in the 1970s, it was a medium-sized church, able to hold around a hundred people. The main sanctuary had two rows of wooden padded pews. The pews had the "giving envelopes" that I often would draw pictures on during the sermons. (Church was a bit of a battle between my father and me when I slouched or doodled.) The children, including myself of various ages, were attending the church's vacation Bible school. We were learning children's Christian songs. I attended the church's summer program three times. My mother confirmed that I had attended it three times and that she had been a teacher in my class during one of the years. She said that she did not know anything about the Bible during a recent conversation, but "I could teach you kids the rosary—of course that wasn't needed."

My second and third times at the church's summer program stand out in my memory. My first experience, I mostly remember drinking cherry Kool-Aid and eating Nilla Wafers during snack times.

There were three songs that have stood out to me when I attended the second time. They are "He's Got the Whole World in His Hands," "Jesus Loves Me," and "Behold, Behold." I may have learned more songs than those three. I have heard my wife teach children at her prior Christian-based private school a song called "Father Abraham." It did not sound familiar to me at all. The songs at my church made a positive impression on me when I believe I learned them when I was nine years old. They were nice to me. While doing some research about these songs, the "Jesus Loves Me[42]" song, I learned, had come from a poem spoken to comfort a dying child. The writer of the poem was Susan Warner (1819–1885). Her sister Anna Bartlett Warner (1827–1915) converted it to a Christian hymn. A man named William Batchelder Bradbury (1816–1868) added the lines

Yes, Jesus loves me,
Yes Jesus loves me,
Yes, Jesus loves me.
The Bible tells me so.

The song became one of the most popular hymns in the world, especially among children.

We also learned a song called "He's Got the Whole World in His Hands[43]." The song was written in 1927 by Master Sergeant Obie Edwin and became a pop hit in 1957–1958. As I learned the words of the song, along with the other kids, I began to take in the lyrics. The song lyrics teach that not only does God have the whole world in His hands, but also "He holds the itty-bitty baby in His hands." This song was popular with the other children in the program.

---

[42] https://en.wikipedia.org/wiki/Jesus_Loves_Me.
[43] https://en.wikipedia.org/wiki/He's_Got_the_Whole_World_in_His_Hands.

Another song that my group learned to sing was called "Behold Behold[44]." The song is influenced by a passage in the Bible. Revelation 3:20 (New King James Version) says, "Behold, I stand at the door. If anyone hears My voice and opens the door, I will come into him and dine with him, and he with Me." This was the song that stuck with me, but it seemed like the teachers at the Bible school were not able to explain its significance. I came away from the first vacation Bible school open to wanting a relationship with God.

I remember as a child believing in God. I did not know who He was. As a young kid, around six, I would talk sometimes out loud to God. (This would continue until I was at least ten or eleven.) I would believe "God" would answer me too sometimes. I saw the George Burns's and John Denver movie *Oh, God![45]* I was at that very impressionable age of seven to eight when I was trying to figure out how to build my own droid and watching the night sky for any sign of UFOs. I wanted to talk to God like John Denver's character did. So I did talk to God. Sometimes, I think I may have gotten answers a few times. I believe God was involved in my life, but I know the enemy was too. I have learned that God, the Holy Spirit, always points believers and nonbelievers to God, the Son, Jesus Christ. My conversations with "God" when I was younger never included who Jesus is, the Savior of the world. I do not believe the being I spoke to, as a child, was God. As years passed, I began to close myself off from a relationship with God.

WHICH DEATH IS TRUE?

I was open to wanting to go to Heaven over Hell. Someone at the church, at some point, preached or taught about Hell. As a child, I believed in Hell. There was a "knowing" that it must be under the earth. After hearing the message, I had a mental image that I believe was influenced by not only the message but also cartoons,

---

[44] www.songlyrics.com/david-kauffman/behold-lyrics.
[45] https://en.wikipedia.org/wiki/Oh,_God!_(film).

like Sylvester the Cat[46]. It was dark, cavernous, and there was a lake of fire. In my mind, the lake was not big. My mind imprinted the lake near my home as being the size of the lake of fire. (That is significant.) As a child, I wondered, *Could people be burning underneath my feet?*

I have heard arguments and proffered thoughts from liberal theologians, secularists, and assorted atheists and agnostics that the doctrine of Hell is false and a way to place undue guilt on people. I am thankful for hearing a sermon or teaching about Hell when I was younger, because it built an emotional guardrail. A wariness that it could be real acted as a staff to this wayward sheep. The enemy would eventually chip at that fear, and in the end, I feared living much more than dying. The enemy would finally get me to disbelieve in a literal Hell, and the emotional guardrail came down. Seemingly, at that point, nothing would stop me.

As years passed, I began to close myself off from a relationship with God. I increasingly used His and Jesus's name in vain with curses of anger. At twelve years old, I bought a beautiful bald eagle kite and told God to "you know what" when the kite was forever lost and ripped to a large tree on the day I bought it!

> I had a thought, when you die, it is like
> lights going out forever. It is nothing. You cease
> to exist. No more pain. Lights out.

That is a compelling *lie* that I woke up to one morning when I was around twelve or thirteen. I thought about it. It sounded logical. It seemed to match some of the lessons I was learning in public school in the early 1980s. In the years that I went to school, organized prayer had been ruled unconstitutional by nine men in black robes (the US Supreme Court). I closed my heart to God more and more. The last time I participated in vacation Bible school at the age of twelve, I do not remember any teachings, just joking around with

---

[46] https://looneytunes.fandom.com/wiki/Satan's_Waitin'.

some of the other kids. One of the kids who shared my first name became a best friend for about one year. I wish you well, Jeff.

I grew up believing that death was that you go to Heaven if you are good and Hell if you are bad. Now, as a preteen, I was believing the demonic lie spoken to me, "It's lights out." No, it is not. I will hold that evidence for when I received Jesus at the age of twenty-one.

> Just as people are destined to die once, and after that to face justice. (Hebrews 9:27)

> For God so loved the world that he gave his one and only Son, that whoever believes in him shall not perish but have eternal life. (John 3:16)

KNOWINGLY

> "But Jesus called the children to him and said, 'Let the little children come to me, and do not hinder them, for the kingdom of God belongs to such as these." (Luke 18:16)

Jesus clearly states that children, including babies, the unborn, toddlers, and school-aged ones, who do not know what sin is go directly to Heaven should their lives pass on Earth. Although babies are born with the same sin passed down from Adam's disobedience, they do not know they are sinning. Many Christians, including pastors, teachers, and laypersons, hold that there comes a point in a person's life when they knowingly rebel against God and engage in "willful" sin—meaning that they mean to do the wrong thing. This age is different for every child, but it tends to be around the ages of twelve to thirteen. Jesus was around twelve years old when He stayed at the Jewish Temple, listening to rabbis, while his parents and other family members unknowingly left for Nazareth. In the Jewish custom, children are ushered into the responsibilities at the age of twelve.

For me, there was a time when my turn away from God and His ways were deliberate. I knowingly got into my parents' cupboard and got drunk on rum and soda. I knowingly walked around my block, with a friend, smoking a marijuana joint his father had given to my friend. I knowingly would rifle through pages of hard-core pornography that teen, who abused me, left for me. I blasphemed God, and some things that I did as a teenager could make me shudder with the thought of how much I deserved Hell and how close I came to be going there!

Ephesians 2:4–5 says, "But because of his great love for us, God, who is rich in mercy, made us alive with Christ even when we were dead in transgressions—it is by grace you have been saved."

Twelve to thirteen is when I knowingly walked away from religion, but I believe there remained a hunger for truth. It just seems a mainline religious church was not equipped to tell me in a way I could understand. The good seed of God's Word had been planted, but as the parable of sower indicates, "Birds came and ate it up" (Matthew 13:4). My heart was open to God, but for a limited time. I grew bored and disillusioned with religion. It seemed to have no answer for my fears and growing sense of inadequacy. So you will see the steps of me walking away from Truth and the consequences it brought on me.

I did not hunger for religion, for righteousness, but for darkness. The attraction to darkness and death increased, but I still had a fear of evil. Around the ages of twelve to thirteen, I inadvertently became an ally of evil to stave off its inherent threat to me. I would begin to submerge myself into what I call the genre of death, including violent movies, books, and music. It was like an unholy baptism, further altering my personal values and philosophy toward everything.

CHILDHOOD'S FAREWELL

In the fifth grade, we were the big kids, upper classman on campus, but then inevitably we were promoted to the sixth grade. Most of the kids in my class would go to what used to be called Sebastian River Middle Junior High School. A few weeks before our elementary school careers ended for the summer, our class visited the middle school. During the visit to the school, we were introduced to the school's band and their director. I had thought Ranee would join, and because I knew Adam was interested, I decided to join during the summer. I chose percussion (drums), because after having pneumonia and being hospitalized for it when I was ten, my lungs were not strong enough to handle the trumpet or wind instrument. At this point in my testimony, many things were going wrong in my life, but band kept me grounded. It kept me grounded because of a sense of shared interests in a talented community of kids who would become some of my friends. I was not just aimless. Band instilled some confidence in me, apart from a growing aggression. Band awakened an ambition in me that was healthy.

My parents drove my brother and me out to a music store in Melbourne, Florida, that sold and rented instruments. They let me pick out a beautiful, new silver-and-blue snare drum, along with sticks and a practice pad. I felt proud to bring the drum in its case to the band's instrument room, like an armory for instruments. My time with the new drum was short-lived because my parents found an antique, used snare drum for a much cheaper price. I turned the new drum in and felt like a "poor kid" bringing a less shiny, clearly older drum to school. I did possess the story that the drum belonged to a man who played in jazz bands. The other kids playing percussion had new snare drums, so I believed (some of the minority kids did not have their own drum, at all) I would grow to appreciate my snare drum.

The first days of sixth grade were so different from elementary school. You may have shared the similar experiences of waking up earlier, meeting in a "homeroom" for attendance, being assigned your own locker, and nearly sprinting between one class to another. I believe I experienced what some mental health professionals would call "adjustment disorder with anxiety." I was extremely nervous during the first weeks and months of my middle school career. I had to take three classes with a large African American female teacher, who, to me, was just mean to the whole class. She seemed to have little patience and did not like repeating instructions if I wanted to clarify them. I did not know that Mrs. Scott was pregnant, and I would never see her again once Christmas break, 1981, would begin.

I was relieved that Mrs. Scott was replaced by Mrs. Alexander for the rest of the school year. Mrs. Alexander was very patient and nice, and my grades improved from Cs to Bs.

The sixth grade had been split into two groups, and unfortunately, Adam, Ranee, and most of my fifth-grade class were in the other group. Another situation presented and had to be faced. The middle school had students coming from three different and diverse areas of Indian River County. African American children from Wabasso and rural white and Hispanic children from Fellsmere were joining white, African Americans (which in the 1980s we called black kids), and Hispanic children from the Sebastian Elementary School my friends and I had come from. Because of my predominantly easygoing nature, keeping friends was not too difficult for me. I, however, was not extremely outgoing, so making friends was not easy for me. I believe that during the first few days and weeks, I was missing several opportunities to try to connect to the students from other schools, because I was experiencing heightened anxiety over adapting to every new experience.

Overall, being in concert band was an incredibly positive experience, but I experienced several verbal clashes and one led to a short-lived but violent fight. In the sixth grade, my band class was in the first period. One early morning, two of the African American boys in percussion were "mouthing off" to me, and at a certain point, I dished some verbal abuse back to them. Before the end of the class, the percussionists were to pack their drums in their cases to be turned back to the instrument room. While I was breaking down my snare drum stand, I suddenly felt the full weight of "TJ," one of the kids I talked back to, on my back. He jumped me! I remember slowly standing up, with TJ still on my back. Once I stood as tall as I could, with a boy who weighed at least as much as me, if not more, I ran backward. The event happened so quickly. I was shocked and angry, and then aggression took over. With TJ holding on, I ran at least fifteen feet and smashed his almost equally thin body into the concrete-blocked wall behind us. TJ let out a pained grunt, let go of me, and fell to the floor. I looked back, briefly, but avoided looking him in the eye. Feeling a mixture of embarrassment and shock that

I would have the strength to do that, I tossed the rest of my drum parts into the case and turned it in. TJ and I never spoke of the incident until we found ourselves playing in the Vero Beach High School Band as bass drummers. During one practice, TJ shared that I had hurt him, and he shared that I had cracked two of his ribs. I apologized and he apologized. I replayed the memory, and at the state of mind of where I was in the tenth grade, I felt some pride. Besides the conflict with TJ, the entire school was on the verge of several fights between members of the different races.

"A race war?" I nervously asked.

Yes, during my sixth-grade year, a rumor not associated with my snare drum incident spread around my middle school that at least two different groups of students wanted to fight. It felt like the entire school, including students, teachers, and principals, was on edge on a certain week when it seemed the students from Fellsmere wanted to fight the students from Wabasso. In 1982, we knew it to be a war between the rednecks and the black kids. The word was widely spread that during the Friday of that week, the two groups would meet and fight. I cannot stress the tension that I felt at this school that week. It raised my anxieties, and I expected a schoolwide, violent brawl. The administrators decided (and to this day it does not make sense to me) to have the entire school dismiss earlier than normal and be gathered in an area that was outside but had shelter. So the students were packed together like sardines, while teachers and administrators guarded us. I remember standing in the loud roar of several hundred students talking at once when… *Thud!* In the back of my head, I got hit by something that sounded and felt like metal. (Brass knuckles maybe?) I do not know, but I thought, *You're kidding me. I get hit?* I quickly turned around, but no one looked guilty. I only saw a kaleidoscope of faces. It turned out the race war did not happen and never happened during the years I attended that school. I, however, internalized the incident. I took note that out of the hundreds of kids, I was the one that got "knocked in the head." I now can see how that may not be universally true. Whoever had the blunt metal object could have hit other students in the head. No one complained, which fed my paranoia about life turning harder against me.

I, true to my nature, did not broadcast and complain that I had been hit in the head! An incident that was supposed to involve dozens of students from two different localities ended with me being a victim.

This incident may have awakened a fear that had to be dealt with. I felt I was targeted by someone because he thought I was weak, nice. That was going to have to change, and during the next few years, I began to open myself up more to darkness. I may have unconsciously reasoned that to be rid of a fear of evil, I would become an ally of evil. After all, "good" does not bother anyone, because it's good.

MY PRETEENAGE
SOUNDTRACK (VOL. 2)

Fear and torment that so plagued my useless existence.

"WHY WON'T YOU DIE, SCAREDY-CAT?"

"There is no fear in love. But perfect love drives out fear, because fear has to do with punishment" (1 John 4:18).

I, however, was walking away from God's love—the One that would deliver me many years later. So fears clung to me. I hated fear. Many times, it made me want to shrivel up and die. I could not let it stay. Fear was going to drive me *insane*. It had to go. Having the "scaredy-cat" label might have been cute when I was younger, but I was feeling serious pressure to develop with my teenaged peers. I experienced a dread about my personal future. I felt an energy that wanted me to break loose, rebel. Yet I feared negative consequences. A beast wanted to be free, but the possibility of mere troubles in life held it in place. I was an unduly, fearful kid.

One Friday night, like most Friday nights, I walked over to Adam's house. When he met me at the door, he said, "We're going to pick up a video tonight. We're leaving soon."

I said, "Cool. What kind of movie do you want to get?"

Adam said that he saw a horror movie the last time he and his family went to Sebastian's one and only video rental store. (For my younger readers, before there were DVDs and Blu-rays, there were movies placed on VHS that you could rent at video stores.)[47]

"What's it called?" I asked.

"*The Gates of Hell*," Adam said.

I tagged along with Adam and his mother and his little sister to the video store. The movie was there, and from the cover artwork, it looked like a zombie movie. Adam's mom rented the movie, and we returned to his house to watch it. I remember Adam and I sat on the floor, and someone turned out the lights, and the movie played.

In the following paragraph, I allude to one specific scene to provide context of how vicious horror movies can be. *The Gates of Hell* was released in 1980. There is a Christian saying, "Be careful little eyes what you see," that should be heeded. My testimony presents that Satan will use anything to turn souls away from God's goodness, and he is involved in one way or another with horror movies.

I certainly had no conscious plan to watch a movie so shockingly violent and graphic that I would desensitize myself to gore and horror, but it seems that it did. The movie was produced by gore-shock Italian director Lucio Fulci. The movie was renowned for having original ideas and some story rather than just having deceased people busting out of graves and attacking people. I do not remember much about the movie, overall. I just remember an infamous scene when some demonic figure causes a young lady to begin to bleed from her eyes and then in excruciating slow speed causes her to vomit her internal organs. That shocked me! When the movie ended, I am quite sure we talked about what we had just watched. I believe I remember also feeling a mixture of fear and excitement when Adam suggested we rent more movies. I was all in.

Interestingly, the next few movies that we watched were also supposed to be shocking, but they paled in comparison. They were a letdown. A definition of "desensitized" is "having been made less likely to feel shock or distress at scenes of cruelty or suffering by over

---

[47] https://www.cinemablend.com/dvds/Grindhouse.

exposure to such images." It seems that I inadvertently accomplished this with one movie!

By the ages of twelve to thirteen, I had watched several horror movies already. A perk of getting older seems to be gaining the privilege to be able to go to bed at an ever-later time. While being able to stay up later, in the 1980s, television shows were changing their standards. Edgier shows were no longer shown at the ten o'clock hour (eastern time zone), but at the nine o'clock hour also. In addition, horror movie commercials would be shown, and some of the scenes scared me when I was ten or eleven, but I would want to watch them too. After my family signed up to receive a premium movie channel, where there was no censorship of movies, I was able to see these movies almost anytime they played. I became a fan of horror movies. I saw movies about mass murders, ghost stories centered around vengeance, and demonic possession of children. I am no longer a fan of horror movies. I have not seen a horror movie since I was twenty-three years old. For me, I learned that they are a doorway of possibly inviting demonic oppression back into my life. What is a doorway for me could be a doorway for you, or it could be a type of music or anything that does not specifically glorify God. Do not forget that Satan wants to know what you are open to. I was open to aggression and vengeance. It seems I would be attracted to other forms of media that could fulfill my growing appetite.

There was a highly effective solution—in fact the only solution—to my fears. That is faith in Jesus who is ever faithful to those who put their hope in Him.

> The Lord is my light and my salvation; whom shall, I fear? The Lord is the strength of my life; of whom shall I be afraid. (Psalm 27:1)

Presently, I have counseled children about how to build inner strength, often introducing biblical concepts that are in line with cognitive behavioral therapy techniques. I have taught the children that the stronger they are on the inside, the less they will feel the need to project strength on the outside (i.e., children may be confident in their abilities and not have to announce their strengths through aggressive behaviors). In middle and high schools, I did not know anything about anything. I see that my major pitfall was not communicating any of my issues with either of my parents. In my secondary schools, I was exceedingly thin, and although I attempted to keep up with my jock friend, Adam, I perceived myself to be weak. Since I thought I was weak, I was vulnerable. To me, it meant that I could be beaten up. That was not a constant threat, but because of my nightmares, being a victim was unacceptable. Opening myself up to more violent media slowly began to make my over-the-top niceness, and goodness become calloused, and a bitterness began to take hold.

It was around mid-1982 that my mother called me out and attempted to redirect me as the word "hate" appeared excessively in my speech. You would think I hated everything. I hate that show. I hate this food. I hate my teacher. I hate this kid, that kid, and especially that other kid! I was feeling it too. "Don't criticize my drumming, you——." Jesus said that good people bring out and reveal to others the goodness stored in their hearts. An evil person, reveals his evil, eventually. "For out of the abundance of the heart his mouth speaks" (Luke 6:45).

Many children and adolescents will say hate or heavier, hurtful words, and though developmentally, it may fall within normal teenage behavior—that does not negate that they are, indeed, speaking about what is in their hearts. I encourage you to listen to your children and call them out if you hear aggressive or ungodly words come out of their mouths. Please, set a positive example as well. As a former child protective investigator, I have been in homes where the parents or children or both used excessive profanity. They don't call it cursing for nothing. Their homes' atmospheres were thick with tension, disrespect, and hatred. All are marks of possible demonic activity.

Atari, ET, Arcades, and a Vacation

In the midst of making uninformed, bad decisions and beginning to reap the first bitter harvests, life was really good during the summer 1982. I felt that Adam's and my friendship was strong. Adam shared with me his interest in collecting some comic books. He showed me and allowed me to read many of his Marvel *X-Men* comics while I was at his home. He had his comics in special plastic bags with white cardboard backing. I learned that his comics were in mint condition, and if I bent a page or damaged a comic in any way, he would kick my butt! I also learned that a beautifully drawn X-Men member, the long red-haired Jean Gray, code named "Phoenix," would cause me to like red-headed girls and women when I was older. Another *X-Men* character Logan or "Wolverine" was an intense antiheroic character that had no qualms about killing enemies from special metal claws that popped out of his wrists. Of course, I took to his character. Having another shared interest with Adam strengthened our friendship through that busy summer.

In 1982, it was a revolutionary year for me and I believe millions of other children and adults with the invention of home video games and arcades popping up in nearly every town.[48] It did pull us into our homes or friends' homes and to arcades or gas stations that had the latest games available. Several times a week, Adam and I and sometimes other friends would ride our bikes to a gas station/convenience store to play Pac-Man. Perhaps a hundred quarters were pumped into the machine. We were spellbound to this little yellow circle that ate dots and were chased around by four ghosts, called Inky, Blinky, Pinky, and Clyde. One quarter gave you three Pac-Man lives, and if he touched a ghost, he lost a life.

Pac-Man was a huge phenomenon that inspired a pop song called "Pac-Man Fever" as well as licensed clothing, toys, a Saturday morning cartoon, and bootlegged knockoffs. It was during this cultural craze that my family went on a cross-country vacation for the first two weeks of June 1982. Immediately, after my brother earned

---

[48] https://en.wikipedia.org/wiki/Atari.

his high school diploma, we set off on the adventure in our light-blue full-sized van.

The notable and relevant memories of that trip include my father, having been diagnosed with multiple sclerosis in 1980, a disease that attacks the nervous system, took medicine that caused unpredictable mood swings and anger outbursts. The beginning leg of the trip, however, was positive. We left exceedingly early in the morning, and after an all-day drive, we stayed at my great-aunt and great-uncle's home in Rock Hill, South Carolina. I remember their backyard being lit up by dozens of fireflies. The visit seemed to be positive, and after visiting a museum, we left for my mom's hometown of Eerie, Pennsylvania. On the way, we were stuck in a tough area of West Virginia. While walking with my mother, I told her I learned that she should carry her purse more casually (she had a death grip on it), because thieves, I learned somewhere, target people who look like they are carrying something of great value. She loosened her grip.

We arrived in Eerie and learned that the northern states were still experiencing cold nights—too cold for Floridians. My parents had planned to stay in less expensive campgrounds, but they decided to stay in motels instead.

One of my famous clashes with my father took place in a restaurant, somewhere in the Midwest. While eating dinner, I accidentally dropped my fork. My twelve-year-old hand quickly began to rise for a nearby waitress's attention.

"No," Dad said very sternly. "Pick it up. You can use it."

"But…it dropped."

"Use it!"

I snatched the fork, and I could not dissociate the thought that this fork landed on carpeted floor. Who knows how dirty the floor is? I obeyed, but the large reservoir of resentment toward my father grew more that day. I did not understand that his disease and his medication could cause anger outbursts. We were probably four days into a two- to three-week vacation, so I just made the best of it and avoided my father.

This is difficult to write, but I was enlightened after I received Christ, that I could be turned against others when I was younger. I have said to others that by the age of five, I hated my dad. By the age of ten, I wanted him dead. By the age of eighteen, I wanted to be the one to do it. Before I met the family of three that possibly came within twenty-four hours of dying by my hand, in Tampa, Florida, my father was my first and only target. By the age of twenty, I wanted to end the Gilbert family line. This meant I had to go too.

Now, getting back to the vacation. When we arrived in Detroit, Michigan, around 11:00 p.m., my father stopped at a red light. My brother and I saw something flash to our right, and we looked out the window. It looked like two flashlights were erratically moving inside a dark store.

"Dad. There's a burglary in progress. Run the light!" I said. About then, the light turned green, and we were off to a motel.

The only other relevant memory was when my mother was driving us back toward Florida. My mother and father were arguing about something, while my father was lying on the back couch-looking seat. The hollering became quite loud, and I felt my usual high level of anxiety. My father sternly told her, "When we get home, we're going to have words."

Without missing a beat, my mother shot back, "I hope it's goodbye!"

Scott and I looked at each other and I mouthed the word, "Wow!"

I understand now that my father experienced his own anxieties, and they could be triggered by vacations. It seemed he worried about money, and although he probably did not mean to, he could cause me to feel like we were all just an expense. This is a trait I have had to be vigilant against in my own family with my own interactions.

At some point during our return home, my mother called our pet sitter. We all learned that my pet iguana "Ingrid" died not long after we left for the vacation. Also, the family's parakeet died, possibly of a heart attack, during one of Florida's infamous electrical storms. The sitter, Mary, seemed devastated to have to give us the news. The parakeet "Tweety" died after lightning hit near our home. My father forgot that my iguana ate hibiscus flowers, and he sprayed insecticide on all our plants before we left. Ingrid was poisoned. Mary buried Ingrid in a coffee can in our backyard. Then she dug it up and placed Tweety's body in the same can. I was upset about the iguana, but relieved about Tweety. I was often tasked with cleaning the parakeet's cage, and I selfishly was okay with not having to do that chore anymore. I wanted to dig up the can after we got home and look at the bodies. I figured the iguana would look like a dinosaur skeleton. I dug their grave and found the iguana's skin was darkened and loose, but it was not skeletal yet. I looked at the remains with frustration and then buried it again. I did not think what I did was odd. I just thought I had to see them for closure and curiosity. I was mad, not sad.

During the summer of 1982, I caught what may have been my last wave of innocence. My brother drove my friend Alex and me to see Stephen Spielberg's *E. T.: The Extra Terrestrial*[49]. It was playing at what had been called the Plaza Theater in Vero Beach. I remember such a strong thunderstorm hit that Scott had to pull the car over, and we were almost late. *E. T.* emotionally rocked me. There is a psychological concept called mirroring. Research, called mirror neuron research, found that some people reflect gestures, complex movements, mouth movements, and emotions." When experts in dance or martial arts watch a performance, their brains are activated as if they themselves were performing. Neuroactivity can mirror emotions, intentions, and sensations of people or animals around us, even in movies, including horror movies.

E. T. was seen by millions of moviegoers, and many of us were so caught up in the story that we cried when the extraterrestrial friend of the main character, Elliot, said goodbye and went back to his home planet. I share, now, a testimonial from someone who was profoundly affected by the movie.

> *E. T.* is one of my all-time favorite movies.
> This movie blew me out of my seat as a kid,
> and still kills me every time I watch it... When

---

[49] https://www.rottentomatoes.com/m/et_the_extraterrestrial.

I returned from seeing *E.T.* for the first time, I couldn't talk for the rest of the day. I laid in my bed and cried for about five hours.

The end of the movie, when E.T. asks Elliot to go back to his planet and Elliot asks him to stay, broke me. I went in to see this movie with no expectations, except that it was made by the same director who did *Close Encounters of the Third Kind*. I mirrored *intensely* to this movie! I was lost in it, and I would feel like E.T. was leaving me. I felt that I regressed in my emotional development for a few months—I felt younger than thirteen. I wanted the doll. I got an E.T. doll. This is embarrassing, but during the beginning of the seventh grade, I could not wait to go home to the doll. Therefore, I believe that *E.T.* was my last "wave" of innocence that I would experience. The draw toward goodness was short, because around October our premium channel began playing *Halloween II*.

9

SCHOOL YEAR OF ANGST

*So deep did a seduction for darkness and
death become a part of who I was.*

WELCOME BACK

The seventh grade at Sebastian River Middle Junior High School brought some welcome and not-so-welcome changes. To my relief, my classes were with almost all my former fifth-grade classmates. Adam was in all my classes, including band. I was promoted to the next level of concert band, and I found an uneasy rivalry with a kid named Robby. He was the drum section leader, and he was not shy about letting me know he thought he was a better player than me. Being in this level of band meant that we would play at the middle school football games. We did not play half-time shows though. During pep rallies, the band played a remarkably simple tune called "Pack Jam[50]." You would think by the students' response that we were a rock band! They went crazy when we played it. Overall, my seventh-grade year was a good year, but it had its own issues too.

The drawback of being with my old classmates was that I had been out of their clique for a year. Plus, I now had to wear glasses, and I was still exceedingly thin, which added to my feelings of inadequacy. One day, I noticed my shoulders were narrow and a bit

---

[50] https://www.youtube.com/watch?v=oXPpng1dQag.

hunched. I stood up straight in class, and as hard as I could, I forced my shoulders down. I've had extremely broad shoulders since that day I was disgusted with my body image. A new boy from New York joined our class group too. He was even more boastful and seemingly self-confident than Adam! I felt jealousy when he and Paul hung out during and after classes. Ranee was also in many of my classes, and that was the year that my crush on her would move on to other girls who were clearly (in my mind, now) out of my league.

On the first day of seventh grade, I had a geology class with many of my prior classmates. The end of sixth grade wore me out with the schoolwork and homework. I was becoming an underachiever. The geology teacher called roll and came to my name.

"Jeff Gilbert. Are you Scott Gilbert's brother?"

"Yes," I said.

"Well, he was a good student. I'm going to expect a lot from you."

"You're not going to get it," I said under my breath, and she did not.

Scott was the hypersocial one in my family. He talked enough for him and me and my parents combined. He never shut up, and to this day, he still talks over everyone. If you discuss a topic that makes him feel uncomfortable, he'll change the subject. He was able to relate to adults well. Me? The subconscious thoughts mentioned from chapter 2, of not being able to utterly understand anyone and that they would never understand me, held me back socially. My fear of evil was decreasing, but my timidity around others was growing stronger! There was a positive event that had happened during the cross-country vacation that impacted my seventh-grade year. My family had driven back to our old neighborhood in Colorado. During our very brief stay, we visited our neighbors in Arvada. While my parents reminisced with the neighbors, my parents spoke highly of living in Florida. It must have had a tremendous impact, because by fall of that year, the neighbors moved to Sebastian. Their daughter Gail became like a big sister to me. They arrived in Sebastian around Halloween and so did the feeling of increased confidence, almost like a mild manic episode that lasted through the season.

Around this same time, our premium movie channel played the sequel to *Halloween*. At the end of John Carpenter's *Halloween* movie, the antagonist mute killer was shot six times by his psychiatrist and fell off a second-story balcony. The final scene had the psychiatrist look at the lawn below, and Michael Myers was not there. *Halloween II*[51], released in 1981, seemed to be an inevitable sequel. I watched it with my mother and brother. The movie began where the first movie ended, and the main protagonist Laurie Strode was taken to a local hospital because of injuries from trying to evade the killer. New characters were introduced before most of them were killed. Many of them were annoying, and I think they were written that way so the watcher had less sympathy for them. I was not as enamored with Michael Myers as I had been the year before, and by the end of the film, the audience was led to believe that the murderer was killed in a fire. I may have experienced a short burst of satisfaction that the killer *who never talked* was back, but I did not know what to think or feel after he "died." (He would return in 1988 for *Halloween 4*[52].) So I believe I came away feeling conflicted. I do not remember experiencing strong feelings of that self-confidence for a few years after. It felt like it went dormant for several years, only to be *completely* awakened in 1988 when I was nineteen.

I had a good time trick-or-treating that year with Adam and some neighborhood classmates. This was the first year I was permitted to go out without parental supervision. It was not all clean fun. I am ashamed now to share that an awkward girl from across County Road 512 and her awkward mother stayed with the group, and behind their backs, we made fun of them. They did not stay with us the whole time, and we continued "cutting up" about other things.

The enjoyable time I had was lost on me, though. It seems during those years, most of the lessons I was learning were negative. I believe the reason the creepy atmosphere of Halloween was weak that night was because I was among friends. I felt valued and a sense of some significance. As a mental health counselor, I understand how

---

[51] en.wikipedia.org/wiki/Halloween_II_(1981_film).

[52] https://en.wikipedia.org/wiki/Halloween_4:_The_Return_of_Michael_Myers.

averse the effects of long-term isolation can bring. It affects a person's mental health, and in the spiritual realm, it gives opportunity for the enemy to tempt a person into various destructive ideas and actions. (You will witness this in my near future.) The lesson of the importance of having and maintaining meaningful positive friendships was lost on me. The more isolated I was, the stronger in the Halloween "spirit" I would be. The reverse was also true.

"I'M TELLING YA"

Adam, my popular friend, began dating a girl, around late fall, who was an eighth grader, and she was in my band class. Holly was a pretty and an approachable girl. She was down to earth and not pretentious and was friendly to everyone. I learned, sadly, that she passed away in 2013, six years ago from this writing. (I had been attempting to find her weeks before I learned of her death through a social media site. I wanted to share how God had been gracious to me.) With me, at least, she left her influence that remains with me today. In the 1970s and 1980s, when someone agreed with someone, they would usually say, "You're telling me." Holly would say, "I'm telling ya," when she did not say anything, but she just agreed. Maybe it's a regional thing or her family said it. I do not know. I just know that at my current age, I have only heard this phrase from her. I liked her saying, so I have used it and I remember how cool she was every time. I dedicate this section in her memory, for several months later, she would be my first date.

In the late fall of 1982, however, Holly was with Adam. My Friday nights routine of going to his house and watching a car-action show called *Knight Rider* had been disrupted. Adam would have her over to watch a video, and then his father would drive her home. Even then, me being no Casanova thought it would be better to take a girl out to dinner and a movie! I do not remember being too jealous. Adam was my best friend during this time, and I would be a jerk if I tried to create drama to break them up. (So I did not create drama.) It did cause me to like Holly more. I will admit. I waited and experienced some boring nights at home. In time, Holly and

I became better friends. Holly and Adam did not stay together for very long. At that age, you could say it was long, but I think they broke up after two or three months. They remained close friends, and she called Adam her "brother." That is when I remember feeling some jealousy, and probably in a pity move, I became Holly's "other" brother. I experienced my first rage attack while on a bus, sitting diagonally from them, alone. I believed I was being ignored or maybe patronized by both. I was standing against the window side of the bench seat. Suddenly I felt a rush of heat, darkness, and anger. I pulled my right leg away from the side of the bus and forced my heel straight back! I felt the violent impact at once. A loud metallic thud reverberated in the bus. I was in excruciating pain, but my anger and pride kept my face strong. (Thirty-one years later, I would need an x-ray on my right foot for something unrelated, and the technician found a hairline fracture on my right heel.) That anger outburst happened a short time after I lost a close four-legged member of my family after a brief illness.

THE SHORT LIVES OF DUFFY AND HIS BROTHERS

Let me take you back to that cool October day in 1977. It was the day the oppression began, but it was also the day our sheltie Heather gave birth to four healthy puppies. Whatever dark thoughts I had experienced after the school bus dropped me off was quickly forgotten when I arrived home and heard high-pitch grunting.

"The puppies are here!" I shouted.

"Shhhh. Don't disturb them. We're getting ready to take them to the vet," Mom said.

I would have to stay home due to limited space in the car. My father's parents—my grandparents from Kansas—were visiting at the time. They went to the vet, and my father watched me. I was so excited, but anxiety came over me as I thought about wanting to keep at least one of them! That would make us a family of three dogs, with our eight-year-old Chihuahua. That would be asking a lot, but really, I wanted to keep them all!

Heather's puppies were initially named Leroy (after his father's name), Peanuts (the runt of the litter), Zeke (who most looked like the mother), and Petey (who had a spot on his face, like *the Little Rascals* dog called Petey). They could fit easily into the palm of my eight-year-old hand. I was not allowed to touch them for several days. Their eyes remained closed for around five weeks if my memory is correct. (All I know is I could not wait to see their eyes!) While I was beginning to have rough days at school and bullies were coming out of the woodwork, I largely forgot my problems when I came home to them.

At first, I took to Petey, but over time, Leroy stole my heart and attention. I never saw his father, but my mother described him as being smaller and being a darker brown than Heather. Heather was large for a Shetland sheepdog. Leroy's, along with his three brothers', expressive eyes opened, and the puppies were big enough to play with. They were also big enough to start to be house-trained, and I would wince when I saw them get their little noses rubbed in their pee, receive a quick swat on their behinds with a rolled-up newspaper, and then put outside immediately. It seemed cruel to me, but it seemed to be effective. They were house-trained before their owners bought them. That was tough. I said goodbye to three of the puppies sometimes after they were bought and I returned from school. I was so glad the family chose to keep Leroy, who my brother named Sir Isaac McDuff or Duffy for short.

Sadly, in a matter of a few years, all of Heather's puppies, except Duffy, would die either by being hit by a car or by being run over. Zeke, who was bought by a rich family in Johns Island, was run over in their posh neighborhood. The one we knew as Peanuts was accidentally backed over by one of his owners in her car and had to be put to sleep. Petey's death stirred sadness and anger in me. I learned while his owner's child was walking him near their home, a pickup driver appeared to purposely swerve his truck and killed the two-year-old dog instantly. I felt so badly for that child, who I had one play date with to visit him and Petey, who was renamed "Laddy." Besides Duffy, Laddy had been the one I was most close to. I think in a very visual way and as I heard all these horror stories, I envisioned every bloody death. Only Duffy made it beyond the age of five.

Duffy had his own personality. He had spirit, and he was hyper as well as a barker. He was not always as affectionate as Heather. He would, sometimes, resist the bullying behaviors of my father's chihuahua. Duffy, while running back and forth along our fence, created a trench. He and the neighbor's dachshund would taunt each other. He was full of life, and then he became sick. It seemed he had been sick for over a week, maybe two. It was evident that he was not well, and my strong-spirit, feisty dog became mean. He must have been in pain or tremendous discomfort. He would nip at me when I tried to pet him. He seemed to get more aggressive the more his health declined. I was beginning to give up trying to comfort him, because he would snap at me while lying down, weak. I wanted him to go to the vet, and finally my parents took him. The day before they took him, Duffy was still weak, but he licked my hand and offered his face to me. That is my last memory of Duffy. My parents took him to the vet, but they came home without him. He was dying of kidney failure, and he had to be euthanized. His organs were shutting down.

I was much more mad than sad. I blamed my parents for not taking him to the vet sooner. I was angry at Duffy for pulling me back into caring and loving him by being nice to me again. A growing discontent was coming over me, and all these deaths had me willingly move toward anger and hatred. Duffy had specifically been my dog. I walked him and helped feed him (sometimes), and he slept on my bed. Suddenly, he was gone. The frustration and anger overwhelmed any sadness. While I write this now, I am feeling the sadness.

FIGHTS

When you walked up to my bus stop in the morning, you never knew what you were going to see or hear. I think my trepidation around older teenagers occurred at that bus stop. There could be arguments between the boys who lived on the poor side of County Road 512. One morning, a group of older boys were bullying a slender dark-haired kid named Tim. I arrived at the bus stop, and the older boys and at least one of the girls were throwing sandspurs at Tim. These weeds that look like the Medieval weapon called the morning star grew in Florida, especially near the Atlantic and Gulf coasts or in fine sand. They are very painful if you step on them, or if you must use your fingers to pick them off your shoes or clothes, they could easily pierce your skin. The kids across the highway were throwing stalks of these sandspurs at Tim, and they were attaching everywhere on his body! By his yelps, I think some were cutting into him. They were attaching to his back, his front of his shirt, and his legs—all over him! He was wincing and crying out in pain and trying to run from them, but they would corner him and throw more stalks at him. The bullies were persistent, and before the bus arrived, Tim was covered in sandspurs. I felt bad for him. I told him I was sorry they did that to him, and I may have tried to remove some of the stalks from his back. That incident happened in the sixth grade. Tim was an eighth grader at the time. The next year, I guess Tim "needed" someone to bully, and guess who he targeted?

There had been a handful of times the bus that took us home was late. One afternoon, our bus was later than usual. This meant there was free time for students to talk, cut up about whatever amused them, and as time passed, frustrations would set in for some of them. If I knew I would be writing of this account thirty-eight years after it happened, I would have paid closer attention to what set this event into motion. I just remember that Tim just started trash-talking to me, and I did have a mouth of my own. No doubt, I said something sharp back to him, and I may have hurt his pride. The next thing I know I am agreeing to fight him once we get off the bus. I had seen Tim bullied and cower several times, so I became overconfident that I could beat him. I did not think that he could be quite battle-hardened from his previous fights. He was experienced, and my last fight was when I was seven years old, trying to keep a kid from stealing my friend's bike. Tim was more than ready, and I had no idea what I was walking into.

I remember Alex and Adam were trying to talk Tim out of fighting me. They knew what I did not. I recall standing on the grassy median on Wimbrow Road, each of us had our dukes up. Tim came toward me, quickly, and in a blur, I saw his arm move toward my line of sight. *Booong!* He connected so hard that I heard the loud thud followed by my ears ringing, and I felt dizzy, as the delayed pain increased beyond me functioning, let alone fighting! Alex and Adam immediately stepped in and stopped the fight. Tim hit me in the left eye, and I had a faded black eye the next day. I guess it satisfied Tim, a ninth grader beating up a small seventh grader, and he never bothered me again.

On a Saturday afternoon, in late spring 1982, I hung out with Alex in my front yard. I had just returned from buying a new fishing pole. My parents were off again, and Alex and I were sitting on a cement bench in my front yard. Everything was fine, even after Ricky stopped by on his bike for a short time.

"Ricky" (not his real name) moved on the corner of my street my sixth-grade year. Ricky, objectively speaking, was a cute kid, and he knew it. He was charming and could make friends with virtually anyone. He was an only child; and his parents, both, had conversations with him, encouraged him, and praised him. Ricky was confident, borderline cocky. I had an uneasy friendship with him. If we were together, either Alex or Adam were there too. Ricky's parents were talented people. They owned a hairstyle place in downtown Sebastian, where I received all my haircuts until I left for an art school after graduation. Ricky played the saxophone in the middle school band, and he was a talented keyboard player. He would play in a high school rock band called U4EA (euphoria) and compete with a rock band I was trying to form. If kids were born winners, Ricky would be one of them. Ricky even dated Holly right after Adam! There was only one flaw. At times, he could be annoying as anything!

Ricky joined Alex and me on the bench. I do not remember the conversation, but I believe we welcomed him. Ricky stood up, and while I was talking to Alex, I suddenly felt something light land on the top of my head. I reached up and knocked and pulled off pieces of the evergreen shrub that grew behind us.

"Stop, man!" I raised my voice.

Then I felt some more drop on my head.

"What the—! Quit! You're picking my mom's plant!"

I turned back toward Alex and heard Alex say, "Stop. Don't do it, man." I felt more of the plant lightly drop on my head.

I felt a rush of anger I had never felt before. In a blur, I grabbed Ricky by his shirt and in one motion threw him into the shrubs! I began hitting him, and he briefly got away and grabbed my fishing pole.

"Oh, please, break it!" I yelled.

Ricky held the pole like a sword and swung it back and forth to block me from getting near him. After my veiled threat, he slightly lowered the pole, and I came at him, not unlike my bully Tim. I pulled my fist back and aimed it toward his face, probably an eye. Ricky tried evading and turned his head, and I struck his left ear, hard.

Ricky cried out in pain, "You—!"

I could begin to feel my anger drain away and pity take its place.

No! He had this coming! Come on, Ricky, fight back! This feels good! Fight back!

"Come on, fight me!"

Ricky stood there in pain. The anger was almost gone.

Don't go!

It was almost completely gone. I told Ricky to go home. I do not know if he was being defiant or if he was in shock that I just did what I did. I picked up Ricky's bike (which was heavy) and carried it across the street and tossed it into the field. Ricky cursed me under his breath some more, and my flash of rage was gone. Ricky got on his bike and slowly rode away from my home. Alex and I talked about what he had just witnessed, and my ego was high. Alex respected me more.

"Good Job!"

A few minutes after the latest short-lived, one-sided fight, Alex and I went next door to his house. Alex wanted to call Holly and tell her what had happened. Holly and Ricky had dated after she had broken up with Adam. Ricky then broke up with Holly. I remember Ricky being melodramatic in the band room the day he planned to dump her, when he loudly and repeatedly announced, "Someone's gonna be pissed!" I do not know if he was trying to build his own confidence up, or he was just being self-centered making it seem like losing him was a big loss. It would turn out that Holly seemed to be fine with the separation.

Alex explained to Holly what he had just witnessed in my front lawn, and then he hands me the phone.

"She wants to talk to me?" I asked, feigning modesty.

"Yeh," Alex said with his Pennsylvanian accent.

"Hello."

"Good job! I wish I were there to see it!" Holly exclaimed.

I gave her my side of the story, and then I felt confident, not Halloween confident, but more of a normal level of confidence. I was blessed that Alex had stayed the whole school year, but he was going to be returning to his mother's home for the summer. (I did not know that I would not see Alex again for thirty-one years when I moved back to the area with my wife and son in 2014.) I knew Alex liked Holly a lot, but I reasoned that Alex would not be around. I did not consider his feelings for awfully long.

"Holly, would you go out with me?"

"Love to," she said.

10

MY METAL YEARS (SIDE A)

A life surrounded by death.

MY FIRST DATES

I had been struggling with feelings of inadequacy and worthlessness during the seventh grade. I refer to the biblical truth that was discussed earlier, "Perfect love drives out fear" (1 John 4:18). I must share that the love of God brings boldness, true connectedness, and rest in His provision and protection. It is being able to be in others' company and to feel adequate to just be there. This is an adequacy through Christ that is empowered by communion and prayer. The adequacy I experience today is unlike the inner frenzy that came around during the fall of every year. Today my adequacy may wane and weaken, yet it is everlasting, especially when I need it to help others. I did not know God at thirteen, and I was stuck with my perceived shortcomings. It ended up impacting my dates with Holly.

The drive to Holly's house was not short. She lived about eleven miles from my home. On the drive there, I thought about and remembered going to her fourteenth birthday party in December of 1982. Adam was there, and some of Holly's eighth-grade friends were there as well. I remember feeling included and not just tolerated. My starkest memory about that night is that at some point, the party moved outside. In the cool December air, we were gathered into a circle, close to one another, and we played spin the bottle behind a structure behind her house. One of my spins of the long-necked soda bottle landed on Holly, and I gave a quick, awkward kiss on the lips. At some point, one of the eighth graders, possibly Holly or her best friend, suggested we play strip spin the bottle. If the bottle, after it is spun, stops spinning in front of you, you take an article of clothing off and then you spin the bottle. I do not remember how long we had been playing it, but I remember my shoes, socks, and shirt were laying on the grass behind me. Holly was down to her bra and underwear when we heard her father call out, "Holly! Phone!"

Holly and all of us frantically gathered and put on our clothes. No one was completely naked. To stall for time, one of Holly's friends asked loudly, "What's the name of your [pet] rabbit?"

In a shaky, raised voice, Holly replied, "Uh, uh, Peter!"

We could not help laughing, nervously.

Holly was dressed and ran to her house to answer the call. I thought, *I like being a teenager.*

Remembering that night, I nervously smiled, as we approached her road turnoff near a volunteer fire station. I rang the doorbell, and her mother answered, and Holly was behind her. Holly was dressed in a long-sleeve collared shirt with dark-blue jeans and tennis shoes. She looked intimidating and nice. She and I sat in the backseat of my parents' car, and my mother chauffeured us to Melbourne to eat lunch and watch *Jaws 3-D*[53].

Bless my mother, she tried to help conversations start by asking Holly questions. I sat in near silence, intimidated by her mere presence. Holly, in a friendly manner, answered my mother's questions. I saw no openings to break in with chatter. My quiet nature was steamrolling me, and the hour drive to the theater was just awkward. I remember looking at the Indian River. US 1 lies along the river, and at some points, the river is a mere few yards from the road. On a clear, sunny day, the river sparkles rays of sunlight on the ripples of an aqua blue. On stormy, windy days, the river can appear sinister, with its dark-gray hues and white caps on the top of waves. I would stare out the window, not taking in its beauty, and daring not look directly at

---

[53] https://jaws.fandom.com/wiki/Jaws_3.

Holly. My social anxiety was off the charts. Holly wore some makeup at school, but I had never seen her like this. I felt unworthy, and it is likely that the subconscious thoughts of not understanding anyone and everyone not being able to understand me were present.

We did eat lunch at a fast-food place. I think at a certain point I felt more comfortable, but I do not remember any specific conversations. Holly did not appear to be uncomfortable or even frustrated with me. Perhaps her expectations were low. I think she may have wanted to reward me for hitting Ricky. We watched the third movie in the *Jaws* series, and she seemed to enjoy it. The night ended, and I walked her to her door. My friend, Adam, had told me that when girls want to be kissed, they look you straight in the eyes and do not move away even if you inch closer. Holly did not give me that look, or if she did, nerves caused me to miss it. (It turns out that Adam never kissed her either, because she never gave him the "look" either.) I did ask if she wanted to see *Star Wars: Return of the Jedi*[54], and she said, "Love to." I walked back to the car and replayed the night with frustration over my fear of opening to Holly.

Anxiety can imprison you in your own head. I have taught some of my patients how anxiety draws us into ourselves and that for some people strictly focusing on others' comfort and well-being can help us not focus on our own fears. I have found that practicing this helps me be aware of my environment, my surroundings, and the person or people that I am talking to. Practicing mental health counseling is like a performance to me. Sometimes I can experience a kind of stage fright before meeting with a client, but when the person or family is in front of me, "It's showtime. Time for me to focus everything, all of my attention, on them." If I had had this knowledge when I was thirteen, how would things have turned out for me? If I did not have that tape recorder in my head reminding me how I could not understand anyone, would I have developed socially more normal? I will never know. I can only use the knowledge, especially the knowledge of God, today in my daily interactions. Mr. Sammons, my high

---

[54] https://starwars.fandom.com/wiki/Star_Wars:_Episode_VI_Return_of_the_ Jedi.

school band director, taught us that we are only as good as our last performance. I recently thanked him for teaching me this and that I eventually took it to heart.

Alex and I had already seen *Return of the Jedi* on the last day of school. I knew the movie well enough, and I knew Holly had not seen the movie yet. I knew there were teddy bear creatures that were cute and called "Ewoks." I thought that Holly would like them and like me for "introducing" them to her. I would learn much later how a fair amount of manipulation takes place during first dates, how most people are on their *best behavior* and do much to try not to offend each other. (I do want to say that I liked how I was real during the first date with the woman who would become my wife. I simply said during a *Star Trek* movie, "Let's make this official. Do you want to go with me?" Seven months later, we were married.) For my second date with Holly, I was being infuriatingly nice and silent!

My brother was the chauffer this time. Like the first date, I did not talk again, and my brother asked Holly questions she politely answered. The movie was playing at the Vero Beach Plaza Theater, so the drive was much shorter. We saw an evening showing and did not have dinner together. I remember looking over at her, peripherally, when certain scenes played. She, and the audience at large, laughed when one of the Ewoks said something that sounded like, "Eechaa wawa," after a stormtrooper landed a laser blast near him and Princess Leia. (I do know some people have never seen any *Star Wars* movies, and I would encourage you to watch them. I have used the movies' themes to teach children to not be ruled by their emotions when making decisions.)

Holly, at that Ewok scene, said, "Oh my god, I want an Ewok!" I thought, *Yes!*

The movie ended as well as that very brief time of bonding over the movie. She told me she loved it and wanted a stuffed Ewok. I thought I would get her one, but the merchandise lagged behind the release of the movie. I walked Holly to her front door again, and throughout the night I again did not see any welcoming looks. So she thanked me, and that was that. Within weeks after the next school year began, Holly was going with a guy I had known since I was five years old. His name was also Jeff, and he would be the one to break Holly out of her shell. Holly and I remained friends through the school year. I did not like Jeff, though. The last time I saw Holly, she was wearing an Iron Maiden T-shirt, and she looked lost and sad. She was waiting for her bus, and I was auditioning to be a percussionist at the high school. My mother sent me her obituary notice in the mail recently. She had died at around the age of forty-three. I had wanted to share with her all the ways God had blessed me and explain some of this testimony to her.

THE GETAWAY

A week or two after the dates, I was excited for the opportunity to visit my aunt, uncle, and cousins in Brandon, Florida. Michael was nineteen, and he drove us across the state for a one-week visit. I was excited to see Wendy, and I had learned that the family had acquired a ferret they named "Reaper." I have been to their home enough times that I can, even now, envision the layout of the four-bedroom house. Uncle Ed, who was addicted to watching sports, sat on a rocking, recliner chair. It was his chair. You did not sit in it, and if you did, you wouldn't sit there for long.

My oldest cousin, the late and great (to me), Kevin had a small bedroom behind the living room (which oddly to me was not used). Kevin was into hard rock music, and I had been exposed to some of his music when the family visited our grandparents in Vero Beach. I remember riding with them, Kevin driving us to the ocean and playing screeching, hard music loudly! My ears would ring after the ride. I believe they were listening to either Kiss or maybe AC/DC. At my age of, then, ten, I could not say I hated it. I was just used to hearing Top 40 pop music on one of our local rock stations. I had heard similar hard rock music when I was about seven years old. I was on my swing set at the Sebastian home, and I could hear some piercing guitar music from across State Road 512. The distance did not make it loud, and I remember, while sitting in Kevin's car, "I've heard this kind of music before."

Kevin's room had a stack of blank cassette tapes, now filled with various heavy rock songs. Kevin also had a boa constrictor, kept in a long glass aquarium. I had a soft spot for reptiles. I preferred lizards, but snakes are reptiles too. He let me pet it. Kevin also had a cage for his ferret, Reaper.

I asked, "I like Reaper. Does it mean anything?"

Kevin stated, "Grim Reaper. The Angel of Death."

"Oh. Cool!"

He explained that Reaper had fallen out of a second-story home of his previous owner and did not have a scratch on him. Kevin stated that the ferret cheated death, and he was called Reaper because of this. Reaper was of the weasel family of species, and they have a gland that causes them to smell badly, like skunks. Like skunks, ferrets can be "depewed," but they never completely lose the odor. Reaper had coarse long dark-brown and tan hair covering its long, slender body. I loved Reaper!

Going down the home's hallway, Wendy's room was off to the left. She still had that creepy canopy over her frilly girl bed, but I had seemingly conquered my fear of evil. The canopy did not bother me at all. Wendy was involved with her middle school swim team, and I would not see as much of her as I had wanted to. She was polite, but the days of us being like best friends were long gone. She appeared to be extremely popular. She was taller than me by a few inches. I thought she was pretty. She was always cute. I put her in the league of Holly. My own cousin intimidated me with her popularity. I was awkward around her too.

Laura, the middle cousin, was closest to Scott's age, and I believe they would hang out together for a large part of the visit. Laura had been in a bad car accident while she was in high school. My mother had told me that her neck hit the steering wheel, and it damaged her vocal cords, irrevocably. She spoke with a raspy voice after the accident, as if she could whisper loudly. She seemed to take it all in stride. She was and remains a very good-humored person. (In September 2017, she would implore my family and my parents to stay at her own home with her husband, because the category 5 Hurricane Irma was threatening the east coast of Florida.) Laura exhibited her kidding nature, and we had a good time. Hurricane Irma would drift within about twenty miles from her home, and Vero Beach only contended with having electricity out for two days.

At the end of the hall was Aunt Ruthie's and Uncle Ed's master bedroom. I had known or thought I had known Ruthie and Ed since we had moved to Florida when I was four. I knew Ruthie as truly the "cool aunt." She had a great sense of humor, and she liked and knew pop music. She was a teacher at their local large Catholic church. (Wendy had her as a teacher in elementary school.) My maternal grandfather had three daughters. My mother was the shy, middle child. Ruthie was the extremely outgoing youngest. Ruthie's interactions made her seem like a peer. During this visit, Ruthie was pouring Ed a drink, and it somehow spilled on the kitchen counter. I did not mean to, but I blurted out laughing, until I looked at her and then at him. Ruthie looked scared and mortified. Ed looked disgusted and angry. I would learn many years later that Ed had been verbally and physically abusive to Ruthie. He had also been strict and emotionally abusive to Kevin. I stopped laughing and never regretted a laugh more.

MUSIC MADE JUST FOR ME

Wendy called me to her bedroom, about the fourth day of our visit. She pulled out a record from its cover. The front of the cover had an illustration of a building with the architecture style of a glass box. It had a gun-scope target on the building, and in the middle of the target was a yellow and orange blaze with dense dark-gray smoke. On the upper left of the record was the band's name, Def Leppard. I remember my mind acting like a computer searching through downloads (memories) of bands' names. There was *Molly Hatchet, Alice Cooper, Led Zeppelin? Could I have mixed that name up, and it was Def Leppard?* No, I would learn that Def Leppard was a fairly new band in 1983 and that this album cover I held in my hands was called Pyromania. (That would explain the burning building, right?) Def Leppard became known as part of the "new wave of British heavy metal." It was a movement that would touch every corner of the globe and reach me where I was.

Wendy carefully placed the needle down on the record. (I thought, I don't even own a stereo. Is this how I can become popular?) I began to hear simulated wind, setting an atmosphere of interest. A lone guitar begins to strum in the midrange. The guitar sounds clean, but powerfully reverberates too. The first heavy metal song I would hear was called "Too Late for Love[55]."

I thought, *This is good! This is what I want to hear! Where has this been? This sounds like it was made for me!*

---

[55] https://en.wikipedia.org/wiki/Too_Late_for_Love_(Def_Leppard_song).

11

MY METAL YEARS (SIDE B)

A force was driving me to want to avenge myself.

GOING TO THE DEEP END

I exploded, "Wow, Wendy! They sound great!"

"I thought you would like them too. The whole record is good!" she said.

She was right and I thought, *Could it be that I would have something in common with her again?* Yes, I did have another something in common with Wendy, for a while. I had an almost insatiable appetite to hear more. My brother and I left our cousins' house a few days later, and I returned to Sebastian quite changed again. I thought this could be the key, or a key, to having more mature things in common with my classmates. I did not have my own stereo, but my heart leaped when I learned that Scott had "Pyromania" on cassette. When he was at work or his community college, I would go to his room, plug his earphones in, and listen to all the Def Leppard tape. I lay on his floor and placed the light-tan cassette upside down into his boom box or portable stereo. Cassettes, for any who may not know, must be rewound to hear the first song. Scott had finished side one, so I put on side two. "Foolin[56]," the first song on the second side, began to play. It started with a melodic, calm acoustic guitar opening; and

---

[56] https://defleppard.fandom.com/wiki/Foolin'.

after the first verse, all the electric guitars, the bass, and drums came fully alive. It was like a drug! I was attracted to the power, the attitude, and the subject matters—all of it!

There I was, hidden away, listening to music I did not know existed. Laying on the floor, I encountered conflicting emotions. The emotions I experienced probably matched many first-time listeners as described by Shannon who is administrator of a social Web fan site. She described that she "really enjoyed what I was hearing, but it scared me... I felt I was doing something wrong by listening to it." I felt the same way—fear mixed with feelings of doing something wrong and also feeling strong. It was a mindset of, "Look at me. Look what I can handle!" The thing was Def Leppard was more of a type of hard rock than heavy metal, and they became like a gateway drug to me for heavier and more aggressive metal music. I also had thought Def Leppard would make me more popular with my classmates, but it would influence me to be more of an outcast and antisocial than before. That was an unintended consequence! Pop music, not heavy metal music, was accepted by most of my classmates. My cousins' town was close to Tampa where heavy metal was more popular. Sebastian, Florida, was stuck on Michael Jackson and the Police, pop music performers!

My newfound love of hard rock and later the more aggressive heavy metal bands put me at odds with the church culture. I would point out that Satan can use country music to form a cheating, womanizing alcoholic. He can even cause a snobbish kind of pride in people who listen to classical music. I have even witnessed well-meaning Christians flash subtle signs of self-righteousness from listening to praise and worship. It is not necessarily the genre, but the individual soul's attractions. That said, heavy metal was directed and marketed toward disaffected youths, feeling alienated and full of angst. I believe it comes down to what you do with it.

A Christian brother, who has a prominent ministry at a church my family attends, shared how a very heavy song against drug abuse helped him make a wise decision. The band is called Metallica and the song is called "Master of Puppets[57]." He said that one day, "I finally listened to the lyrics, and quit smoking pot. Drugs always kind of freaked me out and the song just solidified my fear." One song from this band helped redirect this brother in Christ. Another song from this band, however, influenced me to get over my fear of Hell in 1990. The lyrics indicated that Hell could set you free—free to do what you want, free to enact revenge! Obviously, those lyrics had no significant effect on the minister from my church, but because my heart would become open to all things violent, "Hello? I receive that!"

MUSIC THAT WILL DRIVE YOU MAD IF YOU LET IT

I spent many days for the rest of that summer on my brother's bedroom floor, listening to the earth-rattling guitar, bass, and drum notes of Def Leppard. Then, I began to fall asleep in the middle of listening to the tape. That would bother me. Is there anymore music like this? Any bands that I can trust are good? I did not know. None of my other friends were into the hard rock band from England or hard rock, period! I did not think to ask others or my cousins, so I just kept listing to the same tape. I craved more.

While visiting Nanna and Papa in Vero, Holly called me.

"Oh my, you have to listen to this new group. They're called Quiet Riot! Hold on, I'll play this song I taped off the radio. Hold on!"

I listened, heard her tap the play button, and then a song called "Cum on Feel the Noize[58]" started playing. It sounded very distorted over the 1983 landline, but it also sounded faster and more aggressive than Def Leppard. Honestly, I was not that impressed. The song was very repetitive, but it did have a level of aggression that I could relate to at the time. Sometime later, I heard it on the radio directly, and I was much more impressed.

---

[57] https://en.wikipedia.org/wiki/Master_of_Puppets.
[58] https://en.wikipedia.org/wiki/Cum_on_Feel_the_Noize.

"Cool, Holly. What's the tape called again? Metal Health? Wow. Yeah, I'll get it. Thanks."

The conversation probably did not last too much longer because, well, she was talking to me.

That next Thursday night, my mom needed to go to our local Woolworth, and I tagged along with cash from mowing lawns. She was with me while I looked at the assorted records and cassette tapes. I found the "Q" section and plucked the tape out of the display. I looked at the album cover. It had a man in an iron mask, and he was wearing a red leather-looking straightjacket. He was in a padded cell, and I think I took a deep breath, as I remembered running across children and adults that were in an insane institution when I was younger. It was a special school facility for severely mentally handicapped children and adults located near Daytona, Florida.

It is amazing that I am a licensed counselor, not only because I had once been a misunderstood patient (whose symptoms largely disappeared the moment I finished a prayer) but also because I developed a real fear over anyone who behaved abnormally (I know, "pot meet kettle"). They just made me exceedingly nervous from lack of trust.

Let me take you back to when I was about six years old, and my parents took Scott and me to a rodeo in nearby Fellsmere. I remember that I was returning with Scott from the restrooms, taking in the noises, hoots, and hollers and walking through a desertlike environment. I saw a man behaving very erratically, and it grabbed my attention. I did not know at the time, but the man was clearly drunk. He had been trying to climb a tall fence that was barb-wired, and he ripped his pants. He was hanging from what was left of his jeans!

"What's wrong with him?"

Scott tried to shut my outburst down immediately. "Shut up! Don't say anything!"

"But what's wrong with him?"

It is not like I had not seen people who drank, but this man was acting crazy, and it was a little frightening.

The Halloween night that I was first oppressed, Scott and I were walking along the road by the lake. (This was minutes before I had my first violent vision.) As we were walking, I saw a tall teenager quickly walking toward us. He looked upset. It did not look like he was wearing a costume, and I blurted out, "What are you supposed to be?"

The male youth, wearing street clothes, looked down at me while starting to pass us by and said, "—— off!"

Whoa, his sharp answer startled me and seemed abnormal. Michael again said in a loud whisper, "Jeff, quiet!"

The last time I was exposed to people who behaved erratically was when I was around the age of nine, my parents, brother, and aunt visited the fourth cousin. The fourth cousin from Brandon, Florida, is Gregory, and he was born with Down syndrome. (He is the brother to Kevin, Laura, and Wendy.) The institution/school facility contained mentally handicapped people who did not speak words but to my nine-year-old ears could be quite loud. I remember they were stocky-built, and their movements were scary and erratic. There was a heavy teenaged girl who managed to sit on my dad's head! (She just tackled him and sat.) There was an older male patient who was swinging on a swing. His tongue was out, and he kept making loud noises. I do not mean to be offensive about writing about this experience, but I was frightened by the students. I equated them to being "crazy," and so I developed a fear of strange behavior. I never visited Gregory again.

I held the Quiet Riot "Metal Health" cassette, took a breath, and walked off to find my mother, who was in a nearby aisle. Then I saw an eye-catching display of a novel by horror author Stephen King. The novel was *Christine*[59], and from what I could understand, it was about a possessed car that gets even with the owner's bullies and tormentors. *Sounds good to me*, I thought. I snatched the book and bought the cassette and the novel. This was the point that I believe I truly and willingly walked toward evil. *Look how much I can handle, now! Heavy metal music, horror movies, and now novels!* My peers may have judged me to be a wimp by my outward appearance,

---

[59] https://www.kirkusreviews.com/book-reviews/stephen-king/christine.

but I was going to make my mind and heart hard as steel! *They would mentally crumble at what I can handle!*

I went home and listened to the entire Quiet Riot tape. I loved it! I especially loved the first song, "Metal Health (Bang Your Head)[60]." The song lyrics "warned" me (and every listener) that it would drive me mad. I feared the insane, but what if I let myself go mad? I had seemingly eradicated my fear of evil. *What if I address this fear as well?* This new album had attitude too. The band was from America, based in Los Angeles to be exact, and they had gone through several lineup changes. There were two songs on the album that became a type of soundtrack to my Stephen King novel. They were "Slick Black Cadillac" and "Love's a B——," you know what! The Cadillac song was about a tough car, and the "love" song was about, well, it is about love being a heartbreaker.

The novel hit close to home. The main character was an awkward, nerdy high school student. His best friend was a popular, good-hearted jock (if that does not sound like Adam and me, except I rejected the premise of being a nerd and preferred "outcast"). The awkward friend buys a beat-up 1958 Plymouth Fury that turns out to be possessed by its former dead owner. The nerd's car exacts revenge and kills off all his bullies and tormentors. In the process, the young man loses his awkwardness and acquires a tough, cooler, even cold, demeanor. He learns his car is killing, and he is fine with it.

After buying the Quiet Riot album, I came home a couple of weeks later, and my mother showed me a sales flyer for a local store. There were a few portable stereos on sale. There was one that caught my eye, and I had enough money from mowing ours' and our neighbors' lawns over the summer. Mom drove me to the Luria's store, in Vero Beach, and after picking out a better stereo, she bought it for me. It was a Lloyds stereo and was a smoky gray. Now, I had control of when I could listen to my music.

Around this time, one of my parents saw a drum set for sale in our local paper. Honestly, I do not remember asking for a drum set, but I cannot imagine why I would not want a drum set. We all drove

---

[60] https://en.wikipedia.org/wiki/Metal_Health.

out in the light-blue van, and my parents purchased the set for fifty dollars. The former owner had also played in jazz bands. The set consisted of a bass drum, one tom-tom, a floor tom, a crash cymbal, and a high-hat cymbal. I got my first drum set that Saturday morning.

After setting the drums up in our back porch/Florida room, I plugged headphones into my stereo. I called a "blaster," held my sticks with one hand, and with my left pressed the play button. The "Metal Health" song begins with eight eighth notes, rolling from snare to the toms, and ends with crashes on the cymbals on the counts of one and four (I believe). Well, the moment the music played loudly in my ears, I pounded the drums, and on the first cymbal crash, I hit it so hard that the cymbal and stand went straight down to where my father was sitting! It fell less than a foot in front of my terribly angry-looking dad!

"Take those things off!"

I never drummed with headphones again until I had an electric set at the age of forty-eight. (I wanted to share that story!)

It seems within a few weeks, I was falling asleep listening to Quiet Riot. (One of the band's support crew from England would say, "Quite right," and his British accent made it sound like "quiet riot," and that is how they got their name.) At one time, in early 1984, Scott and I had tickets to see Quiet Riot in St. Lucie County, but the show was cancelled when it did not sell all the seat space. I began to do research, mainly by looking at other album covers at our local record store. There were two bands I decided to take a chance with. I would buy Ozzy Osbourne's "Bark at the Moon[61]" and Van Halen's "1984[62]." Van Halen, to me, was not very heavy at all, so I hardly listened to it and regretted buying it.

I would also regret buying the Ozzy tape. I remember walking toward the lake on a Friday night, meeting Adam, who was also bringing his new portable stereo. While I was waiting for him, I felt uneasy while listening to Ozzy. A song called "Centre of Eternity" played. While listening to it, I felt apprehensive and a little fear. It

---

[61] https://en.wikipedia.org/wiki/Bark_at_the_Moon_(song).
[62] https://en.wikipedia.org/wiki/1984_(Van_Halen_album).

reminded me in a subtle way that although I may have been making peace with evil, I still wanted nothing to do with Satan. I do not believe Ozzy Osbourne is satanic, but he was a humanist, and he did promote rebellion toward God. Most of the heavy metal bands did. That had to be a challenge for the enemy to get me to be open to violence and evil, but not to the evil one. I believe my slightly churched background was influencing me to stay away from any bands, movies, or novels that glorified Satan. I, at that time, did not know if Jesus existed or not, but I respected the concept of Jesus and had no respect for Satan. Here, his minions were influencing me behind the scenes. They were hiding behind the symbols of an ancient pagan holiday.

PLAYING WITH MADNESS

During this time, when I visited different stores' music section, I would see album covers from a band called Iron Maiden. Their album covers had a similar zombielike character with lights shining from black hole eye sockets. (I have learned that radio usually did not play heavy metal songs, so groups would design album covers to attract attention.) A friend I would meet in four years told me that he was "wearing Iron Maiden T-shirts and hanging their posters before I ever heard a single song. Imagery, you know?" My friend, named Johnny, stated that he owned the band's merchandise before he ever bought one of their albums. I was becoming tired of the last two cassettes I had been listening to, but I did not want to spend any more money unless I knew what the band sounded like.

Jim was in my grade, and it was known that he was a heavy metal fan. I asked him if he had an Iron Maiden cassette, and Jim let me borrow a tape of theirs called "Piece of Mind[63]." I had the cassette, and Adam allowed me to take it to his home to play on his parents' expensive stereo system, sitting on their wicker entertainment center. I will never forget Adam putting the tape in and hearing the hiss of his speakers become louder. Then a furious drum intro started

---

[63] https://en.wikipedia.org/wiki/Piece_of_Mind.

a song called "Where Eagles Dare." For me, it was love at first listen. Looking at Adam, unfortunately, I could tell he did not like it and could not handle it. It was like I gained a friend, and my friendship with Adam developed its first genuine strain.

We only listened to the first song, which turned out to be written about the World War II movie of the same name. I went home a little early that day so I could hear the rest of the album. I had never heard such heavy, intricate music. I ended up loving every song on the album. Looking at the zombie mascot, Eddie, was spooky at first, but then I was very attracted to it. I would learn that every song of the album dealt with deaths—death through war or fighting or an insane person jumping and drowning in a pool, death. My prior bands were singing about rock, women, and partying; but Iron Maiden were singing about death. Because of me not seeking and rarely accepting proper perspective from my parents or others, I just took in the message of "death is cool." That is not fair to the band, though. The band is highly intelligent, and they have written music about mythology, world religions, history, and even poems. It is just that the stories that attract their attention are laden with tragedy, triumphs, heroes, and villains; and these various characters either die or fight others and kill. I do not think my parents had any idea what I was listening to or how my openness and the enemy hardened me toward tragedies and deaths. At one point, my parents grounded me for getting a D in a pre-algebra class. I was hidden away in my room listening to three Iron Maiden cassettes that I had bought within a few months of hearing them at Adam's house. They were "Piece of Mind," "the Number of the Beast[64]," and "Powerslave[65]." The band remained my favorite for years—years of misinterpreting their messages.

FRED, THE WIMP

At the end of my nine-week grounding, I was permitted to come out of my room, hang out at Adam's house, and watch after-

---

[64] https://en.wikipedia.org/wiki/The_Number_of_the_Beast_(album).
[65] https://en.wikipedia.org/wiki/Powerslave_(album).

noon TV again. After saturating myself in the music made for me, I was slow to rejoin my family. I was truly becoming unsociable. Do not get me wrong, I had been allowed to listen to my music, do my homework, eat dinner with my family, and join them in watching evening TV during the grounding. I came out of it, however, with a more negative attitude, and it matched a phrase that became popular during the mid-1980s, "—— the world!" Caring brought anxiousness to me. *What if I worked on not caring?*

I remember a classmate having the "FTW" antisocial slogan written between his knuckles, and an aware teacher called him out for it. The student said that the initials did not mean what she thought it meant. He said it meant, "Fred, the Wimp." The teacher did not buy his story, and I believe he received detention.

The concepts of death from Iron Maiden was in the forefront of my mind. It was death in the fantasy realm. It was not obituaries, grieving families, and funeral arrangements. It was a violent ending, sometimes moving on to more. During this time, a new student, a grade above me, joined the school's concert band and drum section. His name was Calvin, and he decided to target me for ridicule. I had an inclination that Calvin could be superstitious, so one morning, I started talking about death. He called me crazy and did not ridicule or talk about me or to me again. I began to take note that strong minds could compete and overcome strong bodies if the mind in the strong body is weak and prone to fear. In simpler words, strong minds can defeat strong bodies.

One day in my eighth-grade science class, the teacher announced to our class that it was Ranee's last day. She was moving out of state. I had not had her in many of my classes that year. Aside for my love affair with heavy metal music, I do not remember having any serious crushes that year. I remember briefly thinking, *Wow, she won't be in class tomorrow, or ever. This is the last time I see her.* I felt more shock than sad. The next day, she was not there. I am not proud, but I forgot her faster than I thought I would. It is possible the not caring anymore attitude that I was working on somehow helped me cope with her absence.

My Second Brush with Suicide

In the ninth grade, I did have one notable crush, a blonde girl named Leigh. She was in the advanced concert band, and she was immensely popular. She was new to the area but seemed to fit in immediately. To set this story up, in the mid-1980s, teen dance clubs were popping up in towns, small and large. I went to one in Vero Beach, and I thought it was okay. I had gone with some friends from band, and I did not have a horrible time. I did not like to dance, because at that time I was about six feet tall and maybe a hundred pounds if I was wet! The drummer in me had rhythm, but my long gangly arms and legs, my self-image just did not lend any confidence to dancing.

One early spring Saturday night, the local Catholic church held a dance for their youth group, and I was invited by two brothers in the band to go. I do not remember participating in one dance, but Leigh was there, and I asked her to dance to a slower song.

"I'll dance the last dance with you," she answered.

So I waited. Song after song passed by. Someone else got the last dance.

All I can tell you is I remember walking toward where my mom was parked. I was upset and was feeling like a fool. I was wearing a blue Members Only jacket, and my hands were in the jacket's pockets. My foot hit against a root of a large oak tree, and I lost my balance and I fell straight down. My arms were still in the pockets, and they could not help with catching me as my chin slammed with the front of my body into the ground. I was mortified and enraged, but I kept it inside. My mom saw my spill and made sure I was okay. We headed home. I remember thinking I was a loser, and no one would ever really like me. I had brushed off Mom fussing over me. At home, I was in bed crying, and I heard in my mind, *Kill yourself. Take the whole bottle of Tylenol PM now. Kill yourself. Light's out. No worries.— them all! Kill yourself.*

I remember agreeing with the thought. While crying, I thankfully fell asleep. The next day, I would not be inclined to kill myself. I was disappointed that the hopes and positive thoughts I had had about becoming a teenager were not coming close to coming true. True to God's Word, "the enemy comes to steal, kill, and destroy" was happening to me, and I did not know it. I was and am resilient, and I had developed a personal philosophy that suicide was a coward's way. But life was getting rougher. Although I had dodged that brush with suicide, I was getting a feeling deep inside that my life would not last long. I was becoming comfortable with that thought. I was also beginning to feel like I was destined for something big before my early death. I was not equating that with Halloween though.

Third grade class portrait

Halloween 1977

Napping, with puppets, Earnie and Howdie Doody

Asleep with Duffy

My family

Posing with my first drum set at 13 years old

Reaper, the ferret, and me at 14

My Kawasaki KE 100

Painting of an album design for Tropical Storm

Heather and Duffy (1980)

The Nissan 310 (Behind me is where a consequential
dream of my grandfather would take place)

Me as the Grim Reaper for a band Halloween party

Mom and me before Graduation ceremony

This was a display of my inner feelings in 1989

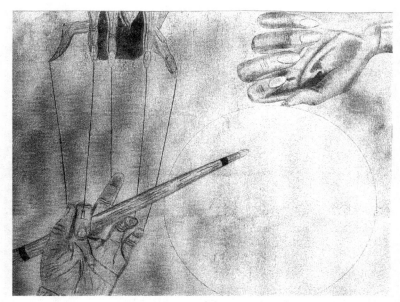

An art project of drawing hands

My first pencil portrait of a man a Chinese farmer

Johnny, and me before Guavaween 1991

My U.S. Air Force security police academy photo

My wife, Fawn Gilbert, during my ten-year high school reunion

Fawn, Aaron, and me in 2019

My parents in 2019

12

ACCEPTANCE AND REJECTION (PART 1)

No hope to help me want to live.

ANOTHER FIRST DAY, WEEK, MONTH, YEAR

I suppose after my brother left to attend the liberal arts college, Mercer University, in Macon, Georgia, home was noticeably quiet. My brother, except for two times a year, had been living and going to school out of state since 1984 (1985 would be my last year of being sexually abused by his friend after he learned that I had told one of my friends). Not having Scott around made me feel like an only child, and home *was* quiet. I continued to either not seek guidance or not know how to ask for it. Again, I felt emotionally unprepared to start a new grade at a new much bigger school. Adam, I appreciated, allowed me to ride to school with him. His mother would drive us almost every day of our sophomore year. Adam would be busy working with his father in his office-cleaning business after school. Our days of hanging out were ending for a season.

Vero Beach, Florida, has a very wealthy area along the Atlantic Ocean and the Indian River. In the 1980s, some children and teens were known as preps, or they were "preppy." Preps wore designer clothes, typically like Izod or Polo Ralph Lauren, and some wore expensive Jordache Jeans. It was a stereotype that preps were stuck-up snobs, but all stereotypes are based on some truth—it just is not universal truth. My brother had influenced me and to a degree turned me into a prep. I just was not stuck up. Vero Beach students seemed to look down on students who came from Sebastian. This may not be a universal truth either, but it felt to me that the Vero students would not accept Sebastian students until the Sebastian student proved some kind of character worth. Beginning my first day, week, and months at Vero Beach High School was like the amount of anxiety and confusion that I experienced at the Sebastian middle school. I felt judged. I felt largely rejected. I felt absolutely lost, being in a class of almost seven hundred peers! Being a member of the band and the drumline brought limited worth to my peers, but I would take anything. I still cared.

Playing for the Vero Beach High School Band, known in these parts as the Pride of the Treasure Coast, was an honor. Performing with one of the best marching bands in America was a mostly positive experience. The drum instructor, who gave of his time voluntarily, was Billy Mann and he was a positive mentor. There were still run-ins with competitive members of the drum-line that caused me to feel inadequate. Once, after being yelled at by the assistant band instructor for missing a cymbal crash, I almost made a gesture that possibly could have brought much-needed intervention. My hands were shaking. I visualized what I wanted to do. In my thoughts, I heard me say, *You know how after some kid commits suicide, a bunch of people he knew say, "I wish we had known. I wish he had given us a sign.' Here's your sign.* And I would throw the cymbal against the wall. I stood there, my hands shaking. I just stood there, and the assistant director went back to starting the song. No one knew.

BITTERNESS SETTLES

About three or four weeks after school started, I felt ill, and I began to have high fevers and felt like I was hit by a steamroller. My mother took me to my pediatrician, and after some tests, I was diagnosed with having mononucleosis or mono, "the kissing disease." It wore me down, terribly. I was able to participate in band and carry the biggest bass drum, but I was almost useless afterward. I would come home from school, watch the *Transformers*[66] animated series, and nap until dinnertime. My first few months of high school, I learned that sleep could be a hobby. Mono makes you exhausted, and part of the treatment is getting plenty of rest.

I had a teacher, God bless her, who would allow me to sleep through her class. I would be feverish and drift in and out of consciousness in the class. I did not tell any of my classmates, and I could hear them talk behind my back—or so it seemed. I could hear them talk about going to parties, getting drunk, and having sex. It infuriated me! (This is a trait of the Michael Myers character that I did not connect at the time.) I did not know one person in this class, except twins that I did not know well from Sebastian. Several were seniors. I remember hearing their stories, whether true or not, and raging on the inside. I think I was jealous. That is an emotion I almost never experience these days. (If I do, it is very shallow and brief thanks to God's redirection of my thoughts, perspective.) But in my adolescent years, I had been listening to violent music with attitude, watching horror movies, and reading horror novels. One cannot expose themselves to hours of negative-leaning media and not escape or evade its negative effects. I grew to hate some of the seniors in the class. I did not attempt to be open or make friends with any of the classmates. This decision bit me when I joined the marine biology class on an all-day fieldtrip to Sea World. It was a dreary, cold rainy day. I remember being alone the entire day, hiding out in shops and restaurants to escape the rain. I was miserable, and rather than blame myself, I hated my classmates. I felt absolute rejection. I even wished I were back at school. A part of me could always remember how I had been popular before October 1977. What happened? Where did that kid go? I could not dwell on that. I was here again embracing the idea that my life could be short. These are my first memories of feeling bitter.

---

[66] https://en.wikipedia.org/wiki/The_Transformers_(TV_series).

TROPICAL STORM

A few months before the end of middle school, a professional rock band that played cover songs performed during an afternoon assembly. Adam and several band friends came back that night to see the band Free Fair, although they were not free. They were an exceptionally good band for a band that did cover songs. I vividly remember the drummer doing a solo that ended with a familiar eight eighth notes that open the Quiet Riot song "Metal Health (Bang Your Head)." After the concert, Adam and some of our mutual friends decided to form our own band. I, of course, was made the drummer. By 1984, I had bought another small drum set and combined it with my first set. My first set was metallic royal blue, and my new set was a mother of pearl gray. I do not remember who came up with the name, but I thought it was genius. Our band was Tropical Storm. It consisted of Adam on guitar, "Phillip" (not his real name) on guitar, and I believe Joe was going to be the bass player. Only Phillip and I were actual musicians, so Adam and Joe committed to buying their instruments and learning to play them. The commitments probably lasted a month.

I loved the Tropical Storm idea, and I did what I could to keep it alive. I wrote lyrics and presented them to Phillip, who would put music to them. I wrote the lyrics to "Tropical Storm," and Phillip added music and sang the song to me. I wrote the words,

> Tropical Storm.
> Taunting us with fear.
> Tropical Storm—Yeah!
> Tropical Storm.
> Taunting us with fear of a storm that grows near.

The tune he came up with was catchy to me. I still live in Florida, and when a tropical storm or hurricane threatens the East Coast, I'll softly sing those lyrics to myself. My songs sounded more like Def Leppard than anything really heavy, and most of the songs I wrote dealt with love—I was hopeless in that area.

Phillip left the band and joined a band called *U4EA* (euphoria). Phillip did not let me know that he wanted out of the band; he just joined another. I was upset with that. I found another guitarist, and my mother picked him up from Vero Beach, and he came to my house to jam and see what we had. That guitarist never returned to my house. It went well, but the band was not forming. It was an idea, some songs, and I painted what could be an album cover, with menacing storm clouds, lightning surrounding the band name, and violent waves crashing onto a beach. Tropical Storm was an idea I loved, but it was a reminder of rejection. There were musicians at my high school, but no one wanted to join. The band that became mine never formed, and I had tied some unrealistic dreams to it.

DRIVER'S ED WITH LUCY AND LIZ

In January 1986, I chose to take the driver's education class. I had my learner's permit since I was fifteen years old. I had been permitted to ride my motorcycle, a 1984 Kawasaki KE100. I had immensely enjoyed riding that bike around Sebastian with a very short-lived friendship, who also had his motorcycle. He had his bike first, and through some manipulation, I split my parents to first obtain a small Honda minibike. Then after I proved I could handle a Honda 50, I worked on my mother allowing me to buy the KE100. At this time, when Cyndi Lauper's "Girls Just Want to Have Fun[67]" song was popular, I was listening to Iron Maiden and reading motor-cycle magazines. I would accidentally kill the KE100 when my friend and I attempted to cross a flooded area known as the mud tracks. The water was deeper than we thought and went above my muffler, and the engine died. When it dried out, it never rode over twenty miles an hour when the top speed had been seventy miles an hour. With the KE100, I was able to learn the driving rules of the road and practice alone. I took driver's ed so I could earn my driver's license without having to test through the Department of Motor Vehicles.

---

[67] https://en.wikipedia.org/wiki/Girls_Just_Want_to_Have_Fun.

My perceived anxiety caused me to avoid certain challenges that I thought were difficult to defeat.

The students who did not practice driving through the orange cones would sit under a metal overhang when it was other students' turn to drive. Sometimes we would be in the portable classroom to watch movies about driving and some about consequences of driving under the influence. Under the overhang, two girls motioned for me to sit with them. If I had not been believing the lies that ran through my head—*No one understands you. You can't understand anyone*—who knows how things would have turned out for me with everything. Lucy and Liz were seniors. Lucy was like the bad girl type. She was not thin, but she was not heavy either. She said that she was half Indian (or Native American is more accepted today). She had attitude, but not toward me. She and Liz, who was white and much heavier than Lucy, were genuinely nice to me. We sat together during the majority of the semester. We were together the afternoon that the Space Shuttle Challenger exploded on January 28, 1986, and after the principal announced the tragedy, it seemed the whole school was in shock and somber. When it comes to interacting with women, my wife has noted that I am (still) horrible at reading any signs when someone flirts with me. Looking back, maybe Lucy or Liz liked me, but I was being increasingly emotionally sealed off from others. To this day, I wish I could have known people better.

THE IRON MAIDEN CONCERT AND SO MUCH MORE!

"I want my MTV!" My area finally received the Music Television channel in mid-1986. That was five years after it had premiered on cable. When we received MTV, they played a show in the afternoon called *Metal Shop*. It was a half-hour show of only hard rock or heavy metal videos. Back then, it seemed metal fans would take what we could get. In late September, while playing the tritoms or triple toms for the Vero Beach band, Iron Maiden released their sixth studio album, "Somewhere in Time[68]." The album cover had the thin zombielike character again, but this time, he was retrofitted to appear like a cyborg assassin. I had become an avid reader of heavy metal magazines, and I learned that Iron Maiden would be having a concert about an hour and a half from my house. I still had money from mowing lawns, and that summer I had worked at a fast-food restaurant. Two of my friends worked at the restaurant—the one-year-apart brothers, David and Shawn. David and Shawn's taste in music was similar to mine, and after learning that my oldest cousin Kevin was going to the show and would take me, I asked if my friends could be taken too. Kevin was very easygoing, and my friends' parents allowed us to travel across state to my cousin's house near Tampa, and Kevin would drive us to a civic center in Lakeland to watch the concert. The concert happened on January 18, 1987. I had plenty of time to prepare.

My junior year was a year when my bitterness was setting in like concrete drying. I had a rivalry with the other junior tritom player. (Tritom players wore a harness with three different-sized drums in front of them, which make three different pitches of sounds. They sound awesome to me.) I received more mocking from my peers, and my ability to relate to others was still mostly declining. A new sophomore girl joined the flag corps, and she liked Ricky, and I liked her. Sarah became a good friend to a fellow junior, Jennifer, who played cymbals. Sarah hung around us drummers, as well as David and Ricky, who were best friends. I never asked Sarah out, and before I knew it, she was dating a trombone player.

In the eleventh grade, students who were sixteen or older and had their driver's license could drive to school and park away from the school. That year, I carpooled with David and Shawn, and it was great to avoid school buses for the last two years of my school career. One morning, on Fourteenth Avenue, near Sixteenth Street, the high school principal (and my former Cub Scout den leader) saw a student walking away from the direction of the school. According to his statement to a sheriff deputy, he took his eyes off the wheel to

---

[68] en.wikipedia.org/wiki/Somewhere_in_Time_(Iron_Maiden_album).

write the student's name down. He did not see that the car in front of me was yielding to make a left turn, and the principal's car plowed into my car's rear! Seat belts were not mandated by law then, and I went forward from the impact, but thankfully, I just bashed my thin knee into the dashboard. Shawn and David hit against the driver and passenger chairs, and Ricky, I think his legs hit his side of the dashboard. In the grand scheme of things, I was not seriously hurt, nor were my passengers. The principal, however, hit his forehead against his windshield, and he received some medical attention. He apologized and explained why he took his eyes off the road. I thought that the kid that was skipping was going to be expelled! (He was not.) My car, a metallic gold Nissan 310, was drivable with a large dent in the rear hatchback. This would be the car's first of three accidents with me behind the wheel. A football player's brother rear-ended me, and after a storm, I hit a large fallen tree branch on a street with no lights after a band practice. I was getting dismayed, discouraged, and a little paranoid about driving. My poor car would be three different shades of metallic gold by the time my brother kept it with him in Georgia. Somehow, I was still permitted to drive across the state, but two of those accidents had not happened yet.

Shawn, David, and I arrived at my cousin's house on the day of the concert. We had been listening to Iron Maiden music the whole way there. We arrived in the midafternoon, and my aunt Ruthie informed us that Kevin would drive us to the show after he got off from work. Inwardly, I fretted and shared my worries with my friends that Kevin would get home too late.

"It's sold out. There will be a line!"

Shawn and David assured me it would be all right.

Kevin arrived, and after he ate, he drove us to the show. I had calculated in my head that he would take I-75 to I-4, which would take us to the Lakeland Civic Center. Kevin went the back way, and I did not recognize any of the roads. It was a much shorter route. We listened to his music on the way, and I tried to relax. (Kevin, God rest his soul, would repeat this favor with me alone at another concert in February 1989.)

We arrived, and I think I experienced some derealization over the kaleidoscope of faces. The other concertgoers had black concert T-shirts, denim or leather jackets, and jeans in various conditions. I wore a green Izod polo-type shirt and jeans with new shoes. I quickly bought an Iron Maiden T-shirt, put it on, and felt uneasy when Kevin decided he wanted to sit far from us in the bleachers with his powerful binoculars. Shawn, David, and I wanted to stand near the stage. We all agreed to a meeting place after the concert. It worked out, well.

There was a strong familiar odor in this huge building, and I realized that my best friend's father had been smoking pot in a pipe when I was ten! Teenagers were smoking marijuana in this huge hall. It was a fun yet angry atmosphere. When the headliner began to play, their elaborate futuristic stage, complete with lights, prop spaceships, and progressive cityscape, was revealed. A song from a movie set in the future *Bladerunner* provided an appropriate addition to the set. Then the band began to play, and we had never heard anything so loud in our lives. (I can speak for us, because David, Shawn, and I experienced ringing in our ears for at least two days!)

I found myself enjoying the concert and being a mere forty feet from the band when I felt someone push hard and fast against me. I stepped as forward as I could without bumping into the people in front of me and turned to see a young man, who had been smoking some drug earlier, pass out to the floor. The young man startled me, and the antivictim mentality kicked into gear.

"I hope that—dies!"

Shawn gave me a bit of a shocked look and he laughed. I meant it. Since becoming a Christian, I have thought about the young man. I believe he survived his overdose because he was not in the papers. I have had thoughts of whatever came of him and feeling bad that I wished him dead. That is part of what God has brought to me—a spiritual concern for others.

The concert ended with the band playing their title song "Iron Maiden," and the three of us made our way out with about 25,000 youths and young adults. My whole town of Sebastian could have fit in that building and still have room for about 15,000 more people!

We caught up with Kevin. He always had a way with words. He said, "With my binoculars, I could count the number of hairs on Bruce Dickenson's chin." He was referring to the lead singer, who sported a three-day-looking beard. Coming out of the concert, which was louder than anything I had experienced, Shawn, David, and I complained that we could not hear anything. Our ears rang for at least two days. We returned and stayed one night at my cousin's home. I briefly saw Wendy, but we hardly spoke. I thanked Kevin for taking us. I drove my friends back to their home the next day. I was now even more enamored with the heavy metal culture.

13

ACCEPTANCE AND REJECTION (PART 2)

I wanted to be set free.

THE INSPIRING BOB ROSS

No sooner had I started high school that I felt pressure all around to think about and choose a college. I had begun to pin some of my hopes on college in regard to dating and other carnal interests. Scott had come home a few times and would share stories of parties at his fraternity, of "getting drunk and getting laid." All the teen 1980s movies were sending me signals that I should shun my virginity, and to be one meant that you were a loser. (I do not know if others experienced heightened anger at how some of the awkward boys were portrayed in those teen movies.) Some of my first thoughts and plans were to seek a music scholarship and attend a college that had a good music program. My brother was probably toying with me when he suggested Princeton University. That was not an option. I looked at a college that my father's sister, "Aunt Marcia," worked for in Hays, Kansas. I also looked at my brother's own Mercer University. Scott was partying to the point that he was failing classes, and it was taking him longer to finish his program. What should have taken around two years took about four. I noticed our meals at home were becoming frozen dinners, and there were no frills anymore. Scott was costing my parents a fortune, and as my time approached to make post-high-school plans, my options were dwindling due to tight finances. Staying home was not an option for me. I would have viewed myself as a failure.

During the summer of 1986, I happened to find an inspiring oil paint, wet-on-wet canvas painter on the Public Broadcasting System (PBS). The artist was Bob Ross, who sadly passed away on July 4, 1995. He painted landscapes and seascapes. I cannot describe how beautiful and *peaceful* his paintings were. He seemed to be a very gentle man, and he was a positive influence in my life. He would say that there are no mistakes, "Just happy accidents."[69] I was sad when I learned that he died the year I would start Bible college.

I had been an avid drawer. I mostly drew animals but would tackle *Star Wars* scenes and some of my favorite album covers. Scott and I seemed to have been born with some artistic ability. If it is a gene, it came from our great-aunt Ruth Newton, who was such an accomplished artist that *Walt Disney* had pursued her for animation around the time he was making *Snow White and the Seven Dwarves*[70]. I was taking art classes along with band classes to help keep my grade point average high. I was doing well in the art classes, and I had learned that a trade school that my cousin Kevin had attended offered an associate's degree in commercial art/graphic design. With my options closing, I filled out an application with my mother's help. A talent recruiter from the school visited my home, and he looked at my personal portfolio. The school he represented, Tampa Technical Institute, accepted me. I felt some relief that in the middle of my junior year, I knew where I was going after high school. The dreams, wishes, and hopes began.

BECOMING SOCIALLY AWARE

I remember rare instances of news breaking into my life when I was younger. I have some recollection of seeing some stories about the Vietnam War. I consider seeing news footage of long lines of cars

---

[69] https://en.wikipedia.org/wiki/The_Joy_of_Painting.
[70] disney.fandom.com/wiki/Snow_White_and_the_Seven_Dwarfs.

waiting for gas during what seemed to have been an energy shortage in the 1970s. I recall, in 1979, American officials being taken hostage by Iran. In the mid to late 1980s, I remember being bombarded with images after horrendous violence had taken place. It was then that I learned the phrase "drive-by shooting."

I felt shock and was aghast at the cruelty of people. It would feed my *unsafe* worldview. I felt helpless to listen night after night about young men, around my age or a little older, shooting other young people to death while driving past their victims. My parents would watch national news, while we ate dinner. The drug-related murders became a phenomenon that brought me awareness. The news cameras would capture images of bloody white sheets covering the victims or chalk outlines of a person with bloody puddles. Gangs, I would learn, were fighting turf wars over drugs. Innocent women and children could be caught in the cross fire.

I just thought, *This is wrong. The killers should die!*

I had watched a series of movies about an armed vigilante when I was around twelve. The films were called *Death Wish*. It was one of the graphic offerings from our premium movie channel. I believe that a spirit of murder pulled me toward justifying this certain kind of killing in order to get me to just accept that I could take someone's life. Once while my parents and I were having dinner, and another news story of gang-related violence played, I said, "In thirty years, America is going to be crawling with vigilantes, and I will be their leader."

I said it with conviction and with a grandiose tone. It fit in with the suspicion that I would die through violence, and I would be greater than I was at that point of time. Two things were true—I was vehemently against the shooters and the drugs. My turn away from drugs happened while watching a short, early 1970s documentary about drugs. In the ninth grade, my life management class played a short film called *Dead Is Dead*[71]. It depicted the reality of addiction to drugs, including showing people use needles, people vomit some thick white liquid, one man was shown having extreme diarrhea and

---

[71] educational-film.fandom.com/wiki/Dead_Is_Dead.

soiling himself and much of the restroom he was in, and it showed dead overdosed bodies. The film shocked me! True to my nature, I did not talk to my parents or others about it. My mind snapped shut on the thought of using drugs forever, which was one decision I could be proud about.

One Friday morning, I saw a story on the front page of our local newspaper. It was drug related. I read that a young man, I will call T, was arrested and charged, along with an accomplice, for murder. The young man had been in my world history class. As a favor, I had driven him home a few times. He lived in a poor area of town. According to the newspaper, a man had given his mother's watch for crack cocaine. The man obtained his crack, but he returned to the dealers the next day. One of the dealers was T. T and the accomplice beat the man who returned to try to get his mother's watch. The man was beaten and kicked to death. Waking up to that news shocked me! It was the beginning of what I perceived to be an awfully bad day. I was self-centered, so I did not think of the victim or his mother. That is to be expected when you emotionally withdraw from others.

It was my day to drive, and I picked Shawn and David up at their home. It had been a dreary, rainy day. I pulled up to the juniors parking area and found someone's car in my spot. It just added to the day. Classes seemed to be more difficult. The day was rough. After dropping David and Shawn off, I went home. I remember standing near the dining room table, and I pulled my glasses from my book bag. One of my lenses were not attached to the frame, because it was only held together by fish string, and it broke. I could not fix it, and I felt heat rush to my head. I lifted my leg in a jiujitsu stance (because I had a few private lessons from a martial artist a year before), and I kicked the dining room wall. A heal-sized deep dent was the result. My flash of rage turned to terror. Dad was going to kill me! I thought up a story and used it, and they bought it. The surviving dog, Heather, mother of Duffy, got excited and jumped on me. I lost my balance, and I fell. My shoulder dented the wall. I say thankfully my parents believed. People remained none the wiser, including me.

Just Not Your Kind!

David and Shawn drove me home from school one spring afternoon, and David put a cassette in his car stereo. His speakers hissed, and then a fast, furious barrage of drum notes opened a song called "Wake Up Dead[72]." The band was and at this writing is Megadeth. The song, and every song after, blew me away! I was an instant fan. Some of the songs sounded downright scary! (Picture songs that could sound like a horror movie soundtrack made with electric guitars.) I would learn that the main founder of the band, Dave Mustaine, had been raised in a Jehovah Witnesses family, but he turned to witchcraft for a time. Dave Mustaine played lead guitar and was the vocalist. His vocals were not clean operatic notes, but a cross between talking and singing, with a snarl, but with emotion. The music was fast and aggressive. The style of music had once been known as speed metal, but today it is known as thrash metal.

"Dave this is awesome!"

I had remembered seeing a short news documentary about up-and-coming speed metal bands on MTV a few months before. I remember one young band member who spoke out, looked directly at the camera, and described a particular song. He said that his song was about a boy meeting a girl and the girl meets the boy. The boy falls in love with the girl, but the girl does not love him. The boy kills the girl. The young front man, with blazing red hair and an ungodly intense look on his face, made an impression on me. While the members of my then favorite band Iron Maiden gave me the impression that they could get along with their fans and even maybe like me, Dave Mustaine gave me the impression that Megadeth fans had to earn their respect from the band.

A song called "Peace Sells[73]" largely explained Mustaine's philosophy. He talked to God every day. He paid his bills and went to court when he was summoned. If he did not seem kind, it was because he was not *your kind*.

[72] https://en.wikipedia.org/wiki/Wake_Up_Dead.
[73] https://en.wikipedia.org/wiki/Peace_Sells.

That was it! If I did not mesh with you, that was your problem, not mine! Megadeth taught me it was okay to not get along and it was okay to be at war against the world. I would buy their "Peace Sells... But Who's Buying" cassette and later their "So Far, So Good... So What!" tape.

I want to inform you that Megadeth indeed became another negative influence in my life, but their two founding members are born-again Christians today, and their music is still edgy, but has positive messages. While living my life, I did not know how influential the band's messages would be to me, but looking back, I see clearly now. This is not the last reference you will see of this band in my story.

BAND HALLOWEEN PARTY

Before the horror movie icon Michael Myers would become inadvertently my total focus of attention, I was fascinated by the concept of the angel of death. Iron Maiden's albums often would have a shadowy Grim Reaper in the background of their albums. On October 29, 1987, the high school band held a Halloween party in the cafeteria. It was to be a party that encouraged everyone to wear a costume. There was even a costume contest. I had come a long way and had so much further to go from being the eight-year-old in the hobo costume. I decided to go as the Grim Reaper. I bought a black cloak and used a realistic-looking ceramic skull as a prop. I fashioned a scythe from a long pole and cardboard with an aluminum-covered "blade." I remember putting the white liquid makeup over my face. I colored all the skin around my eyes black, and when I closed my eyes, they looked like a skull's eye sockets. The most tedious part was drawing in teeth over my whitened lips. I was quite proud of my appearance, but I do not remember expecting to win first place in "scariest costume."

At six foot four and weighing around 120 pounds, I made a fairly realistic angel of death. While I remember the party, I do not remember how others were dressed. I was feeling Halloween strongly. I do remember a blonde blue-eyed girl from the flag corps hanging near me. Her name was "Nicole" (not her real name). Maybe being in the costume made me more attractive and maybe I felt confidence behind the costume. She wanted to know who I was, and she realized I was the tallest member of the drumline and band. In a surge of self-confidence, I asked her out and she said yes.

I would make the mistake, apparently, of sharing the good news. I do not remember who I told—it was not more than two. The news got back to Nicole, and she changed her mind. She accused me of bragging about going out with her! I was devastated, and I had just met her. I wrote a letter expressing how hurt and confused I was, and another girl in the drumline, KC, convinced me to save my dignity by not letting her read it. So that was that. I continued to see her at the marching practices and football games, and it was like a knife twisting in my heart—a heart I allowed to grow soft. I would eventually think, *I won't make that mistake, again.* I imagine some of her girlfriends may have talked her out of going on a date with me. Otherwise, I had no idea what really happened. It was fairly clear she was ashamed of me. I had been an outcast.

OF METALLIC MIND AND SKYSCRAPER BODY

"This is the last will and testament of Jeff Gilbert. I, Jeff Gilbert, being of metallic mind and skyscraper body do bequeath the following to…" In the school newspaper, *Arrowhead*, seniors were encouraged to do a mock last will and testament and to have a creative, fun time thinking and writing what you would want to leave your friends. The opening lines were usually the most creative. Instead of writing about being of "sound mind and sound body," I almost immediately came up with metallic mind and skyscraper body. It fit me to a T. I was almost the tallest boy at the school, and my mind and heart were being hardened like steel.

High school turned out to be a more challenging experience than middle school. It seemed the older I became, the more of an outcast I became. I was communally delayed, and many of the friends I had from middle school socially left me behind. I am not sure I was aware of this at the time, but I would experience depressed moods for days and weeks, and then I would feel normal, for me. The social issue bothered me. I would hear, around every Thursday, conversations between the more popular kids at school.

"Hey, man. Are you going to Chris's party?"

"Yeah, dude. I'm going to get wasted!"

After the high school football season, the band had off on Fridays. Adam, my friend since I was ten, would be at these parties or working with his father. It was crazy to go through the week thinking school was a drag, but then the weekend comes, and what? Stay home. Listen to some Iron Maiden or Megadeth, but what else? I hated loneliness. Depressed moods would settle into my weekly routine. It was not a clinical depression—it was more situational.

Resentment and anger would simmer below the surface of me. My music, honestly, did not help the situation. Their messages were also full of resentment, and I thought *my* bands are too sophisticated to just party. Long after becoming a Christian, I would learn pretty much all the rock bands were partying. Some bands had an image of being deeper than that!

The anger I was experiencing, I would learn after getting a master's degree in psychology in 2012, was largely an unhealthy type. It seems that there is a healthy anger and unhealthy anger. People with healthy anger strongly *prefer* people treat them with respect, do not belittle them, and do not get in the way of them reaching their goals. The ones with healthy anger feel intense anger, but they do not lose control of their thoughts and actions. The people with unhealthy anger *demand* to be treated a certain way, not be insulted, etc. A person who "demands" has an inner motivating force that demands satisfaction. These are the types that often escalate disagreements into aggressive arguments and violent confrontations. I want to remind you of my confrontation over Ricky placing pieces of my mom's plant on my head. That was a clear example of unhealthy anger. My anger was in its infancy at this time.

Rejected and Accepted: For What?

I thought about if I wanted to include my senior prom story. I took Tina, another senior, who was in the flag corps. Tina was a petit brunette who was a straight A student. I do not remember when she caught my eye, but I remember it was on a charter bus the band used for away games. She wore her red-and-black skirted uniform. She was also on the dance line, and on the middle song of the halftime show, the girls shed their skirts, and underneath one learns she and the others were wearing the leotard version of their uniform. It was eye-catching, and they let us know they knew it, by flirting looks they would give.

I was not thinking of taking her to the senior prom, but that event was about a month away. I wanted to take her out on a date, instead. I asked her out after my jazz band class. Tina turned me down. I was not devastated this time, but I was not happy about it either. This may sound insulting, but I thought I had lowered the bar of my standards enough. She said, "No thank you," with an, "I'm flattered, but…," expression and slowly turned around and walked away.

Three weeks later, the dust had been settling from that crash and burn when Tina came into the room where I was putting the drum set away.

"Um. Would you go to the prom with me?" she asked.

I do not remember saying yes, but I had to have said yes. I remember feeling confused.

Why? She just turned me down! What? Is she desperate? I thought.

I did not want to take her to the prom. I wanted to go on a date. Apparently, I said yes. I told my mom and she said I had to go. The more I thought about it, the more I did not want to go. I thought, *Why does she want me to go? Was she hard up for a date?* Perspective changes everything, and I took it to be like an insult when I could have been flattered and made the best of the situation. I could have showed her that she chose wisely by making the night feel special for her. That was not who I was at that time. I was going to show her why it was a good idea she turned me down the first time. I was going to make the night awkward at best.

Early after accepting her invitation, I wanted to not go. The whole thing became complicated. I had to pick out and rent a tuxedo that would somehow not clash with Tina's teal dress. (I would learn that teal is a vibrant bluish-green.) I had to get a corsage. It just seemed to me that a date would have been easier. I experienced a lot more than second thoughts, but my mother would not let me out of it. At some point, someone decided that we would go out to dinner with another couple, and that couple, from my point of view, took charge of everything. They decided where we would eat. It was expensive, and the food was not worth it to me.

During the prom, which had a Chinese dragon and New Year theme, many of the songs were rap or hip-hop, even though rap music was a young genre in pop music. Dancing to rap was awkward. Tina and I and the couple we were with did not stay long. (I think I had one slow dance with Tina.) The three decided to drive to Melbourne, which was about forty miles north of Vero Beach, to eat breakfast at Denny's. I just went with it. I remember filling the gas tank of my father's Toyota and hearing Lita Ford[74]'s "Kiss Me Deadly" song, not even thinking about Tina and how the night could end. Tina and I followed the other couple, going 110 miles per hour, trying to keep up and not lose them. We ate our meals, and I began to dread driving Tina back to Vero Beach and then driving back to Sebastian. I also began to imagine listening to Iron Maiden on the way home, and that desire won me over. The loner, outcast was nowhere near to be open to positive changes at this time. I let Tina know that I did not want to drive her home, and I asked the other couple to drive her home. They did. I left after unconvincingly telling her I had a good time. From my memory, she did not seem upset, but I was not good at reading others facial expressions then. We did not speak again during the rest of the school year. I hoped that Tina has forgotten me. I had to have contributed to her not enjoying the prom. I feel bad about that. I would contact her and apologize in 1990 about a month before the rampage God stopped.

---

[74] https://en.wikipedia.org/wiki/Lita_Ford.

14

PREPARING FOR A BRAVE NEW WORLD

Hope to help me want to live.

GRADUATION OR "THE END OF HELL"

It had been a long fourteen years. My school career did not start off being a hellish experience. The early years were actually great, most of the times. I remember my next-door neighbor's grandson and my best friend, Alex, and I starting kindergarten together. We had different teachers, but we were together during lunch and recess. I remember being moderately popular. I remember my mother going with my second-grade class to a planetarium museum as a chaperone and a girl named Cathy squeezing my mom's hand, because Cathy was afraid of the dark. I remember a friend who was into World War II movies, because his father had served, and we would jump from the swing sets and pretend we were paratroopers, hitting the ground when the teacher's head was turned. Then third grade started, and some kind of oppression began. Except for the bullies and having a crush on Jeanie (the "mommy" when we played house in first grade), that year was a blur. I did not pass an end-of-year standardized test, and after resisting instruction through summer school and having a bad attitude, I was held back. That is why it was a long fourteen years. As high school ended, I felt a conflict of emotions, from relief, to dread of experiencing more loneliness, to having hope that the commercial art school would be a new start. "Give me hope! Let me be normal!"

The graduation ceremony was held on Saturday afternoon, June 4, 1988. My parents, of course, attended. I was aware that almost right after the ceremony, my parents would be driving their '84 Dodge Aeries and my brother's and my Nissan 310 to see Scott's graduation. I was going to miss my car, and it was the last day I drove it. My parents would drive both cars to Macon, Georgia, where Mercer University is. They would be gone for at least three days, and I planned on practicing doing what I wanted. My father would graciously let me use his '80 Toyota Corolla, while Scott drove the three-toned golden car.

The ceremony itself was surreal. It seemed that this would be the last time that I would ever see most of my classmates from Sebastian Elementary and the middle school. The ceremony was held at the Vero beach High School football stadium. The temperatures were pushing into the low nineties, but the concrete bleachers were radiating intense heat. The concert band played "Pomp and Circumstance," and I remember thinking the year before that that would be the last time that I performed that traditional song with the band. I was proud, but disappointed that the next Macy's Thanksgiving Day Parade, the classes of 1989–1991 would be performing. My class missed the invitation by one year!

After receiving my diploma, I drove home, and my parents picked up the Nissan and departed for Georgia. I called Shawn and David to see if they wanted to hang out or anything. I picked Shawn and David up, and blasting one of my Iron Maiden tapes, we headed out to a convenience store in Wabasso. We bought some snacks, and at some point, one of us decided it would be a cool thing to smoke a cigar as a celebration of what we had accomplished. David dared me to take a deep drag from the stogie, and I did and immediately coughed up a lung! It was funny to us. I thought about how this was our final semifree summer. I would be starting a job delivering pizzas within a week or two. Shawn would be going to my brother's college, Mercer University. We reflected on some of our past experiences and shared some of our hopes for the next year. Hope was not a dirty four-letter word at this time.

HERE'S JOHNNY!

I had occasionally watched *the Tonight Show*[75] with my mother on Friday nights, while my father was usually sleeping on the couch. During the 1988 summer, I began to watch *the Tonight Show* every weeknight. I do not know why, but I began to pay attention to the suits Johnny Carson wore. I noticed he dressed sharply. I believe the catalyst for this attraction to dress well was when my parents brought me a Brooks Brothers sport jacket they had bought while visiting Aunt Patty and Uncle Bob in Boston. It was a dark-gray tweed jacket with flecks of blue intertwined. It looked very sharp with dark-blue slacks. During the summer, I went shopping for similar suits and sports jackets that Johnny Carson wore. I knew I would have to work when I started the commercial art school. I did not know what job(s) I would have, but it turned out that my second job in Tampa required that I wore nice suits. I include this to point out that I had hope. I was trying to fit in with my perception of societal norms. Scott's prep influence was quite evident still.

THE ANGRY, ABSENTMINDED PIZZA DELIVERY MAN

The week I graduated from high school, I found a help-wanted ad for a local Italian restaurant. "Pizza Gio's" (not the real name) was looking for someone to deliver pizzas on Thursday through Sundays, four o'clock until ten o'clock at night. I was paid four dollars per hour, whether I delivered a pizza or not, and I was given a dollar for every pizza I delivered. The customers would bless me with tips. On a busy Friday or Saturday, I could earn $50 in tips alone! In 1988, this was a big deal to me!

---

75 https://en.wikipedia.org/wiki/The_Tonight_Show_Starring_Johnny_Carson.

Pizza Gio's was a mostly positive experience. The restaurant was family-owned, and the location I worked with was run by the owner's son Rob. I worked with Rob, his girlfriend was the waitress for the restaurant, and Tom prepared the pizza. Rob and his girlfriend were approachable and open, and I perceived they were working to help me open up more. Tom appeared to be standoffish, like I could be. I felt he did not like me, and I did not know how to respond to that, except to stay clear and not talk to him. He was nice from what I could see. He just was not friendly toward me.

Delivering pizzas in the years before GPS was very tricky. The kitchen had a large map of Sebastian, and Rob or his girlfriend would have me write down the directions on a notepad, and I would jet off to the destination. Even with written directions, it could be difficult to see addresses when it was dark, and many areas had few streetlights. I would become stressed at returning to the shop and having one or more orders to deliver. I listened to a lot of Megadeth, especially the "Peace Sells… But Who's Buying?[76]" album in the car. I did not realize it or notice it, but I began to become aggressive, full of attitude! I have explained to people that my temper was like a volcano, and there came a point when it erupted and kept erupting. While driving and stressing about finding my next address, "Mount Gilbert" began to release ash and intense heat. (It was not even erupting yet.) I was alone and free to be angry. No one was present to stop me or scold me. I also remember saying some violent things to other motorists—some even threatening. At one point, I said in a voice (remember I had practiced ventriloquism), "Iiii oughta kill ya, and I think I will!" through clenched teeth. That phrase made its debut during that job, but it was few and far between at first. Within two years, I would be saying the same, similar, and more detailed phrases in a voice that was not purposely changed but was lower and raspy, demonic. I still did not talk to anyone about my increasing openness to violence.

Rob and his family were nothing but kind and patient with me. (If they knew the stuff I was saying from my heart, they probably

---

[76] https://rattlehead.fandom.com/wiki/Peace_Sells…But_Who's_Buying?.

would have called the authorities on me.) Rob remained supportive, and he knew I could only give him four months because I would be leaving for the commercial art program in late September. I watched how Rob and his girlfriend treated each other, and I hoped, hoped to have a meaningful relationship one day. I left Pizza Gio's under mostly good terms. I had accidentally left two delivery pizza bags on my roof and driven off leaving them to eventually fall, hence the absentminded part of this section title. One was never found. Rob and *his* Tina bid me farewell, and I never saw them again.

DAD HAS THE "C-WORD"

I have not heard my dad's voice in thirty-two years. Honestly, I do not miss it. I am sure he has missed his ability to speak all of these thirty-two years. Around late Spring 1988, Dad developed a raspy voice. The old saying could apply that he had "a frog in his throat"—except it was not a frog. My father was diagnosed with cancer of the larynx around July of that year. I remember he immediately began radiation treatment, which he received in Shands Hospital, while he stayed at inpatient housing through Winn-Dixie. I do not remember having a family meeting, being explained what was going on, or praying for healing. I was either left in the dark about much of the details or darkness enveloping me caused me to not care or demand answers—or both is possible, probable.

My father had not smoked since I was born, and it was unlikely that smoking was the cause of his particular type of cancer. Dad had been taking a lot of medicines for his multiple sclerosis, and one pill could have, they learned, cause cancer. Dad had a low, booming, and authoritative voice. That voice had kept "scaredy-cat" alive within me, while resentment and anger at being afraid invited vengeance and aggression. My dad's radiation treatment was not successful. While I was just settling into the art school, Dad's larynx and some lymph nodes had to be removed. He and my mother would later tell me that he "died on the table twice." Some huge, negative events had happened to me before they reported this to me, which could explain why I largely felt numb before, during, and after they told me. Dad had to use a robotic-sounding voice for a long while. He eventually received prosthetic instruments that would help him speak, but not with his voice. He seemed weaker and vulnerable. Instead of appropriately pitying him, I felt less vulnerable and stronger.

FATEFUL MOVE

At some point, I would have to find a place to live while attending art school in Tampa, so my mother and I drove across the state to explore my options. This was huge. The longest I had been away from home had been five days during band camp. Other than the camps, I might have stayed over at Alex's, Adam's, or another good friend's during some Friday nights. This was me, without any supervision at all! I had already been saturating myself into negative things, but now I would have no limits. I would also be responsible for holding at least a part-time job, preparing my own meals (breakfast was waffles and vanilla ice cream for a few weeks), and attending the art school, doing all it required for graduation! I felt anxious about where I would be living. If I had known all that was waiting for me, I am sure I would have stayed home.

My mother and I arrived at the main campus near lunchtime. I remember the main campus's appearance was unremarkable. It resembled a large section of a strip mall. We walked through glass double doors and headed to the administration area. There was a bulletin board that had some housing opportunities. My mom and I were looking at the roommate wanted postings, when a medium-built young man introduced himself after begging our pardon.

"You looking for an apartment? Because I have a really good roommate, and I'm leaving school and I don't want to leave him hanging. I'm Robby. I'm looking to help my roommate get another."

I noticed Robby had a faded shiner, like I had a day after my fight in the seventh grade. Robby partially explained that he was dropping out of school, and his roommate was upset that he was leaving abruptly. I remember his roommate, James, explained why Robbie had the shiner. I do not remember if Robby explained how he allegedly harassed a girl in his class and a few boys followed him home and assaulted him. That is how I understood it.

We followed Robby to the apartment, which was about a few miles from the main campus. I felt excited to see where I might be living. We traveled from Busch Boulevard to Fletcher Avenue. The apartment was not far from the University of South Florida and University Square Mall. I believe I remember my mother being a little concerned that the apartment was near a college. She mentioned that the surrounding neighborhoods could be rough. Robbie pulled into Fredericksburg Apartments. I had no expectations, so it looked like it could be livable. They were clean gray-block structures. My campus was several more miles away, but it was not an unreasonable drive. We only drove by the apartment to see if the area would be safe enough. Robby had provided his roommate's name, James, and phone number before we parted ways.

My mother and I returned home to our modest one-story house that had been our home since 1973. I was told that James would be home that night, around six o'clock. I called James around six thirty, and he answered the phone. I have told this testimony at various venues or to individuals for about twenty-eight years. I tell people that it seemed that "Christians were coming out of the woodwork." That is not to be disrespectful today, but to explain my past disrespectful mindset. James was the first born-again Christian I met, one of many!

James only seemed to want to know if I was a Christian.

"I'm looking for a Christian roommate. Are you a Christian? Robby wasn't," he asked and stated.

I paused very briefly and said with some conviction, "Yeah. I'm a Christian. I go to church every Sunday." I lied. I did think, though, that I was a Christian because I had gone to church.

James seemed to relax a little after I told him something, I knew absolutely nothing about. James's voice was not high, but it was preppy. He sounded like a decent guy, and by the end of the call, James offered me to share the apartment with him. We said our goodbyes, and we committed to follow through with details. I hung up and wondered why he was hung up on having a Christian roommate?

LEAVING THE LIVES I KNEW

I worked a few more weeks at Pizza Gio's, while my father continued to receive radiation treatment about five hours away, and I said goodbye to Shawn, David, and Adam. Shawn would attend Mercer University. David would remain in Sebastian, working at a funeral home. Adam would stay in Sebastian temporarily while working at a high-end sight-and-sound shop. Adam and his girlfriend would eventually move to Orlando, and Adam would be a support, if I knew how to receive it.

Leaving home is a rite of passage, but it seemed so big to me! No one really prepared me. I did not give them a chance. At some point, my drum sets would be sold, along with my BMX-style bike, my ten-speed skateboard, and my video games. I felt a strong mixture of nervousness, sadness, and optimism. I was leaving the few friends I had, neighbors, and my grandmother, Mom's mother, Nana. Papa died my junior year of high school after he had been initially hospitalized for a bleeding ulcer. His Medicare coverage apparently ran out, and he refused food or drink after he was placed in a local nursing home. I believe he died of organ failure from dehydration. He was seventy-six.

I was also leaving my "lives." The changes that would occur within a month would engulf me and drive me toward that *fiend* I described in the first paragraphs of this book. I was leaving the me who had been popular and spirited, the increasingly awkward child who was fortunate to have any friends, and the lovesick but increasingly frustrated teenager. Now, who was I going to be? I *wanted*, but I did not know what I wanted or needed.

The time came—the weekend of September 10—to move to Tampa. My mother had a coworker Andrea, and her friend help transport my bed, computer desk, a dresser, and my Fischer boom box on Andrea's truck. They followed my mother's car and my father's Toyota. I was mostly optimistic. *I'm going to learn how to do art, like a professional. I'm going to make real money.* Not much thought went into who I would associate myself with, what my values were, or how I would handle seemingly (to me then) unbearable stress.

15

YES, HE'S BACK!

A mission sent from hell.

FREE TO BECOME

What was I free to become? Would I become a well-paid graphic designer? Would I be part of a friendship among four outstanding artists? Would I remain a minimum wage retail sales associate? I did not travel to Tampa to become what I would later describe to be a potential homicidal maniac. Equally true—no one sets out into a destructive path. They have to be *misled*.

I do not remember what I listened to on the way to the drive to my apartment in Tampa, but at some point, I turned on a Tampa radio station. I only remember one song from that drive. A local Tampa station played Elton John's "Rocket Man[77]" as I was merging onto my main road, Fletcher Avenue. I do not pay attention to lyrics, and my wife would vouch for that. So for this chapter, I looked up the lyrics for "Rocket Man" and was struck that the chorus described someone leaving far from home, being gone for a long time, and "I'm not the man they think I am at home." Of all the songs I had to have listened to, "Rocket Man" is the one that I never forgot.

We arrived at the apartment, and we all moved my bed, dresser, computer table, lamp, and boom box into it. I thanked Andrea, her

---

[77] https://en.wikipedia.org/wiki/Rocket_Man_(song).

friend, and my mother. I was not an ingrate yet. I could sense Mom's sadness, and I knew she had to return to her and my father's home with him not there, only the surviving sheltie Heather waiting for her. Andrea and her friend left soon after delivery, and my mother stayed and left about an hour later. She gave me a kiss on the cheek, like she always does.

After she left, I made myself a sandwich, after my mom had bought some groceries. I was alone and free, and to me, I never tasted a better sandwich. I thought, *I'm free*. I would remain alone through the weekend because James would not return to the apartment until around eight o'clock Sunday night. My roommate would go back to his hometown almost every weekend. His home was an hour and a half away. Mine was three hours away. During the weekend, I did not fret about being alone. I watched his TV and listened to my music, loudly.

Some say you never get a second chance at making a first impression. James arrived back at the apartment at around eight at night. James was a few inches shorter than me, but his 6'2" looked more filled out than my 6'5". James had dirty-blond hair, wore wire-rimmed glasses, and had dimples in his cheeks when he spoke and smiled. James may be the first true Christian peer I can remember meeting. He looked peaceful and confident. We talked for about three hours. He filled me in on his last roommate's drama and per- ceived faults. He and I discussed what we wanted to do with our future, respective degrees. (James was in the electrician program, and I was in the art program.) I was on my best behavior and my normally easygoing self. James seemed to accept me. Eleven o'clock came, and James had to go to bed. He worked at a bank, in a high- rise, in downtown Tampa and had to fight I-75 traffic to get there by eight.

That Thursday night of my first week, James informed me of seeing a sign for free kittens at a plant nursery down our street.

"Why don't you go by there, and if it looks okay, pick one up."

I had never owned or raised a cat, but I loved all animals. "I will."

Friday afternoon, I drove about a block from our apartment and pulled into the nursery. The nursery had assorted plants leading

155

to a small shacklike store. The ground, even in the store, was covered with mulch. I saw at least a few roaches (and I do not *do* roaches). I asked to see a kitten if they were still giving them away. An older lady handed me a gray tabby kitten. It fit in the palm of my hand easily. I thought it was a female, and in my head, I named "her" Carrie. I named her after a horror movie and a dream I once had. (The cat turned out to be a boy, but was answering to that name, so the spelling was changed to Cary, like the late actor Cary Grant.) I brought Cary home and bought dishes for him. He melted my heart, like the puppies had. I played a little rough with him too as if he was a puppy. James came home that Sunday night, and he seemed to be happy with Cary too. Cary took to me.

I could not help paying rent without a job, so the next week, I went job hunting. The first place I applied for hired me. Rax, a fast-food restaurant that served roast beef sandwiches, called me back and offered me a job. I told my mother the good news, and she ran it by Aunt Ruthie, who lived near Tampa. After Ruthie learned where the restaurant was located, near the Tampa Bay Buccaneers stadium, Ruthie gave me advice to not accept the position. Ruthie stated that it was a high-crime area because of strip joints down the street. Drugs and prostitution ran rampant on that road. So I applied at a couple more places, J.C. Penney and Toys "R" Us. The toy store hired me, and I started as a $3.35 an hour minimum wage sales associate. I was actually excited to start. *So far, so good, Tampa.* So I was a commercial art student and a sales associate so far.

October 10, the first night of school arrived. It was about a thirty-minute drive from the apartment. The night classes started at six and ended at ten. I believe we bought the art equipment we needed for the first quarter. I bought a cardboard portfolio and a tackle box, which held all the equipment. It was, to me, exciting to be buying professional, commercial art gear.

The first quarter teacher was a pretty young woman who resembled Bernadette Peters from the early 1980s. I noticed and would continue to notice that a student, around her age, flirted with her. (They would end up marrying after their divorces were finalized.) I would estimate there were around fifteen classmates. We all sat at large interlocked drafting tables/desks in a spacious office setting. There were two rows, and each row faced each other. A space between allowed the instructor to walk and inspect work or answer questions. I looked around and saw a few people who could be placed in the same outcast category as me. Two seemed to speak very easily to each other, and it turned out that they were high school friends who enrolled together. I would learn their names were Mike and Johnny. Next to them was a pretty redhead Christian named Kim. I never heard her say a negative thing about anyone. Across from me was Dan, who would marry the teacher by around Christmas. A long-haired, wire-rimmed glasses-wearing, man in his midtwenties sat next to me. Another long-haired but thinner young man sat near as well. A heavier redhead sat near the one who wore glasses. I did not take in all the classmates on the first night, because I felt panicked when we were asked to draw free hand, anything we wanted to draw.

The first night of school was an occasion to experience inadequacy. I remember looking around and seeing the other students' astounding works of art. I felt like I was out of my league. I was, but I am proud to say that I took the approach of accomplishing art like I did to learning drum music parts—I took it seriously and I practiced. Back to that night, I just swallowed and thought, *Too late to quit. Just stay with it.* When I was not working at Toys "R" Us, I was usually working on a project or practicing. There was a week when my new routine was disrupted.

While watching TV with James, a commercial for a new Halloween movie played. *Halloween 4*[78] was going to be released in October 21. James did not know about me having an on and off obsession with the holiday or the *Halloween* movies. My eyes probably widened, and my ears become more attentive as I asked James if he wanted to see it. (*Ah, freedom to see what I want to see.*) The wise saying "careful little eyes what you see" was not in my awareness, of course.

James said, actually enthusiastically, "Yeah, I'll stay here that weekend."

---

[78] en.wikipedia.org/wiki/Halloween_4:_The_Return_of_Michael_Myers.

THE RETURN

A week after school began, the teacher asked the class, "Junie needs a ride home every night. She lives near Fowler. Can someone take her home?"

Blast my weakness for girls! I looked around, and there were a few cute women that could be Junie. I raised my hand. I took a chance. "I go near there. I can take her."

Ms. Peters turned to a heavy young woman that I had judged to be childish in the class and said, "Jeff will take you then."

I thought, *You know. You could get to learn who people are so you know who people are in this kind of situation!*

I drove Junie home and I want you to understand who I was then, I am not that now. I had been hardening my heart and mind. I would not be rude today, like I could be then. Junie did have a high-pitched childish manner about her. (That is just observation.) I was cursing myself for offering her these rides. It was taking me out of the way by an additional fifteen minutes. I just complained like mad on the inside. On that Thursday of the first week of driving her, Junie asked me if I would be mad if she did something. I do not remember answering, but the next thing I knew, she leaned toward me in her seat and planted a kiss on my cheek. (That had to have taken some courage.) Junie, before I had a chance to react, bolted out of the car and quickly entered her mobile home. I felt like I was in a horror movie or psychological thriller. I remember staring straight ahead. I was not flattered. I was enraged! It was roiling on the inside of me. A snapping was taking place. I drove home, and my memory of that night fades. Spiritually induced blackouts were beginning.

The next day, I worked at the Toys "R" Us, and James and I went to see *Halloween 4* after he came home from his job. I do remember being excited and looking forward to seeing it all day. I had thought the murderer had died in *Halloween II.* (*Halloween III* had nothing to do with the first two.) I remember being briefly disappointed with the opening credits not including a jack-o'-lantern with the piano music theme playing. I feel no need to share any scenes or any of the plot. I am walking a thin line between explaining how different media were influencing me and avoiding promoting these media sources. If you have never seen *Halloween* movies, I think you are better off not watching them. I just want to share that I believe it was after the movie that I *fully invited* evil into my life.

James had driven us, and I remember distinctly the drive home. I was behaving erratically and as if I was having an episode of hysteria. In my memory, I could see me from my point of view, but I could also perceive me from my right side. I kept repeating, at least three or four times, "Yes! He's back! He's back! He's back!"

I raved about the Michael Myers character surviving, being back, and even living at the end of this movie. I felt the night, the coolness, the dampness. (Tampa had cooler, more fall-like weather than the Sebastian area.) I felt that Halloween atmosphere that I had felt at the age of eight very strongly. James must have looked at me like I was crazy!

Earlier that week, I had innocently asked James to tape *Halloween I* and *II* on his VCR. James agreed to tape them. The week after, while James was at work, I watched the movies when I was not working at the toy store. I remember watching them over and over, and then I do not remember anything else about that week, including functioning at work, at school, or with interactions with James. I do not remember driving Junie home that week. I must have functioned adequately enough because I did not have any negative feedback from anyone. I just did not and do not remember anything, until…

The first thing I remember was hearing a familiar song, and I was sitting in my car, apparently getting ready to pull out to go to school. Megadeth's "Into the Lungs of Hell[79]" somehow pulled me back to reality. It was like waking up to a place unexpected, hearing familiar music, and realizing you had plans you do not remember making that could ruin several lives!

When I came to, hearing the heavy metal song, I had planted ideas along with mental images or violent visions embedded in my mind. I thank God that an instrumental song with Hell as its theme

---

[79] https://en.wikipedia.org/wiki/Into_the_Lungs_of_Hell_(Megadeth_song).

seemed to have pulled me out of a trance. In a trance, voluntary functioning may be diminished or suspended. I, of course, did not credit an evil, spiritual influence, but my then "holy-day" Halloween. I was *supposed* to take the Toyota up to eighty miles per hour, release Junie's seat belt, quickly reach over to the passenger's door handle, open it with my long right arm, and shove her with my left! I saw how the scenario was supposed to work out. I saw Junie's wide-eyed, surprised look just before she is flung from my car. The vision continued briefly and "showed me" that I was supposed to go home and grab our butcher knife. I was supposed to stab anyone I saw while walking on the sidewalk near my apartment. It was all laid out, complete with visuals. I "saw" one young man's pained surprised look after I plunge the blade into his chest.

The song pulled me back to reality, and I rejected those plans. I did *not* do it. It freaked me out. Days of my memory were not there, and they still are not! I do credit the Megadeth song for stirring up that awareness of a lingering fear of a literal Hell. Megadeth has a special place in my life, and I am thankful that the two founding members are serving Christ today.

The next night started the weekend, and Cary and I were home alone. James again visited his mother and brothers. Although I resisted, fairly easily, following through with the ideas of what was described above, I still felt Halloween strongly. I looked out the kitchen window and watched the breezes make the oak tree leaves sway and whisper like when I was eight. It was cool enough to have the windows open. I believe I remember wondering, *Is Halloween a spirit?* Maybe another trance occurred. Two concepts were swirling around in my mind. Perhaps my yearning to feel significant influenced me to not reject that "I am the physical manifestation of Halloween, and the movie *Halloween* was prophetically written, and I was to be the fulfillment."

These spiritually induced trances were dangerous! I think of the many heinous crimes that have occurred by others to others and understand when people gasp and think, *Why would someone do such a thing? How did he think to do that? He's sick!*

Throughout His Word, God admonishes us to be alert, aware, and sober. An idle or easily influenced mind could be filled with doctrines of demons, a warning the apostle wrote in 1 Timothy 4:1. On October 28, 1988, I did not know the enemy had me trapped like a python coiled around its prey. My ignorance had me locked into ever-increasing delusional thoughts.

INVADER

A few weeks later, I woke up to James saying loudly in my ear, "Wake up, Jeff! We've been robbed!"

"What?" I answered with a clearer mind than I expected.

James in forced speech, heightened with anxiousness, exclaimed, "Someone broke in last night! They took my wallet and my disc player!"

I got up and followed James into the living room where the CD player was missing. (He did not steal the TV or the VCR.) I eventually learned that the thief took my watch—one that displayed constellations and phases of the moon. It was a gift, and I actually had cherished it.

"James, when I put your shampoo back, were you awake?" I had run out of my shampoo and had borrowed his until I bought a new bottle the day before.

"No, I didn't hear you put it back. I was asleep."

Fear and a very creepy feeling came over me. After James went to bed, I stayed up for a bit. Just before I went to bed, I placed his shampoo at the open entrance of his room. When I did, I heard some movement. I was not in a talking mood, so I just placed the bottle down and went back to my room. My door was closed. The movement I heard sounded like someone who was awake, moving in the room. I believe I heard the burglar! That realization brought an enormous amount of fear.

James had contacted the Tampa Police; and an officer came, took our statements down for the report, and dusted James's open windowsill for prints. I, honestly, felt anxiety and I had difficulty going to sleep for what felt like a long time. Tampa could be rough, and I was still living in an unsafe world.

Unplugged

If some people do not like situations, many people figure out how to make the best of them or mature ones seek to learn from them. Me? Back then I began to feel unbearable stress, and I did not face the situations. I began to dissociate, disconnect, or *unplug*. I remember meeting my parents at my aunt and uncle's house in Brandon on Thanksgiving 1988, and a strong emotional wave washed over me. Emotionally, briefly, I felt like I regressed, feeling like a child.

I don't want to live here, anymore. I don't want to go back to work tomorrow. I want to go home. I'm done. I'll quit school. Thoughts were running through my mind. I wanted to go home! The inner voice sounded like a boy of about eight years old. I would begin to hear that kid a lot more. I sat back and stared straight ahead and unplugged my emotions. I felt sadness and anxiousness drain away, until I felt emotionally numb.

Leading up to when I felt like I could not take it anymore, I encountered a lot of stress at the art school. I was gratified that I was being taught techniques that were helping me crank out works of art that were genuinely good, but every Thursday, a big project was due. In early November, the class had to do a still-life drawing. I may have dodged a bullet, so to speak, when I did not throw Junie out of my car, but I had a sincere obsession with the pagan night. I went home and carved a jack-o'-lantern, a dark cloak resting to the right and a butcher knife (my mom's) resting against the pumpkin. I took a photo with exceptionally low lighting, and when I returned to class, I drew and shaded my macabre work. As my drawing began to take shape, a student named Mick said under his breath, "Someone has seen too many *Halloween* movies." (You think?)

When you live a mere few blocks from University Square Mall, wouldn't you find yourself going there when you had nothing else to do? Well, I visited there at least a few times. I looked at a store devoted to knives and cutlery. I want to say it was a Cutlery World store. I thought our kitchenware was lacking. I was upset that our butcher knives were much smaller than the ones in the store. Moving deeper into the mall was a large music store. I chose to take a chance on another new heavy metal album. I bought Metallica's "And Justice for All[80]" cassette.

Metallica is a band similar to Megadeth in that they are a thrash metal band, but Metallica had a more humanist theme to their music and lyrics than some of Megadeth's paganism themes. I thought, at the time, they were a great band. They were aggressive. I remember sitting at my computer desk in my room and listening through the entire album, while James again was at his mother's. A song called "Dyers Eve[81]" reflected how I was feeling. A young man no longer home felt life was too difficult to complete. The young man in the song curses his parents for not adequately preparing him. In the end of the song, he ends his life. I did not want that for me at the time. I was struggling, and looking back, except for the Junie issue, I was *not* doing horribly. I was holding down a job. I did leave Toys "R" Us, and a department store called Burdines hired me. (This is the job that required that employees wear coats and ties.) I was keeping up with my art projects. I was learning to pay a share of my rent, electric, and food. I, however, still was not seeking proper prospective. I had just begun on my own, and I was writing myself off as a failure! Hours and days of being alone opened me up to more demonic influence. There was still a resistant part of me. On the new album, a song called "One[82]" has a line that has the singer call out to God after being severely wounded during a war depicted in a movie. I would sing in my car, "Hold my breath as I wish for death. Oh, please God help me!" I did sing it as a prayer. I was lost.

In early December, the class was going to meet at the night campus and drive to an art museum for a field trip. I, along with others in the class, did not know how to get to the museum. Everyone was going to follow the teacher and try to keep up with each other. Traffic lights began to not cooperate with me. I was in front of the student with long hair and a mustache, who I'll call Duane. I was coming up to a light that was red but turned green, and I kept going on my

---

[80] https://metallica.fandom.com/wiki/...And_Justice_for_All_(album).
[81] https://metallica.fandom.com/wiki/Dyers_Eve_(song).
[82] https://metallica.fandom.com/wiki/One_(single).

merry way. As I was coming up to my green light, a car blurred into my sight, and I clipped the driver's left rear. Our cars were dented, but drivable and street legal. Duane and Shannon, who were carpooling, briefly stopped to make sure everyone was okay, and then they drove on to the museum. They told me they would let the teacher know what happened.

The accident happened near Tampa Bay, and the place appeared to be an industrial area. It had to be around 7:00 p.m. I saw no pay phones or traffic that could help. The person who hit me was a middle-aged woman. She suggested I find a phone to call police. I walked off and felt like I walked several blocks before I came to a pay phone. (This was long before cell phones were available and phone booths were near sidewalks.) I called the police and made my way to the scene of the fender bender. When I got back, I saw the red-and-blue lights from afar. As I walked up, I learned that the other driver gave her side of the story and that it was a lie. She told the officer that her light was green, and my light was red. (This was before traffic lights had cameras to verify evidence.) I was given a ticket and told that I could contest it. I drove home mad and shaken.

I later asked Duane if he remembered how long "our" light was green, and he answered that it was green for at least a few seconds. I asked Duane if he would be my witness and he agreed. (I won the case five months later.) It was through this incident that the ice was broken between me and the other four artists who had become a tight knit of friends. For the first time, I was a part of a group of good friends with similar talents and similar interests. Plus, I was the only one who lived away from my parents. My apartment would become a sanctuary and a place for parties. That seemed to be a positive.

In late November, my mother told me that Aunt Ruthie told her that Kevin was going to go to a Metallica concert in Lakeland, Florida, where I had seen Iron Maiden with my high school friends. Kevin offered for me to go with him on January 18, 1989. This was something to look forward to.

Another thing to look forward to would be moving out of our apartment and finding another one. James informed me that our lease was up in February and that we would find another place to live. James was concerned about our apartment being broken into, and the burglar was never caught.

The year 1988 was ending. It seemed to be closing on a hopeful note, and although I continued to consume negative, dark media, I did not dwell on what had almost happened that Halloween. I know I went home for Christmas, but I cannot remember a thing. (Now, I can look at the baby in a nativity display and say, "I know that baby! That baby, turner Savior of the world, saved me!") The next two chapters—the years of 1989 and 1990—will be much darker. The enemy was finding me to be an increasingly useful vessel. Unbeknownst to the enemy and me, light and deliverance were on their way.

16

MY MIND

Compelling lies I believed.

FEELING AT HOME

My cousin Kevin came through for me. If he were still alive, I would want him to hear that. The band Metallica were coming to play in Lakeland, and Kevin invited to take me. We purchased our own tickets, and he drove me to the concert after he got off from work on February 10, 1989. I had been let go by Burdines after Christmas because I was hired for seasonal help. It was not a permanent job. I would be free that night and the next day. Kevin had to work the next day.

Kevin and I pulled up and parked, and we saw several black-clothed young men and women drinking outside of their cars. I remember hearing one rambunctious guy scream, "Metallica!" Here I was in the same venue two years past seeing Iron Maiden with my two high school friends. Last time I was here, I felt like I was more than a little out of my element. This time, I felt at home. I was comfortable. I was among other angry, aggressive outcasts. The atmosphere was dark.

The concerts were awesome! I have to give the bands their due. Queensryche opened up for Metallica, and they were amazing. Queensryche's singer had the voice of an opera singer. They were one of my favorite bands. They came from Seattle, and their politics were definitely progressive. In spite of that, I appreciated their talent.

I did not want my ears to ring like it did after my first real concert, so I stuffed some cotton balls in my ears. Despite that when Metallica opened with their first song, I found I had never heard anything so loud! The band played their set, which took about two hours. Kevin turned to me near the end of the concert and motioned for me to follow him. We were leaving early because Kevin had to be at work in the morning. I remember walking outside of the arena and still being able to hear the band, albeit muffled! I thanked Kevin for taking me and drove to my apartment after we arrived at his home. That was the last outing I would have with Kevin. Kevin died in 2010.

Around midnight, I arrived at my apartment to a friendly meowing Cary. I was in a good mood until I opened the refrigerator to get a drink. There was a nasty note written by James taped to the sweet tea container. (James was a little passive-aggressive, and he would leave me notes when he was displeased about something I did or did not do.) Apparently, my undiagnosed attention deficit hyperactivity disorder inattentive-type-self made the punch and tea in the wrong containers. God forbid my carelessness! Yes, James and I were having some clashes. I did not think I was a slob, but James kept things more organized and cleaner than even my mother. We had just moved to a new apartment, which was exciting, but he seemed to be distracted and easily annoyed.

James and I started clashing a little bit not long after I moved into the old apartment. I do not remember cursing or using profanity around him, but why would I not? I was a sinner, not a Christian, and I was steeped in aggressive, angry media. James ran afoul of me when he said, "Because you listen to heavy metal, you're going to Hell."

Whoa. Where did that come from?

I remember answering, "I don't believe you go to Hell for what you listen to, but who you are." (Obviously that conversation happened before I almost threw Junie out of my car!) I was annoyed that

James would judge me. I had already learned of his pet sin, and I knew it was his weakness. It damaged his witness to me.

James did try to reach out to me. He took me to his hometown, introduced me to his mother and brothers and his friends, and took me to his church. I remember the people being much louder than my old Methodist church. I sat through the sermon, but I do not remember one word—I am not sure I heard one word! (The enemy can render one deaf, blind, or mute.) I remember looking up and seeing the pastor crying! Tears were running down his cheeks. He was weeping. I heard inside of me, *What a faker!* A slight empathetic mood that was rising in me was shoved aside by those words, and I felt like the pastor was trying to build sympathy for a big offering. For all I know, God may have told him that a possessed visitor was in the church. The pastor could have been praying for me or any other lost souls in that building, but the enemy within convinced me to dismiss all of it, including James's efforts to reach me.

MY FIRST ART GIG

I had left the sales position at Burdines under good conditions. They said they simply did not need me anymore. I would start to look for another job. My parents, God bless them, were helping me make ends meet, but I needed to find work. Sears hired me for a position in their men's department. While meeting the store manager during orientation, I told him that I was a commercial art student. The store manager informed me that their display department was looking for another artist. He asked me if I would be interested, and the next thing I knew, I was working with the display team. I felt so proud! Here I was, an art student being accepted for a commercial art position before graduation! Hope, which was not a dirty four-letter word to me, yet flooded me!

I started the next Monday, and the art supervisor showed me what he wanted me to work on and how to do it. He took me to a room with an old projector, and it cast a large image of the words "Sears Furniture Express" on a wall. There was a huge piece of paper that spanned the projected words and had room leftover. The supervisor gave me the task to trace the letters and words onto the paper in a twelve-foot version and an eight-foot version. I felt anxiety about starting the project. Not only would the letters be traced, but also I would be painting the letters in black paint. While working on this project, the supervisor would have me do other tasks, like design displays for mannequins in the men's and women's departments. This included having to undress and redress a female mannequin, which was awkward, embarrassing, and an arm fell off it!

I completed the furniture signs and all the displays (so I thought), but Friday afternoon, the supervisor told me I was too slow. He said I spent too much time on the signs and that the other team members had to cover other projects that I did not get to. He fired me. I was crushed! Negative thoughts assaulted me, and most, if not all, were my own. I thought, *Fired. You can't do this. Fired.* My disjointed thoughts were that I could not do the commercial art job. I was not fast enough. I drove home at around eighty-five miles per hour, zipping in and out of tight spots, not caring if I died in a fiery crash.

Mr. West, the Sears men's department manager, called me later and let me know that he still wanted me for his department. I was grateful and accepted. I started that following Monday. I worked full time and had to wear suits. I worked with a few of the other associates and thought everything was going okay. On Friday afternoon, Mr. West asked me to follow him, and as we went up the escalator, Mr. West pointed to the first floor and gave me a lecture I will not soon forget.

"Look down. You see that? That is your subdepartment, and it looks like Hell!"

Mr. West explained that he hired me to run the underwear, socks, and work clothes subdepartment. I looked down, and it was in shambles. T-shirts, underwear, and socks were not put back properly. It *was* a mess. Here's the thing. I do not remember him telling me throughout the week to work that section, ever! So I was left with two possibilities. One, Mr. West wanted to get me back for not taking his position. Two, I may have experienced another trance and never directly heard the supervisor. I do not think it is two, but it is possible. I just do not want to think that Mr. West would set me up for that very discouraging moment.

I stayed with Sears for about six months. It was not a bad experience. One of the articles I sold was coveralls for mechanics, the outfit that the Michael Myers's character wore. I did not think anything about it at the time, but later I would "need" one of those outfits. I ended up quitting the position at my mother's suggestion. The company had approved me for a short vacation so I could attend David's (my friend from my high school) wedding. Mr. West later disapproved my time off because the company changed the weekend, and they were going to perform the annual inventory. I protested, but he refused to budge. I was extremely disappointed, and my mother told me to leave the company. So I clocked out, left, and drove back to Sebastian to attend the wedding. (In hindsight, that seems to be an irresponsible action, but I think I would do it again. My next job had a Christian who was real, and her witness of Christ's love would eventually succeed in reaching me. You will see.) I would find another job within about one week.

WEARING ME DOWN

"Whatever is true, whatever is noble, whatever is right, whatever is pure, whatever is lovely, whatever is admirable—if anything is excellent or praiseworthy—think about such things" (Philippians 4:8).

If I had been following the Apostle Paul's admonition, I would have avoided a lot of emotional upheaval. I, however, would have foolishly scoffed at such a proposition. Whatever is pure, lovely, and noble flew in the face of what I was submerging myself into, the genre of death.

Duane, Johnny, Mike, and Chaz seemed to welcome me into their circle. Shannon and a tall, lanky student Mick would join us during some of the breaks. (Mick looked like Batman's enemy, the Joker.) Those that smoked, smoked. I usually grabbed a Snickers bar and a soda to carry my fast metabolism through to an eleven o'clock dinner. In spite of being among friends, who shared my interests in death, horror movies, and some heavy metal, I felt like I was among my kind, except I would still feel out of place. I was feeling disrespected (yet I do not think I was being disrespected), and inadequacy called out for a correction, a retribution.

It was during these several months in 1989 that I began to have intrusive thoughts, many of which I did not agree with. Some of them, I did. Aggressive and interesting (to me then) thoughts and phrases started running through my mind, similar to me as a preteen beginning to say, "I hate," because it was in my heart. The phrases were lighting on me. I would accept them and begin to live them. One was, "Respect me in life or in death. Yours!" I share these not only for added context but also as a warning if you detect thoughts that "exalt themselves against the knowledge of God" ever running through your head (2 Corinthians 10:5).

During the spring and summer months of that year, I was experiencing mood swings ranging from depression, anger, and rage to some manic-like good moods. The good days I labeled as my "It's great to be young and insane" days. The bad days I could not get to sleep. I was apathetic. I felt empty and numb. Anger was increasing, and hopelessness was trying to settle in. Phrases would rise up, and I would hold onto some of these. "Do unto others before they do unto you." It was a direct affront to Jesus's Golden Rule, to treat others as you would want to be treated. I liked the thought of being psychotic. Why not? I was dwelling on thoughts of one day having a do-over and following through with what almost happened the past Halloween. I remember outside of class while talking to one of the art friends, I blurted, "I wonder what it feels like to stab a rib cage? Would the knife break through or stop?" The friend, who was himself twisted, made no big deal about it. The friends joked around a lot and rarely took anything seriously. One afternoon before seeing a movie with Johnny, I said, "I have the will to kill, but lack the guts." That thought was my own after the enemy had been working intensely on me. I noted I wanted to do something violent, but I was not mentally ready for it. My parents' style of parenting—to make it clear that consequences come with negative behavior—had made it more difficult to just go on a rampage. There was too much hope in me still. There was one phrase that came that now sounds ridiculous, but I glommed onto it. It was, "I am saving my anger for a scary day." That one felt like directions. I needed to not lose my temper so much and to store wrath up for a scary day? Halloween? It was around this time that I began to resign myself to the idea that I would go on a rampage on that night. I just did not know when. The night came every year, and I still had nowhere near the certainty that I could go through with it, but my mind was being assaulted with violent thoughts, slowly at first.

"That's Not Good"

Sometime during that summer, I must have begun to reach out to Adam, who was living with his girlfriend while attending the community college. Adam is probably the closest friend I ever had. I frequently hid out at his house from the age of ten until around fourteen. We truly confided to each other—or at least, I did to him. So I began to call him. He could tell I was changing. During one conversation, I began to tell him about some of the aggressive thoughts I had been having. I began to refer to myself separately from "my mind." I would say something like, "My mind is saying this…" Adam was taking an introduction in psychology class, and as I continued to refer to my mind as something separate from me—my personality—Adam said, "It sounds like you have a split personality." He also said, "That's not good." I remember many of our conversations for the next year had Adam saying, "That's not good." He stayed with me, though. He did not know how bad I was. No one, including me, knew. During that summer, we rebonded over our comic book collecting. (The art friends were comic book collectors.) Plus, that was the year that Tim Burton's *Batman* was released. There was a revival in the comic book world. Adam did make me feel welcomed.

One of the things that was *not* good was when James's mother and brothers visited us, and the apartment was packed with his family. I thought about killing them. I envisioned James coming home and finding his family dead, a bloody mess. I think I laughed at that thought but was inwardly shocked and rejected it. James and I clashed more frequently, and he was still leaving sticky notes, correcting me. I came home from my new TJ Maxx store job, and James left me one about me keeping Cary (the cat) in my room. I wrote a note back telling him, "Eat—and die! And Cary's staying with me!"

Maybe after that was when James distanced himself from me and became unfocused. He began to skip classes, and he started hanging out with a seventeen-year-old girl and her mother on their front porch at the apartments. It was obvious James wanted a relationship with the seventeen-year-old, but I believed it would not end well. Not long after James made his intentions known and rejected (apparently, because I was not there), James dropped out of his electronics program, quit his job, and moved back to his mother's home. If I had an ounce of empathy, maybe I could have encouraged him to continue in his program. My increasingly grim behavior certainly could not have helped James's situation. So I needed to find a roommate.

CHANGES: SOMETHING'S COMING OVER ME

The visions or dreams of me being an old man alone in the depressing motel room began around this time. Why was he alone? Because he was antisocial. Why was he poor? Because he was a failure, a loser. Why was he alive? Because he didn't have the guts to go through with it. Go through with what? A rampage. This would weigh on me.

I remember James's decision to move being a shock, even though I felt something had changed. I feel bad for him now. He had a roommate that was what some have called demonized or possessed. It is possible the Lord removed him for his potential safety. He left. He left me to pay for the furniture because it stayed. I would also have to cover all the rent, unless I found someone quickly. James allowed me to pay for his half of the VCR. James left Cary with me, but I think he took another kitten he had found. He called it Gizmo. Cary never got along with the kitten, so I was glad James took the kitten.

173

James had barely left town when I found out that one of the transfer art students needed to find a new place to live. I will call him "Stewart." Stewart was from Canada—I believe it was Toronto. He seemed to be an easygoing young man. In a stereotypical way, he would say "eh" a lot! Stewart had a full-time job. He worked as a security guard. He enthusiastically agreed to move in, helping to pay for half of the appliances that James had left. Stewart moved in, but we rarely saw each other. He worked midnight shifts and slept during the day. I worked part time, and once insomnia released its hold on me, I would sleep at night.

During free time, I would go to the University Square Mall and look in their music store. While in the store one day, I found lyrics to a song by *Megadeth*. (Remember I am not good at understanding lyrics unless I can read them.) It was called "Good Mourning/ Black Friday[83]." As I read the lyrics, I learned that the song seemed to be about a guy who loses his mind and maims, kills, and mutilates people with a hammer. It is quite a vivid picture the song presents. The song at that time now meant something to me, and before long, I would call it my anthem. "Friday" began to compete with Halloween. Fridays were once a week. Halloween was once a year.

While I believed I was becoming more psychotic, I had to do what I could to make ends meet and stay in the art school. An opportunity to work at a retail designer store that would be opening in a month presented itself. Aunt Ruthie let my mother know about the position. I applied, and TJ Maxx of Brandon, Florida, hired me. It would turn out to be a job that held the greatest consequences for my life. I thank God I was hired by that clothing store.

The store would not open for at least a month, and the new hires were helping receive the products and organizing the store. I worked in receiving and actually bonded with the department supervisor. He had long hair and was a heavy metal fan. As opening time approached, I was needed in the men's department. The men's department supervisor was Jack, and he looked to be around his midtwenties. Another guy named Dave worked in the depart-

---

[83] https://rattlehead.fandom.com/wiki/Good_Mourning/Black_Friday.

ment, but he appeared to me to be lazy and to patronize others. The store appeared to be brand new, and with employees working in an open, honest environment without customers present, a camaraderie was built among the employees. I had my supervisor David and two women from the store came to my apartment. David and the two women stayed the night. Nothing happened, and I did not pursue anything. We were friendly as a group, and I would develop a bit of a crush on one of the women, who were around eighteen years old. I was twenty.

After the store had opened, I thought everything was going well, but around mid-October, I received a notice that I was being laid off, and I was crushed! David was staying. I drove home and called my mother, who voiced her shared disappointment. While speaking to her, I grabbed a butcher knife from its holder. The lights were dim. While she was talking to me, I put the tip of the blade into my then skinny rib cage. I began to press harder and felt the pain.

Press harder! I heard in my head.

No, it hurts! It sounded like the eight-year-old me.

I pulled it away, frustrated that death was still scaring me. I shoved the knife back in its holder, and my mother encouraged me that the store may hire me again as the Christmas season started. She was correct. They did.

Not long after being laid off, my group of friends and I enjoyed participating in a Latin-influenced Halloween parade and festival in the historic district of Tampa, in Ybor City. The festival was called Guavaween. We ate at a pizza place and watched the parade of costumed people throw candy and beads at spectators. I could feel the intense, aggressive boldness, but I was having fun with my friends. We returned to my apartment, and I remember watching some movie that Chaz had brought. It was supposed to be a sexually explicit, soft porn movie, but I found it boring, and anger started rising.

The group was Johnny, Mike, Duane, Chaz, and Mike's girlfriend. I remember some young man coming to my apartment and arguing about Mike's girlfriend "Missy." Johnny, who plays things cool, remained calm. Duane and Mike rose up and told the young man to go. The young man did go, but the verbal altercation had me on edge to the point of wanting to be violent. The man left, and I eyed Chaz's costume prop, a machete. I had carved a big pumpkin earlier that day. I asked Chaz if I could use it on my jack-o'-lantern. Chaz agreed, and he followed me. I set the pumpkin on a closed dumpster and swung the blade clean through the jack-o'-lantern. I did not know why, but I did not think one simple swing would go through the pumpkin that easily. Darker thoughts arose, but details are not necessary.

I would have preferred to not share this incident, but it has relevance for later. I took the two halves of the pumpkin, put fake blood along the "cut," and set it in the hallway for Mike and Missy to see. They were making out in my roommate's bedroom. They did not see the evidence of my weird episode until later in the morning. I took a photo of the jack-o'-lantern, not knowing I would use it within six months. As I had mentioned, there are parts of this testimony that is very embarrassing. This was one.

In early November, my classmate Mick made it known that he needed a new place to stay. Mick was largely part of my group of friends. He joined us during breaks and could communicate fluent "comic book fanspeak." I thought about how nice it would be to split rent and electric into thirds instead of halves. Stewart hinted that he thought it would not be a good idea, but with James out, I was the alpha male now. I believe Stewart reluctantly agreed. I decided to allow Mick to move into the apartment. That decision would lead to me accepting my "identity" and accepting my mission. The enemy would give me a target. "That's not good."

THE TARGET

Mick moved in and had not been there for more than a week when his presence tainted seemingly everything! I remember getting up early to go to work at TJ Maxx. It was my second time with the retail store. I came out of my room and found Mick under a blanket with a woman. I knew he had been at a local club. I did not think he would bring a woman home! I was morally challenged then, and my judgment was very suspect. I thought, *Okay. Why not?* They were asleep when I left for work around 9:00 a.m. She was there when I got home. Mick introduced her to me. I will call her "Marie" for this story. Marie, I would gradually learn, was married and had a two-year-old son. The husband will be called "Mac." Apparently, Marie was experiencing a rough time with Mac, and she began to stay in my apartment too. She was of Cuban ancestry and was not unattractive. She had long, wavy brown hair and wore glasses. I thought nothing of any potential negative consequences. I just let her and Mick stay.

That next Friday night, Johnny and I had seen a movie and went to my apartment because it was not late. When we got there, Marie and Steve were at their respective jobs, but Mick and one of his other friends Doug were in the living room. Around nine, Mac, Marie's estranged husband, called. He spoke to Mick, and the argument from my side sounded like Mac was (understandably) angry about Marie staying with Mick. Johnny took the phone at some point and told Mac that his name was "Frank Holiday." Johnny also sounded like he was having an angry conversation with Mac, except the anger was all on Mac's side. (Johnny was and is a good-humored man.) Mac demanded to speak to me, and Johnny handed me the phone. Mac sounded like he was drunk, slurring his words and tripping over a few. I remember him accusing me of keeping his wife from him, and then he said, "I ain't joking! I'll kill you, bro! I'll—kill you, you little—!"

I felt fear! A fear I thought I had put to death years before crushed me. Did I hear the eight-year-old kid say, "Oh my god, he threatened my life!" Initially, there was no bravado. There was no, "Oh yeah?" It was a Dorothy looking down at Toto and saying, "We're not in Kansas anymore," kind of moment.

No, I can't be afraid! had to be among my flight of thoughts.

Mac hung up, and I would learn through Johnny that Mac threatened Frank's life and Mick's. Johnny went home. He seemed unaffected and his normal, amusing self. (Johnny looked and could behave like the late comic, John Belushi.) I, however, felt shell-shocked. Marie came home, my home. She, Mick, Doug, and I sat in the living room, replaying the conversations for Marie. Marie "trash-talked" Mac. Mick and Doug would begin to talk about how they wanted to get Mac back, maybe even kill him.

I began to feel a slow, at first, filling of darkness, violence, and rage. Then it was like a rush of something that felt like it had to get out of me and would tear apart anything in its path if it ever did. Through clenched teeth, I heard a raspier, slightly lower voice come from me. I said, "No one is going to touch Mac. He's mine. If anyone touches him, I'll kill you." With that, I buried scaredy-cat again. That night, Satan gave me a target.

STAYING BUSY AND OFF-BALANCED

I returned to my parents' home for Thanksgiving. I had gotten home the Wednesday before the unique, blessed American holiday. I had to leave early after Thanksgiving dinner. Tomorrow, I would have to work Black Friday in the women's department of TJ Maxx. I do not remember anything about the visit, not even the sheltie Heather slowing down with age. She would die before I visited again. I drove back to my two-bedroom apartment off Hillsborough Avenue in Tampa. I arrived and found my mother had left a message for me to call her when I got home. (That is the modus operandi to contact home after arriving at a destination that is far from said home. Scott would have to collect call and ask for Heather to let my mom know he made it to his destination safe and sound.) I called her, and she let me know that after I left Sebastian, Ranee, from my elementary and middle schools, called—yes, the girl I had a crush on in fifth through seventh grades. It turned out that Ranee remembered me because I was so nice. I must say, as darkness was slowly and then quickly overcoming me, I could still be "nice." My mother told me that Ranee said she also lived in Tampa, and she asked me to call. I felt emotional as memories of a believe-it-or-not more lighthearted time swirled within me. I did call, and I do not remember the conversation, but she invited me to her apartment after the upcoming holidays. I would experience several weeks of ups, downs, and some self-sabotage behaviors.

With James returning home and Stewart having a laid-back nature, I threw some parties at the apartment. I had two after James left. During the second party, I experienced a violent vision, which resembled a medieval execution, and I'll spare any details, but playing in Satan's domain is no game. During and after the vision, I became exceedingly drunk before the many of the invited arrived. I missed the rest of the party, but the participants gave me positive reviews. I decided to hold another party in December 16. I designed invitations using my growing commercial artist skills. It was part of a Christmas tree branch with a bulb hanging off it and the reflection of a rum bottle bouncing off the bulb. Yes, without Christ and hope, Christmas meant nothing to me. Drinking opens your mind to possible increased demonic activity, and no one should drink that much! Today, I would go with what God says, "Do not get drunk on wine, which leads to debauchery. Instead, be filled with the Spirit, always giving thanks to God the Father for everything, in the name of our Lord Jesus Christ" (Ephesians 5:18). I will be sharing more scriptures pertaining to the subjects at hand in order to shed some light in some extremely dark months.

Mick, the new roommate with the live-in girlfriend with the estranged husband, never paid a dime in rent, but Mick could earn some good will by bringing me *Halloween* movie-themed gifts. (I did not ask for anything.) Mick would gift me with two official *Halloween II* and *Halloween 4* theatrical posters. It is possible the enemy was using my new roommate to spoon-feed me evil from my almost fully fledged obsession. Fall of 1989 was a blur of activity. I would find myself at some point ordering and receiving the soundtracks to the first two *Halloween* movies. Let me just say that the music helped fuel my growing obsession and provided an atmosphere that I could visit often. If my Hell had a soundtrack, it was that music, and being in it for eternity was preferable to life on Earth.

During that fall, Johnny would date Shannon from our class. Shannon frequently came out with the rest of us during the school's breaks. She did not fit in well, but I do not believe I was fitting in so well either. The short time Johnny dated her, I began to see her a little differently. Similar to Adam, I was not jealous, and I created

179

no drama. I believe that it was Johnny who ended things with her. I added her to be invited to my upcoming Christmas party. I would end up missing most of the party because of work. When I arrived, it was in full swing, and some were already leaving or had already left. Shannon was still there.

I was, interestingly, angry to learn that one of Mick's friends had been reading tarot cards in my bedroom. The "reader" had left, but the atmosphere of my room felt different. Shannon had not seen me upset, and she stayed for several hours after the party ended. We stayed on my bed, just sitting toward each other and later resting on our sides. It remained innocent through the night, but I wanted to let her know that I wanted her. Shannon had piercing dark-brown eyes, arched eyebrows, and long, wavy red hair. She, at that time, was on the heavy side but not obese. Usually not my type, back then, but I was self-centered, and I honestly thought of using her to get me out of Virginsville. That night through to the sunrise, we talked the whole time. (I am fairly sure she did most of the talking, but I did a fair share.) She left the next morning. I asked her out to see *War of the Roses* in her hometown of Lakeland. We would see it on the following Thursday. The angry yelling between the main characters in the movie caused my anxiety and an undercurrent of anger to grow. It was like I was having PTSD symptoms related to my parents' infamous, to me, arguments. (I do not argue with my wife of twenty-three years. We really do talk it through.)

I had followed some of Johnny's advice to "treat her like crap and she'll love you for it." I had been observant enough through the year that Shannon was a feminist and would not like doors to be opened for her or to receive a bouquet of roses. I thought that was stupid, but I went with it. It was after I took her to her home and we talked, leaning against my father's Toyota, that I said, "Remember, at the party and we talked in my room. I wanted to do something with you." (Yes, that is exactly how my smooth self said it!)

"Jeffrey! Why didn't you say something?" she asked with more intense interest than I thought.

"I didn't know if you would want to."

"Yes, why not?"

There was no opportune time or place then, so without actually doing anything, our relationship changed. I drove home and that (then) pesky hope was rising within me. When I wrote earlier about my natural desire for normalcy and having genuine relationships being a threat to the enemy, I meant it.

I would drive home for Christmas, learning that my father was taking his Toyota Carola back and that my parents had bought a 1986 Nissan 200 SX for me. Like my dad's car, it was a five-speed. It was a light silvery gray "sports car" with headlights that flipped up when they were on and down when they were turned off. It was a very cold Christmas Eve (it snowed in Tampa, flurries), and after visiting my parents' church, we went to my high school friends' Shawn and David's Christmas Eve party. I had not seen Shawn in about one year, and he noticed my speech being more aggressive.

"I could off him," got a laugh out of Shawn. We had a few drinks, and Shawn shared about his girlfriend (who he would later have a successful marriage with). I felt more confident, since I believed I had a faithful, at least, date in Lakeland. That is all I remember about that trip. I had to, gladly, drive a "sporty" car back to Tampa. I had to work the next day. To me, retail was a pain, but I was thankful to be working there. My days there were numbered, and I did not know it. I also had no idea that a new cosupervisor—a young Christian woman, who was going to the then Southeastern College of the Assemblies of God—would change the course of my trajectory. She would start a spiritual tug-of-war.

17

"I'm Worse. I'm Real"

I began to ponder these things: the intriguing atmosphere, the night, the death threats, the movie and its character, and me.

All your life long you are slowly turning...either into a heavenly creature or into a hellish creature: either into a creature that is harmony with God, and with other creatures, and with itself, or else into one that is in a state of war and hatred with God, and with its fellow creatures, and with itself. To be the one kind of creature is heaven: that is, it is joy and peace and knowledge and power. To be the other means madness, horror, idiocy, and rage... Each of us at each moment is progressing to the one state or the other.
—C. S. Lewis

TWO NIGHTS

I feel it would be a good place to evaluate where I was progressing at this time. I was devolving into a kind of madness and idiocy. I was believing the feelings that accompanied the thoughts of being attached to the ancient pagan holiday, Halloween, or what I would begin to call Samhain. It was a Gaelic harvest festival. What I would hear and learn is that the nations of Ireland, Scotland, and nearby surrounding lands saw the dividing line between the living and dead being at its thinnest between October 31 and November 1. Many of the modern activities, like trick-or-treating, carving jack-o'-lanterns, and the rarer and darker underground practices of trying to contact the dead and human sacrifices, had its origins in Samhain. Well, my *idiocy* and *madness* believed I was shadowed by the Druid lord of the dead, Samhain[84]. *He* watched over me and would not allow me to grow socially or to be normal. He wanted me to bring *his* holiday back to its dark origins. Halloween sounded weak, so I referred to it as Samhain and welcomed "his" presence into my life. (What could go wrong?) Well, the other two features of C. S. Lewis's evil creature, *horror* and *rage*, would be the result.

Changing the term to Samhain seemed to bring a seriousness to it all. Willingly being open to a spirit meant, apparently, that the enemy could move against me in a more conspicuous way. Before, he was attempting to communicate using my inner voice in my head, occasionally saying things my literal mind/self disagreed with. Now Samhain could speak and not *play off* that his thoughts were mine. In a short time, I would feel like a member of a one-man death cult. Whether I knew it or not, I was into the occult, and leaving that kind of life is difficult. The following experience with Shannon that I am about to discuss was when demonic influence increased and became pushy.

In anticipation of the next occasion Shannon and I would be together, I bought protection in case we did have sex. The pop culture had spread the message that safe sex was the responsible thing to do, so I complied. I drove over to Shannon's home in the afternoon after work. We talked in her bedroom and kissed. Since she had been a heavy smoker, I found myself tolerating it, but barely. At some point, while clothed, both of us, I was on my back and she was on top of me. I remember at some point she called me a wimp, and I instantly bucked and threw her off of me. She was surprised, but not even mad! She even seemed more respectful. My anger outburst was a horrible gesture I have never repeated.

---

[84] https://www.ancient.eu/Samhain.

Shannon and I went out to eat at a well-known taco fast-food restaurant. We returned to her home. He parents were not home. I was self-conscious about pretty much everything. Shannon and I kissed again, and we started going a little further. Shannon suggested I drive her back to Tampa to my apartment, and I agreed. I do not remember what we talked about on the way to my apartment. We arrived and no one was home. We went to my bedroom, and once it was obvious what was about to happen, I went to the restroom to undress and Shannon undressed in my bedroom. One of the last thoughts I would have was, *This is it.*

I'll skip any specifics except to share that while in the middle of the act, I heard in my mind, *This is wrong. This is dirty. She's a slut. Kill her!* It repeated several times, and it distracted me, and as being as vague yet descriptive as I can, I could not finish. I was not impotent. I just could not concentrate to finish. In reality, Shannon was fine. I just felt conflicted "hearing" that, now, insistent voice in my head.

After a while, I think I gave up. The weird part for me is I did care, more, afterward. I did not know what to make of any of it. I even said something that sounded like I blamed her. Of course, I did not tell her about the commands I heard, not audibly. I never heard these things audibly. It was an awkward drive back to Shannon's home. My lack of empathy blocked me from realizing that I had hurt her feelings. This was December 31, early in the morning. I was supposed to come back over to ring in the new year later that night. Shannon actually said something complimentary, and I thought all was well. We kissed good night, and I drove home and nearly had a road rage incident after a faster car flashed his "brights" on me while on the treacherous I-4. I began to chase him, but he was faster.

After working a later shift at the clothing store, I drove to Shannon's home. I arrived around ten thirty. Shannon met me at my car. My difficulty with reading ulterior motives and not wanting to think about being manipulated caused me to miss Shannon's intentions for me that night.

"Jeffrey, it's late. You worked late. You've gotta be tired. I think you should go home," she said.

I heard words of concern, not "I don't want to be with you now. Go away!" but that is what she meant. I was dense, so she used different words to get rid of me. She became a little more insistent, and her suggestions of being tired started causing me to feel tired. I agreed to leave. She gave me directions, but I made a wrong turn. Instead of heading toward the "American Autobahn" I-4, I turned toward State Road 60. It took me out of the way and meant I might be on the road when New Year's happened. I moderately sped. I made it back to the apartment by about eleven fifty. No one was home. I had never felt so alone. I dragged my portable stereo out to the living room and put in Megadeth's "Peace Sells" song. I sang at the top of my lungs, running through the points about the song. "What do you mean I ain't kind, just not your kind." I was emotional and the enemy hated that. A few minutes after midnight, Mick, Marie, and Stewart came home with snacks. They wished me a happy new year. I appreciated it, and my dark mood lifted.

I called Shannon later, near noon. Her voice was more direct, firm. She talked on (and she could talk a lot), and I thought I heard, "I was with someone else last night. I don't think this is working, Jeffrey. I don't want to go out anymore."

I replayed instantly what I primarily heard, "I screwed you over." Chills ran through my entire body as if that eighty-degree New Year's Day had dropped instantly to the thirties. I did not feel anger. I felt like I was freezing. She did not have to give me details, but darned if she did! She was with a 280-pound guy at a party she and her sister went to.

"Jeff, I love when I am with you, but when you are gone, I don't miss you. I don't care."

Did I speak anymore? Did I slip into another trance? I just heard rejection, and the human part of me died a little more.

LOSING IT

The following Monday night, I returned to the art school. Shannon was there and exhibited behaviors that communicated that she was simply fine. I admit that I remember feeling awkward and my heart ached. Before Shannon and I did anything, my feelings for her were weak. After that night, she began to mean more. Johnny noticed I was down, and during a break, he talked to me. Johnny rarely takes anything seriously, but he has shown an extraordinary amount of care when he thinks he can help. I do not remember what we spoke about specifically, but he attempted to cheer me up.

During the next break, Shannon walked up to me, and she said, "Come on, Jeffrey. Come walk with me."

Having little self-worth, I followed her out of the building. We walked beyond the building where the art school is, and we were coming up and about to pass the next suites of buildings. Shannon had been talking and not apologizing when I heard in my mind, *Drown her.*

I thought, *What?*

Drown her.

Am I hearing what I think I'm hearing. Drown her? There's no water here!

Drown her.

Shannon and I walked past the building, and I saw a large retention pond about a hundred feet away!

What the hell? No, I said to myself.

I resisted and freaked out that I distinctly heard, "Drown her," and I never drove or walked in this area to know there, indeed, was a body of water that I could have drowned her.

We walked back to class and I left class early. I played Megadeth's "In My Darkest Hour[85]" on the way home.

About two weeks later, on a Saturday, I drove to Ranee's apartment after we spoke by phone again. Her apartment was off Dale Mabry, but her area was far north from the Buccaneers stadium. The location was considered to be safer. Dale Mabry is a congested highway, and businesses and apartments line on both sides of the road. All the colors and signs were blending, and I began to feel lost. (Finding places would have been much easier had GPS existed then.) I thought I overshot her apartment, and I turned off into a long strip

---

[85] https://en.wikipedia.org/wiki/In_My_Darkest_Hour.

mall. I drove through the parking lot and stopped to get a look at the address numbers on business doors. I glanced up, and off to my left was a huge costume store. I remembered a conversation I had had with Mick. He said, "They sell Michael Myers masks. Look professional too." I looked to see the nearby intersection and its street name and made a mental note. I looked at the address I was looking for. I was still south of my destination. I moved my "new to me" 200 SX back into the traffic.

About ten minutes later, I finally saw Ranee's apartment name to the left. I turned in and parked. I can say I do not remember thinking back about our times in elementary and middle schools. I walked to her apartment and knocked on the door. Ranee opened the door. I was struck, immediately, by the activity of roommates… friends? My undiagnosed ADHD grabbed my attention, and then I looked at Ranee. The last I saw her, she was thirteen. I saw the nineteen-year-old version, and she was still Ranee. She was always on the thin side, and her dark-brown hair was still wavy and long. I may have "unplugged" again after the Shannon debacles. I did not feel intimidated, but I did not know what to say either.

I was at her apartment for around an hour. I believe we talked about what we were currently doing, and I gave a cleansed version of my Tampa experiences. Ranee stated that she had to go by her mother's nail salon in nearby Lutz. She invited me to follow her, and I could meet her mother. We drove to Ranee's mom's business, and I met her mother. Her mother had brilliant-bright blonde hair. I was struck by the contrast. She was genuinely nice, I remember that. Ranee had also been very hospitable. I hope that I was nice. (I did have that in me still, just not as much when I was a kid.) I stayed at the store for about fifteen minutes, and it seemed the right time to leave. Ranee had given me one of her senior photographs. I still had her number, and I think I gave her mine, but I would not talk to her again until the week after I received Jesus. She was among three people that I called to share my good news. I said goodbye and headed back to my apartment.

In January 26, I drove back to the costume store I had discovered during the trip to see Ranee. I pulled into the parking lot, and thoughts started running through my mind. I think they were my own, but definitely influenced by the demonic powers that were encroaching on every area of my life.

I'm twenty, sick of this world. I'm done. I'll give me a chance. I'll review the quality of life when I'm twenty-five. That's it, not a year longer. Twenty-five. If my life is still—, I'll kill myself, whether I kill anyone before or not.

What? I could really go on a rampage soon, and if not, by twenty-five, I have to kill myself if my life still—.

Okay. Five years is a long way away, though.

(This thought was demonic.) *Then do it soon.*

With that, I got out of my car and walked into the costume shop. Mick had told me they had Michael Myers masks for $39.95—well, he said for forty. He also said that the mask was "almost exactly like the real one." It was too *intriguing* for me to pass. I stepped into the store and saw a kaleidoscope of colors and shapes, a lot of red, grays, and blacks and some whites from skull masks. I asked the clerk if he had "the mask." That is the title of that type of mask. He pulled it down from a shelf. The mask was encased in a Styrofoam head, to keep its shape, and was in a plastic bag. I paid the initial price and would pay a much larger price. I took it back to the car and headed home.

I arrived at my apartment and brought my mask in to show Mick and Stewart. I put the mask on, and it fit well. I peered at Stewart and Mick. We were standing around the secondhand dining room table.

"You're not becoming him, are you?" Stewart asked in a tone that sounded like he was wondering if I really *was* going crazy.

"No, of course not," I said.

I, however, heard in my mind, *I'm worse. I'm real.*

I took the mask off, brought it with me to my bedroom, and put it back over my head. I looked in the mirror in my dim light, and I saw what it looked like.

"I'm worse? Really?"

Years of having a delusion thrust in me were coming to a head.

"Could I? In this?"

First of *countless* scenarios began to rise in my thoughts. What a terror I could be. I had mental images of people seeing the dark-blue coveralls and the iconic white mask and me towering over them, and they would see a flash of the blade.

When someone opens their life to demonic influence, you never know how far into Hell the enemy can drag you. It seems that Satan and his fallen angel companions will at times need permission to increase their influence in your life. Christians often call it "opening a doorway." In a way, it means you asked for it. God is quite merciful toward his children, and He will make mighty moves to protect them, but sometimes He will allow negative consequences to a certain point. His goal is to bring the wayward sheep back into the fold. For nonbelievers, you may find you have no protection at all. Remember the lionesses in chapter one, and how Satan is constantly on the hunt. That is why I called that section "Fair Warning." Apart from faith in Christ, the lost, like me in 1990, are without spiritual and even physical protection. My fall could really affect others.

It seems Stewart, Mick, and Marie were having clashes during the day when I was at work. Stewart decided he had enough of the living arrangement and was planning to drive Mick and Marie out of the apartment. I came home one afternoon before school and saw a "Stewart-illustrated" calendar, counting down the days of the month of February. Every page had a message indicating Mick and Marie would be "evicted" from the apartment. I felt I did not want them to leave. Mick proved useful. When they ignored and jeered the prospect of moving out, I joined them. Stewart's "evictions" would come, but not through his calendar and pressure.

LOST

I try to remember what I thought when I woke up a few days later, and I did not move around or walk like *me* anymore. I easily recall I did not consciously decide that I would "now" move like a character from a slasher movie. I remember I was aware that the movements were different, but it felt natural. It really did. I remember thinking that it was cool that I was not taking my normally long, quick strides when I walked. I was walking much slower and with a slight sway (very similar to how the actor portrayed the antagonist in the first *Halloween* movie). I was stalking, not walking. Stewart was correct in his concern. I was becoming him, but worse in my mind. The thing was, I did not want to give my secret away to everyone. Now, I walked weird! I would become a kind of spectator, while my "Myers-like" persona would, at times, take over.

Mick and Marie came by my workplace, TJ Maxx, to visit me. It was a nice visit. I was leaning against a women's underwear bin (because the company placed me in the women's department), and Mick saw an attractive female employee.

"Whoa, who is that?"

In my new natural movements, I slowly swiveled my head to the right.

"Whoa, you're moving like him now!"

I felt my head slowly swivel toward his nervous smile.

"Yes! He's been moving like this for two weeks!" Marie exclaimed in what sounded like genuine concern.

I simply said, "Shelly. That's Shelly. She's cool."

Thankfully, my voice stayed at its same tempo, but it was slightly lower and a little raspy. I did not mind that, at the time. I fed off Mick's fear, whether it was real or feigned. (It sounded real, but I felt like I was locked away in my body watching half of this stuff—much, I admit, met my approval.)

A couple of Friday's later, Johnny, Mike, and I planned to buy a heavy, heavy liquor and drink it all somewhere in Riverview. Johnny lived in Riverview. When we were in the store to buy it, we were walking away from the aisle when I felt like a "pouring" of anger and violence fill me up. I "sensed" anger and rage, but I was not angry. I was actually excited to be hanging out with Mike and Johnny. I would find that the enemy did not want me to have fun, because that brought hope, which brings a determination to live. It was thrusting its anger onto me.

A legal-aged friend of Johnny's bought the liquor, and we drove off to try to finish it. It did not take me too long before I was drunk. My memory and my sight became very fuzzy throughout the rest of

190

the night. Here is what happened. One of the friend's trucks became stuck in mud, and somehow, I became the one to drive another friend to get tools so another truck could pull the first truck out of the mud. I drove to someone's house, and I vaguely remember not getting out of second gear the whole way there! My passenger picked up some tools, and I drove back. (It should be obvious that today I would scream, "Don't drink and drive!") With very blurry vision and muffled cheers from the others, I looked up to see the truck be freed from the mud. I do not remember anything else from that night. I woke up in Johnny's home with a horrible headache. I had to call in sick for a ten o'clock open time at the Maxx. The supervisor was not happy. A few days later, I opened my trunk to retrieve a T-square for class when I saw a nice large clawhammer in my trunk. (I did not even remember or think about someone throwing tools in my car and leaving their hammer.) I took and kept the hammer and named it—yes, I actually named it—Friday. I named it after the Megadeth song "Good Mourning/Black Friday." It was the song about the fiend that kills and mutilates people with a hammer. Plus, one of my favorite scenes from *Halloween II* involved a hammer. In addition, I reasoned that if I were caught with a hammer under my car seat, it's a tool, not a weapon. (I was a lost fool, and I was delusional as well.)

Marie's car was not available for her to use for a week, or so. One night with Mick, I drove her to her drug store job. On the way back to the apartment, I had to stop at a traffic light. Mick had his window open, smoking a cigarette. I was staring straight and slightly down.

Hey, look up to your right, I heard in my mind. My neck turned quickly, for a change.

They're making fun of you!

I listened and looked to see two young men yelling out of their window homosexual slurs. Instantly, several things happened. I forgot Mick was even with me in the car and that the two could have been talking about Mick. My neck turned back toward the steering wheel, and almost simultaneously, I reached for the hammer, as I saw a mental image of me grabbing the hammer, racing around my car, and striking the other driver with the claw, repeatedly. I reached for the hammer, and it was not there. I felt a panic mixed with the highest amount of rage I had experienced so far!

I growled in a scream, "Where's my—hammer? Where's is it?"

The light turned green, and I heard laughter coming from the car next to me, as they took off and I was fretting over my hammer being missing. I do not remember if Mick tried to calm me down. I tell you there was not one hesitation about what I wanted to do to those two men. I had rejected hurting Junie and Shannon. Had I lost the ability to resist? For that instance, yes.

Where was my hammer? Well, a few nights before, my commercial art friends found my car unlocked at school, and they broke in and "messed" with everything. They turned my lights up (they were the flip-up type), they turned my stereo volume to its highest level, they pulled my car seat in, and they possibly saved my life when they hid the hammer somewhere else in the car.

I drove home raging on the inside. Two sleeping pills finally relaxed me enough to fall asleep in anger.

JESUS LOVES YOU

I woke up ticked off, still! The anger would not die down. I came out of my room and again saw Marie and Mick underneath a blanket. I showered, dressed, and ate in ire. I drove into Brandon to work in anger. I was not walking like myself still. I was assigned to work in the women's department and fill in at the dressing rooms during someone's lunch. At some point, while watching over the dressing rooms, I sketched a clawhammer that had blood dripping from it and streaks on the wall. (Even after receiving Christ, I kept that sketch as a reminder until one of my dogs chewed it to pieces in 2000.) The anger continued.

The new cosupervisor, who was a Christian, walked up to me, being her professional yet cheerful self. I remember hanging up new dresses on a stand-alone round rack.

"Jeff, how are you? Could you work a double shift today?"

I believe I said no, and I remember feeling the anger intensify, but I cannot remember what else I said or if I said anything else. I recall seeing her walk away toward her office.

I continued hanging new dresses on the rack. I think I started to feel bad about how I handled Diana when I heard, not in my head, but everywhere, *Go and tell her everything.*

Now, at the time, I did not know it was God. It was a sound that was not audible, yet my body felt like it had an eighteen-inch woofer speaker in me. I rattled and trembled as He spoke. The voice seemed concerned, seemed involved, but in a positive way. I could not disobey the voice. I walked to Diana's office and knocked on her door. She invited me in, and I did not know what to say. *Tell her everything? I feel like I can't even talk!* I pulled my sketch out of my uniform smock and unfolded it, placing it in front of her.

"This is what I want to do to people," I whispered with a rasp.

Her eyes focused on my gory drawing, and she looked up at me like I was a person drowning in front of her. Her concerned eyes that looked at me with such pure love were her arms reaching out to me. She paused and maybe took a deep breath.

"Ohh, Jeff, Jesus loves you. He died for you. He did this to set you free!"

Every time Diana said Jesus, I would hear screeches, like nails on a chalkboard. Did I hate His name so much that it irritated me this way? No, I would learn a year later that it was literally at least two demons screaming! (Wait till you learn how they react to the Christian counselor I would meet in eight months.)

Diana began talking and brainstorming how I needed help. She got me to promise I would tell my mother when I got home. She continued to look at me with the love of God. She told me that my life would feel like a tug-of-war from now on. I began to feel very depressed. I blew it. Now people will know. "What's going to happen?"

After I arrived home, I sat on the couch in the dark. The shades were closed, and it was late winter. The sun was almost down. I picked up the phone, an old-fashioned rotary dial, and spun the dial to my parents' number. Mom answered.

I do not remember the small talk, but I do remember saying this, "Umm. Get ready for a bombshell."

Mom suspected something had been going on. "What?"

"I want to kill people. I want to kill myself."

"You're kidding," and I do not remember too much more, except after hanging up, I sat in silence in the dark. The Halloween boldness was growing, while I felt more depressed.

The phone ringing broke the silence.

"Hello. I am looking for Jeff Gilbert."

"This is he."

"Jeff, I am with the Tampa Suicide Hotline."

Yes, a suicide hotline called me!

The woman from the crisis center explained that they have a working relationship with a psychotherapist. She asked if I would be willing to speak with him if he agreed as well.

A shrink? Myers had a shrink too, I thought. I told her yes. The enemy within did not seem to have a problem with me seeing him. The woman and I ended the talk, and I continued to sit in the darkness. I thought about death. Then I had an idea. I would get Stewart (who was in his room) to act panicked and incoherently say, "Oh, my god! He cut himself. He's dying. He's not moving!" (Lay it on Stewart!) I stood up and slowly stalked to his bedroom door, and my right hand raised to knock on the door. I was inches from knocking on his door when I honestly felt a tug. I do not remember if my hand was tugged, my conscience was tugged, but something was tugged! I brought my hand down and shuffled back to the couch.

The woman called again. She stated that Morris Gus agreed to see me, and we set up my first session for the following Monday in the afternoon. I thought, *Wow I have a shrink now.*

At this time, my behavior was worthy of serious intervention. I had days and nights of feeling like a caged tiger. I would experience that sensation of being filled up with anger and rage whether I was in a mood within normal range or not. When I was walking to my apartment's mailbox, I would look down and see a shadow that did not look like my tall, thin body. At least on one occasion, I walked the residential area behind my apartment complex. I noted homes that had dogs, porch lights, or other security measures. I just looked and played scenarios in my head. When my own anger was too intense, I would frequently walk to the closed burger restaurant in front of our apartment. I would punch or kick the metal back door, thankfully never breaking my hands. Things had been happening in plain sight, and it took God to begin to bring intervention. It made it a more precarious time.

18

WHEN?

I, now, lived in a deception I accepted.

YOU'RE DARKNESS

The prospect of being a patient to a psychotherapist brought a sense of fulfillment to the Michael Myers's lore. I drove to a multifloor office somewhere closer to downtown Tampa than my apartment. His office was up one flight of stairs. The facility was bright, and there were many windows allowing sunlight to invade most of the offices. I brought a drawing of the character I was finding myself emulating. Since I was elementary school age, I would draw characters and objects that I loved. I brought my drawing to give him a visual of what was going on inside of me.

I met Morris, and he resembled John Hammond from the *Jurassic Park* movies. He was well under six feet tall, stocky build, and had a trimmed white beard. Morris was nice enough. He wore Hawaiian shirts and khaki pants. The enemy within me did not resist me seeing him. I would learn that he was an atheist, and he would block my mother's attempts to stir a faith in God within me. I believed I was agnostic and really focused my thoughts and devotion to Samhain (which I will repeat that I renounced my sins, including idolatry). My mom would beg me to pray, and I would foolishly say, "To what?" Morris would use the psychodynamic theory in his therapy. This older model of therapy could and usually did take years to have symptoms decrease through an understanding of the traumas incurred during the early years of one's life. Today, cognitive behavioral therapy is found to be an empirically evidence-based therapy. It is the type I have used and currently use and many clinicians use during the 2000s.

Morris planned to see me weekly. I do not remember much about most of our sessions. I do remember that I must have let off a lot of steam during the first session, because my anger level was low. I think I began to walk normally again also, but that would change back and forth several times. I would end up seeing Morris for about six months. His atheism, in the end, strengthened my cause. (I would share with him that I received Jesus a week after I had. He politely rejected, but God only knows if he ever believed. It has been thirty years and I do not know if he is alive.)

It is challenging to discuss who is, now, a friend for life and former mentor Diana. It is because I think so highly of her, even though we lost contact around 1999. Even in 1990, I respected her, but she was a powerful woman of God. Her intervention was not received well. It is remarkable that Diana could offend me, yet her life was perfectly safe. She was off-limits. She could make me angry, but the enemy within was silent about her fate. In short, Diana was protected by Almighty God. What a blessing to be able to share that today I am off-limits, and I have tangled with other peoples' demons. Getting there was a whole separate adventure that will be discussed soon.

The store manager, Pat, had allowed me to continue to work at the store, but she gave me several conditions. The main one was that I was to only speak to her about my issue and anything having to do with my therapy. I think I complied for a few weeks. On a Friday in March, when I happened to be off, I drove to the store to pick up my paycheck. Diana was the lone supervisor in the office. She invited me to sit down, and she talked. I do not remember what I said for Diana to say, "You're darkness," but I was actually honored! I thought, *She recognizes the true me.* During the conversation, which was mostly on Diana's side, she asked me a question that stirred heavy resistance within me.

"Jeff, if you were to die today, do you know where you would go?" she asked a common American Christian evangelism question.

I am not sure if I humored her or I really considered the question. "I haven't killed anyone yet, so I guess... Heaven?"

Her expression looked like I was about to step in front of a speeding bus. Her eyes expressed even more love and concern, and it burned into my mind.

"No!" I heard her say, but do not remember what her answer was. I felt uncomfortable and unnerved.

When I drove home, I had just turned onto State Road 60 when I heard, *Who the hell does she think she is, telling you where you're going?*

I simply thought, *Yeah!* and I was upset with Diana. She and another supervisor would call me later, and I spoke about meeting with the psychotherapist. Pat called me into the office the next day and let me go for "medical reasons" and for breaking the agreement. As much as I could at that time, I enjoyed working at TJ Maxx. I immediately felt aimless and discouraged and knew I had blown it. I did not want to think that Diana could have set me up, even when the thought crossed my mind and I felt anger. Diana was not finished with me, thankfully.

MARIE

As you could imagine, having a semiattractive woman, Marie, living under the same roof stirred interests in me. I was horrible at reading others' emotions or thoughts, and I do not know if she showed me special attention to keep her in my good graces, or she was conflicted and did like me, at least a little. I remember after the Shannon debacle, Marie would hold my hand when we grocery shopped. She had a peculiar saying like Holly. Marie, when she would explain anything, would start with saying, "Not for nothing, but..."

For about one week, Mick left her with me, while he visited a friend on the east coast of Florida. I came home from the art school at about ten forty-five at night. I found Marie in my bed watching my TV. After I ate my takeout food and showered (discreetly—Mom raised a gentleman), I lay down in my own bed. I wondered if once *the Tonight Show* was over she would stay or go to the living room. She stayed. I had some carnal thoughts that I reluctantly put down. *I can't screw Mick over, but...* I woke up and Marie had been awake and had performed some basic hygiene. She came over to me and kissed me, pretty forcefully.

"Don't fall in love with me," she said.

I thought, *Well, when you do that, what do you expect?*

I remained a good boy. I think I was walking and moving normally. Samhain was leaving me alone and letting hope stir so he could steal more later.

As Mick returned from his visit, I drove to my parents' home for spring break. While I was there, Mac and Marie's two-year-old visited that week. The child's name was Mac Allen, and after he threw a glass at Mick and hit him near his eye, Mick responded very negatively when he spanked Mac Allen so hard that he left a hand-shaped bruise on his buttocks. Florida's version of children protective services was called by Mac (I assume). I returned from Sebastian, and my apartment felt different, full of tension. Mick was under investigation for physical abuse of the toddler. I was incredibly oblivious of what was happening with these two roommates and how my life was in potential danger because of them.

BROKEN INTO

I came home after school, and Marie was at her job. It was a Thursday night. I had eaten my lone meal for the day. (I was eating once a day at this time.) For some reason, I did not want to go to bed. I stayed up. I was drawing on a sketch pad the *Teenage Mutant Ninja Turtle*[86] Leonardo. (*TMNT* was a popular comic book at the time. I still have that drawing in my portfolio.)

Around two fifteen in the morning, while just finishing up the drawing, a knock came at my door. I opened the door and my heart seized when I saw Mac and another man, about the same age, with him. My door was cracked just enough for my cat to slip past me. I

---

[86] https://en.wikipedia.org/wiki/Leonardo_(Teenage_Mutant_Ninja_Turtles).

thought,—, *Cary!* Cary had been declawed. I could not bear to have him be out there defenseless. I had to get him back. I stepped outside to try to gather Cary. Cary had already made his way to the front parking lot. As I stepped out, Mac closed the door behind me. Now I was trapped outside with them, and Mick was inside.

"I don't have a beef with you, man. He hurt my kid. You know where I'm coming from? He hurt my kid. We don't want any trouble with you, but Mick...," Mac said and trailed off. His cousin, I would learn, Tom, agreed they were there for Mick.

You know, I don't care. He's been a—mooch and trouble, I thought and was interrupted when Mick peeked his head out of the door and called out to me.

"Phone, Jeff! It's important!" he shouted out from the safety of the apartment.

I turned to Mac, with Cary now in my arms. "Listen, I am going inside. I don't care what you want with Mick. I just don't want any trouble in my apartment."

"It's all right, man. Like I said, we only want to talk with Mick."

"I'm going inside to take this call, but I'll be back out." I lied.

I carried Cary to the door and we both went in, while my heart was pounding. Mick was in my room and motioned for me to come to the phone in my room.

"Hello?" It was Marie.

"Jeff. Call the cops now. I know Mac has his gun with him. Call the cops!"

So I dialed 911. I explained the situation the best I could. The operator calmly stated she would send someone out to us.

As I hung up, I heard a jingling at my front doorknob. "I locked it. I know I locked it. I told them I was going to lock it!"

I walked out to the living room just as Mac and Tom (his cousin) let themselves in and casually walked past me, mumbling, "I just need to use the bathroom."

"Yeah, okay." I tried to casually respond.

I felt terror and like I was trapped again. As Mac and Tom walked in the direction of the bathroom and my bedroom where Mick was cornered, I went into the kitchen and looked at the butcher knife holder. *Shhhink.* I smoothly pulled out my blade. I raised it up, and then I thought, *It's not* time. *I'll be the one who goes to prison, not them. That's not an option.*

I decided I was not ready yet. I put the knife back and immediately heard slapping noises coming from my room. I made my way to the bedroom to try to break it up, stop the beating taking place. I turned into my room and was additionally horrified to see Mac and Tom standing over a crouched Mick, trying to block their punches. I pulled Tom away from him, and he turned and pushed me hard into the wall, tearing my *Halloween II* poster.

He shouted, "Did you call the cops,—?"

"Yeah, I called the cops!"

Tom pushed me as I came off of the wall right into a large pile of laundry. I fell into it, and in a blur, Tom was on top of me. He repeatedly punched me in the face. I heard a voice screaming, "Stop! Stop!" and it was me!

You sound so weak. Samhain was coming back.

Tom got off me, but simultaneously, I felt a hard punch in my lower back. Mac hit me! The next thing I heard was them running and a loud crash in my living room and then the front door slamming and a car squealing away! I stood up and made my way to the bathroom. I looked in the mirror, and it looked like a balloon full of blood popped in my face. Fury slowly began to arrive. The stalking replaced my walk again, and I made my way to the kitchen.

Shhhink. The knife was in my grasp, and I felt that filling of rage as I raised it again, more for defense than offense.

Mick came into the kitchen. His nose had poured blood on my bedroom carpet and was still streaming. His nose was broken. I stood, near catatonic, with the butcher knife raised. Mick sounded shaky. "Put the knife down, Jeff. They're gone. Please don't hurt *me*." I was flattered by his fear.

My raspy voice responded, "I'm not going to hurt you."

It took fifteen minutes for the cops to arrive. If Mac decided to use his gun, Mick and I could be dead and in Hell. The cops stopped Mac and Tom at, of all places, an Assembly of God church parking lot. Another officer transported Mick and me to witness that the two they caught were the ones who they were presumably charging with breaking and entering and aggravated battery. It was like a movie. The patrol car flashing lights were harsh to my eyes, but I stared with pure hatred. As far as I was concerned, we were both as good as dead. I thought, *Not only am I going to kill you, but also I'm going to torture you first.* I did not share that with the officers, of course. After saying, "Those are the men who broke in and attacked us," I went silent. One of the officers drove us back home. The rest of that night is another blank.

ADD TWO MORE TO THE LIST

Mac and Tom broke into the apartment on early Friday morning. Late Saturday morning, Marie was on the floor of my bedroom, packing the clothes she had and discussing the recent events. As she was talking to me, I found that she was talking about returning to Mac. Emotions were churning within me. I felt confused. Then reality set in that by returning to Mac, she was returning to my enemy. I remember initially feeling hurt, listening to her no longer speaking as an ally. This young lady had helped feed my hatred for Mac, and now she was returning to him? The emotions overwhelmed me, and I ran (yes, I could run again) out of my apartment and punched the outside concrete wall. My fist was numb while I struck it. When I returned to the apartment, Marie was no longer living there. She was with the enemy. (With my current background in social services and counseling, I now understand that Marie was ordered to not allow any contact with her son and Mick. Marie chose her son over her tryst, and that was the moral thing to do.) In 1990, I was an all-or-nothing thinker. Marie was becoming the second target.

Later that week, Marie came back to the apartment, and Mac brought her. Marie needed to pick up something she had left. I had strategically placed steak knives around the apartment for defense. My heart seized again when I saw Mac outside the front door. I grabbed one of the steak knives and walked in front of Marie and turned my back to her so she could see I had a knife in my grasp. Mick and his friend Doug were in the living room.

"Mac, stay outside! Don't come in here!" Marie shouted.

"Hey!" Mac shouted toward me. "I got the picture. What's it supposed to mean, huh?"

At some point within the past few weeks, I had dropped the photo of the bloody jack-o'-lantern I had taken the night my friends and I had gone to Guavaween. I left it on Mac's lawn, wondering what response would come. I had been disappointed that he did not immediately respond. At his mentioning it, I felt some delayed satisfaction.

"What's it supposed to mean, huh?"

It's my promise to you, Mac, I thought to myself.

I was in silent mode and did not answer him but had the steak knife ready if Mac came into the apartment.

Mac obeyed Marie and stayed outside. (Plus, if law enforcement had to respond to another of his break-ins, I imagine he would be looking at spending a longer time in jail or prison.) Marie retrieved what she came for, and she and Mac left without incident. I was silent and was furious.

Anger, rage, and hatred, these are too weak of words from what I felt after Marie had brought "the enemy" back to my home. While Marie was retrieving what she had left behind, she protected Mac from me. On a certain level, I thought that was cool, but it dawned on me that she was on his side. While the event was occurring, there were no thoughts of restraint when it came to Mac. After she left, Marie and the toddler became targets. At that point, I was a mass murderer waiting to happen.

I remember all of us who were left, Mick, Doug, and I, were brooding in the living room. We were also drinking a lot of beer. I remember the conversation between Mick and Doug being complaints about what had happened an hour earlier. I remember drinking several cans of beer, but not feeling the least bit affected yet. While they were talking, Mick brought out his butterfly knife and Doug brought out his throwing knife he named "Miranda." The two were on the living room floor, about six feet away from me. I was sitting on the couch when I heard me say, "I'm feeling left out." I stood up slowly and unhurriedly stalked to the kitchen. I pulled the butcher knife out of the holder and sat back down on the couch. I was wearing jeans, and I placed the tip of the blade on top of my thigh, slowly pressing down and feeling some pain. Cary walked over to me, and I lashed out toward him! Thank God, Cary flinched back, and my knife missed him by centimeters! He came toward me again, and my knife missed again. Cary perfectly moved out of the way, and I felt glued to the couch. In my head, I may have heard the eight-year-old voice shout, "Don't hurt, Cary!"

Then I remember hearing a noise like when you cup your hands slowly over your ears. It was similar to when you put a large seashell up to your ear to "listen to the ocean." There was a *shhhhh* noise followed by a soft thud and then not a sound. I was rendered deaf! I remember slashing down toward Cary one more time, and then I do not remember anything until I heard the thud and *shhhhhh*.

I could hear and "see" again. I looked over at Mick and Doug when I heard Mick say, "Don't let them get to you, man. You're a good guy. They aren't worth it." I looked at Mick and Doug, and they were crying over me! Tears were running down their faces. Suddenly I felt sick to my stomach, and I made my way to my bathroom just in time. I think I fell asleep there. My butcher blade was left on the couch.

The next day, Mick and Doug told me that after the third time I stabbed down toward my cat, I switched the knife over and slashed through the air.

Mick said, "You slashed at your cat several times, like Michael Myers when he was shot and was blind!" He demonstrated what I looked like, and I was astounded at not remembering it.

BY MYSELF BUT NOT ALONE

I let my parents know what had happened, and they made two trips to my apartment to survey the damage, all the damage. At some point, Stewart was locked out of his bedroom, and he kicked his door, which ripped part of the doorjamb from the wall. Then, Stewart hammered nails to pin it back. It looked horrible. Stewart also had an anger outburst and punched the aluminum bifold closet doors, leaving it a mangled mess. It looked like the crushed cage from the first *Jaws* movie. Of course there was also a one-foot radius bloodstain from Mick's nearly broken nose.

My parents also came to inform Stewart and Mick that I was moving out, alone. I had found a nice one-bedroom apartment at Bay Pointe North apartments. It was humbling that I was unemployed again, and my parents were paying for everything now. Stewart saw the handwriting on the wall, and he was already on his way to another place to live. I think Mick ended up living with Doug. My father had learned of my homicidal and suicidal ideations, and my mother told me that he said he loved me. I said, "Too late." While my parents were at the apartment and in shock at the amount of damage they were inspecting, Mac called! He started his, "Name the place and time, bro," bravado. I told him where and when in quite a raspy voice. My parents heard. The plans to move were expeditated before Mac killed me or vice versa.

The next Saturday, I went with my mother to get a moving truck, and I had a brief moment of emotional regression again. I think I said it out loud, but I am not sure.

"I want to come home. I can quit school. I'm not working, here. I can't… I just can't handle… I want to come home."

We got the van, and I moved out of the apartment. I left the key. It was not the most honorable thing I have done. I admit. By Saturday afternoon, I was alone in my new apartment. Well, Cary was with me. I was proud of this apartment. The carpet was light shag and almost white. The generously sized kitchen was to the right after going down a hallway. Beyond the hallway was a great room that easily fit my dining room table and the couch and chair James had rented. To the far end of the living room was a sliding glass door to the back porch. To the right of the living room was another long hallway that led to the bedroom that I slept in one time. It gave me the creeps, and I slept on the couch the rest of the time. The end of the hallway was the bathroom with a large mirror.

Cary took to the apartment. He seemed calmer at first. I did not sleep well the first night. I woke up Sunday morning, around nine, and thought about church. I thought if I were home, my parents would be going to church. Sundays were feeling empty. If I had the VCR, I would have watched *Halloween* probably, but the landlord at the last apartment somehow got it. I set my boom box on the end table next to the couch, and like a fool, I would go to sleep listening to a *Halloween* movie soundtrack before bed. I set the mask over one of my band trophies, set on my computer table, along with an air-brushed-effect jack-o'-lantern illustration. It was dark, except for the glow coming from the triangular eyes, nose, and tooth-gapped smile. It became my purposeful alter to Samhain.

I remember I started living at the new apartment in May 1990. While I felt more comfortable sleeping on the couch, almost nightly I would wake up between two o'clock and two thirty in the morning. I made an almost immediate connection that it was the time that Mac and Tom broke into my apartment. I frequently had nightmares of starting a rampage and searching for Mac. The dream always ended before I found him, which caused the intensity of my determination to want to take his life to increase. Living alone, I could go days without speaking to anyone. Before I was accepted by the apartment complex, I did speak to the secretary and told her I was going to art school. That was a good thing.

LIKE SLEEPING FOREVER

Not many weeks after the move, I drove to Kennedy Boulevard to a large art store. I needed to stock up on supplies and buy some extra cold-press boards. One would be used to draw a portrait of Ranee from her senior year portrait. The final semester was all about fixing or improving works so each student's portfolio would be as marketable as possible. It had been a good day. I even think I was walking normally. I returned home, listening to one of my Megadeth tapes.

After arriving home, I watched some TV, still not having a bad day. Around 11:30 a.m. I began to have this thought run through my mind over and over, *Take two bottles of sleeping pills. It'll be just like sleeping forever.*

I almost immediately agreed with it. It sounded so good. I decided (strangely) that I would finish the show, which ended at noon. I would go across the road to a food store and buy the PMs. I planned to open all of my windows so my body could be found relatively soon. I did not want to leave Cary with my stench. I would leave a note of how to contact my parents and wait for the end of the show.

Riinngg. Riinngg.

"Hello?"

"Hi, is this Jeff Gilbert?"

"Yes?"

It was Jen, the front office worker for the apartment complex. She told me that the apartment was going to be updating their logo. She asked if I wanted to present a design, and if it were accepted, I would have a month's rent for free. I thought about it, and a sense of significance started streaming into me and hope followed. I decided I would earn a month of rent for my parents. The thought of killing myself was fading for then.

She called about ten minutes before the end of the show.

"Yeah, I'll start working on it. Thank you," I said and meant it.

Diana must have been praying for me, and that tug-of-war was for real.

The apartment's board did not accept my design, but it was too late. Hope did push back on my suicidal tendency, temporarily. This is why I have a poster in my agency's office that reads, "The deadliest weapon against depression is HOPE."

If you ever feel an overwhelming hopelessness and suicidal, please let someone know. Speak to a minister and/or contact a suicide crisis center. Please!

NEVER CRY AGAIN

On a Sunday afternoon, I was flipping through channels. I landed at one that had the actress Sally Field and her character saying goodbye to younger girls, who I figured out were her other personalities. It was the movie *Sybil*, a movie adapted from a book about a woman who had sixteen different personalities. (She had what used to be called multiple personality disorder. Today it is called dissociative identity disorder.) The movie originally came out in 1976. I remember my mother watching it, and I saw the "previously on *Sybil*" recap on the second night, because it was a two-part movie. The scenes I saw scared me. As I watched, what appeared to be the final or near the final scene, I "mirrored." Mirroring is the psychological phenomena when one emotionally attaches to an event or media, and they live and feel emotions not their own. I became emotional, and tears welled up in my eyes and ran down my cheek. Then intense anger welled up, and I clenched my jaw and my fists. An insistent thought overwhelmed the moment. It was a *knowing* again. I was to put on the mask and uniform and stare in the large bathroom mirror until I could not see me anymore. I slipped on the dark mechanic coveralls and zipped it up the front, and as I put the mask on, it rubbed against my wet cheek. In the dim light, I followed my directions. I stared into the mirror. The white mask appeared to glow in the low light. The eye holes, shaped like human eyes, hid my eyes. It did not take long for me to no longer see me. I saw *him*—my protector, my strength, my pride, and my destroyer. I knew what had to be done. I was being called to put the terror back into Halloween, and I could avenge myself with Mac, Marie, and Mac Allen. It is possible that that short cry was the first one since the teen dance when I never got the last dance. How weak was I back then?

19

SOONER THAN EXPECTED

On the night he gave to me.

THE ATLANTA TRIP

On the week of July 9, 1990, my twenty-first birthday, I spent about a week with my parents in Atlanta visiting my brother. It was probably during the trip that my mother realized how different I had become. I would hear from my Christian counselor, about two years later, that my mother told him, "I just want my son back." (As a counselor, I have heard those same words, and I smile inside and think, *With God, all things are possible*.) I must have been quite the sight back then. I rarely went outside during the day, so I was exceptionally pale. I ate two meals a day, if it was a good day; otherwise, I ate one big meal a day. I remained exceedingly thin. I remember during the trip I was slowly stalking and not walking my normal long strides again. I would also learn from Diana, a few years after I received Jesus, that my coworker friends had been calling me "the walking dead." (I was so hurt to hear that, but I could walk like a zombie, so I kind of earned it, right?)

I do not remember anything of the ride to Atlanta or the ride back to Tampa. I wonder if I was in a long spiritually induced trance or if I dissociated during the trip? We celebrated my birthday, and I legally ordered a rum and soda for the occasion. These were among the times that my emotions were out of order. I did not easily socially reciprocate also. I remember my dad being disgusted by my seeming ingratitude. It was as if I was incapable of simply saying, "Thank you." It is worth noting that the Apostle Paul foretold of a time and level of rebellion toward God that a generation in the last days would be characterized as an ungrateful generation. "But mark this: There will be terrible times in the last days. People will be lovers of themselves, lovers of money, boastful, proud, abusive, disobedient to their parents, ungrateful" (2 Timothy 3: 1, 2). I just would not say thank you, and I must say I am seeing these character traits in many people, young and old, today. (For Dad, thank you for everything.)

We returned to the hotel, and after we turned in, I remember having a dream. I slept in the same room with my parents. In the dream, I walked down a hallway in the hotel wearing the mask and uniform. I turned the knobs of every door. They were all locked. It was very real, and if I did not know the gear were back in Tampa, I would say the dream was no dream at all—it was real. When I woke up, I felt contradictory emotions. I felt shaken at the dream but comforted that my "protector" made an appearance of sorts. After visiting with my brother and visiting some large flea market in the mountainous area of Georgia and me searching for a scythe and not finding one—not one—we headed back to Florida.

I Don't Have to Die

Around August of 1990, I woke up and moved normally again. I did not feel depressed or angry. If I had any thoughts of hopelessness, helplessness, and worthlessness, they were very few. I actually felt normal, for me. I did not know the meaning of the word yet, but I felt joyful. I was in a good humor. The oppression, it seemed, lifted. It is like having your soul and spirit crushed under tremendous weight that impacts thoughts, emotions, and actions and the weight and all the darkness are just *gone*. My mind was free to think for itself for a change. Mike, of the Mike and Johnny duo from the art school, noticed.

"Aren't you happy for a change?" he pointed out to anyone who had joined us during the class break.

"I don't feel like I have to die!" I positively said as I tried to explain that all the thoughts of death had lost their allure. He looked at me like I was crazy, which was ironic.

My oppression lifted for a week or two. It was nice. The constant pressure of going on a rampage seemed to release its hold. During those two weeks, I had the opportunity to think about what I could do after graduation, which was two months away. I began to dare to think about my future. I looked at continuing my education at the University of South Florida (USF). I thought about similar carnal plans, yearning to be normal again, like the thoughts I had before I graduated high school. Then the Samhain atmosphere returned with all the power and grimness I came to know so well. As that dark spiritual storm returned, it sank in that I could have only two months left to live. A new emotional struggle launched. There was some resistance from the human side of me. I just wanted to be normal.

THE CEMETERY

I do not remember setting out to visit a large cemetery near one of my old apartments, but I found myself there. I stopped my car at some point deep inside the graveyards. There were lines and lines of headstones. Some were large and had some artist's touch on them. I admired the designs. Some were plain. Some had touching messages, and many just had the dearly departed's name and birth and death dates. I think I was attracted to the cemetery because I came to try to scare myself away from death—my approaching death. It did the exact *opposite*. I got out of my car and was immediately struck by how quiet and peaceful it was. A light, steady breeze whispered through large shade trees, which brought relief and comfort from the harsh August sun. *This is nice. I could stay here*, I thought.

I studied some of the peoples' names and dates of birth and the dates they died. I pictured my own headstone having my name, James Jeffery Gilbert, and my dates being July 9, 1969–October 31, 1990. I accepted that and desired that. I found I did not mind the thought of being forever in a tranquil environment such as this.

Yes. This is the year. Time to prepare. You're going to die after all, I thought without resistance.

The oppression came back stronger than ever, but I had had a chance to think about alternative positive plans just a week ago, and now there was a conflict. After I returned home, I figured out how the day of rampage could play out.

You Stole My Thunder!

In late August, the real world crashed into mine. An exceptionally high-profile case of serial murder took place over four days in central Florida. The killer took four women and one man over a few days. From my then twisted point of view, the killer ruined my year. (My thoughts could be exceptionally calloused.) *1990 was supposed to be my year, wasn't it?* I was possibly screaming in my head. I would be seen as a copycat if I went forward with my plans. 1990 was ruined, and now I had to figure out how to stay in Tampa. My belief was that the midsized city was helping fuel my rage, which equaled strength, and my three main targets lived there.

I watched with great interest how the media, local and national, handled the stories of the murders. My hardened mind played scenarios of the bodies I would leave behind. I regretfully admit that my thoughts were centered on me, my targets, and the fact that I had to stay on earth for another year!

(Today, of course, I feel horrible for the families and friends of the victims of that terrible week, when Satan successfully prompted another man to kill.) The killer was ultimately charged, convicted, and executed for his heinous crimes.

Tug-of-War

I may have come to accept that I needed to wait a year, but Samhain did not. Remember, I had been sleeping on the large dark-brown couch. It was long enough to support my tall body. It was wide enough to almost "feel" like a single bed. Not long after I began to apply the brakes to my 1990 plans, I woke up with a sharp pain starting at the back of my neck and stretching the full length of my back. I woke up wincing in pain. It stung. I raised up and slowly made my way to the large bathroom mirror. I took my shirt off and turned my back to see why it was hurting so much. I saw deep slashes in long X formations running down my back.

Demon, I heard in my mind, loud and clear.

There's no such thing. If demons are real, God is real. It's where they're talked about, I unconvincingly thought.

It just happened to be Monday, psychotherapist day. I drove to Mr. Guss's personal office, which was much smaller than the facility I initially met him at. I told him about the scratch and lifted my shirt to show him. He began to come up with some explanation, any explanation that did not include anything spiritual. I do not remember all of his possible causes, but he lost me at, "Maybe there is a pin or something sharp in your couch and it scratched you."

I asked incredulously, "So I rubbed up against a pin and created perfect long Xs in me?"

Demon.

I never told the psychotherapist the thought that sounded loud and clear in my mind and that I immediately disagreed with, but found it difficult to reject.

"What the—is happening to me?"

My neighbor and dear friend from Colorado, Gail, recounted that she had found her mother crying and praying for me. The mother told Gail that my mother called and told her of my scratches that came from nowhere. The more people were learning about me, the more than I could imagine, and they were interceding for my soul.

Diana, God bless her, continued to keep tabs on me. I would not be surprised if she had been praying for me, and later I would learn that she, and later my college, was praying for me. Things felt more tense. She would invite me to church I believe at least three times. The last time she called, I happened to be laying on my floor with the old-fashioned long-cord rotary telephone. It rang. Cary was sitting nearby flicking his tail, contentedly. Diana called and invited me to go to her church. Instantly I grabbed the phone cord with both hands, while I cradled the phone. In a flash, I wrapped it around Cary's neck and began to pull the cord tighter. I may have heard, *No, don't hurt Cary,* in my mind in the higher voice.

I stammered quickly, "No, thanks, but no."

I felt more in control and less panicky, and I unwrapped Cary. He looked at me and walked away. After hanging up politely with Diana, I decided Cary could be in danger. I had always loved animals and found them more enjoyable to be around than most people. Here I was becoming a monster that could even hurt animals. At a certain point afterward, I began to train Cary to run from me if he ever saw me in the mask. I squeezed his paw while wearing the mask, and he learned to avoid me in the mask. I am not proud. It was a horrible thing to do, but I wanted him safe.

During the final year, which was when the bulk of the oppression was taking place, I was still functioning well at the art school. I had raised my skills close to the level of my peers and earned a first place for a design for a point of purchase display. Our class took a course in photography, the old-fashioned film type of photography. My circle of friends had taken photos at a local fair. We gathered many good shots of the rides lit up at night. Johnny had an idea of taking pictures at a satanic church in Riverview, Florida. I drove and Johnny and Mike rode with me. The "church" was located on a desolate road. There was a high berm that was about twelve to fifteen feet high that led to the property. It looked like a high, steep grassy hill leading to the property. We climbed up and found we were on the backyard of the church. It was around eight at night, and it was completely dark, except for some back porch lighting that partially illuminated the yard. There was a large tree about thirty feet from where we stood. There appeared to be a hole and either a few pieces of twigs or, of course we thought, small bones from a sacrifice. I believe that started an uneasy feeling about being there. We took some photos of the scene and the church structure. Then a calm warm breeze that had been present all night became a cool brisk wind at our backs. This seemed to make us more uneasy. At the same moment we turned away from the wind that came from nowhere, three Rottweilers (I am not kidding all these things happened) appeared in the lighted area near the tree. We were behind a tall chain-link fence, but the dogs started running toward us, barking. Mike started running and Johnny turned to jog, quickly. I was in stalking mode again, so I turned but could not run. I did not feel fear either. I had my car keys, and Mike and Johnny made it to my locked doors. Meanwhile I could hear the dogs passing me and making their way toward the front gate. My car was parked to the side. I finally made it to the car with Mike yelling, "Would you run? Come on,—run!" I made it to the car, and the dogs arrived at their gate, going crazy on the other side! Mike was so mad at me, but I could not run. After I received Christ, I reminded Mike and Johnny why I could not run.

A TIME FOR MALICE

The fact was that the college murders did change my plans, but the force described in the first chapter was still trying to get me to go sooner. Things would go smooth when I obeyed, but if I did not, there would be friction. I did have free will. Several times I would wake up around 2:00 a.m. or go to bed with the thought, *Go to Mac's*. I obeyed at least three times—that I can remember. I did inspect the terrain and security of his home from my car. One day, I was walking back to my apartment from the mailboxes and heard in my mind loud and clear, *When you go to Mac's, check his doors to see if they're locked.*

I stopped in my tracks, *Are you crazy?* because I had decided to hold off on Halloween that year. This was a thought I disagreed with. I was not mentally prepared! The "thought" referred to me in the third person, so it was what I believed to be a spirit linked to Samhain. I thought I was not going that year, but when Satan wants you dead, it is now not later.

1990 was changed to hold off on the rampage. That was my decision. I, however, had threatened Mac, and I felt pressure to follow through. I decided I would try to mess with him. What I decided was foolish, and pretty much everything I was doing then was self-destructive in one way or another. I decided to take an idea from a scene from a well-known horror movie. I would type on an old typewriter the word "DARKNESS" line after line, page after page; but like a weird word search, I would type an "I" and much further "will" and further "kill" and "you." I was my own loose cannon, and my actions would one way or another throw me into a trial by fire that could lead to incarceration, institutionalization, or death.

OCTOBER 28, 1990

Chaz, from the circle of friends, recently moved near my first apartment and invited me over for a Halloween party. It was going to be on Sunday, the twenty-eighth. I accepted the invitation. We had all graduated from the commercial art school, with associates in science degrees in early October. I had not engaged in any activities. So I planned to go. Two days before, I remember buying a medium-sized pumpkin, and I carved it. I left for the party, and the jack-o'-lantern was in the apartment. The party was a quiet affair. Chaz had a couple of friends over, and we watched a horror movie. I found the movie boring, and the theme was about Satan. Chaz did not drink alcohol, so I had a few colas, and we ate some pizza. Around eight, I thanked Chaz and drove back to the apartment.

I arrived to find the jack-o'-lantern rotting, almost completely black on the inside of it. I remember feeling distressed, distraught, and terribly upset that it was "dead." I took it outside and threw it away. I came back into my dark apartment and felt alone, depressed.

It had been about two weeks since graduation, and I was pouring what hope I had into getting into the University of South Florida. Hope was becoming a dirty four-letter word, but Diana and the Bible college she attended had been praying for me. I felt like I was embracing USF and planned to just get through Halloween. I cannot overstate how much I wanted to stay in Tampa. Some of my actions still remained self-destructive. It was minor things, like reading a long horror novel and watching a show about horror movies. Then the phone rang.

"Hello?"

"Hi, Jeff," my mother said and engaged in some small talk. Then she dropped a bomb on *me*.

"Jeff, we've been looking at all the costs with the apartment, electric, food, and we just can't afford you to stay in Tampa. You're going to have to stop seeing Morris Guss, and you're going to have to come home."

My heart sank, and hope was pouring out of me. I could not believe what I was hearing. She told me to call the psychotherapist and to cancel tomorrow's appointment and that I would need to prepare to move by the weekend. A flight of negative thoughts swirled in my head—all these friends I will leave and the city that revealed my destiny. I felt darkness approaching me.

"Okay," was the only thing I could say. I was at my parents' financial mercy. I said bye at the end of the brief call and hung up the phone.

The moment the phone clicked, I heard, *Go for the kill.*

I said out loud, "Okay."

I called Morris. My hands and my voice may have been a little shaky. Morris answered.

"My parents told me to cancel tomorrow's appointment. They're making me move back. I'm done. I'm going for the kill." (Give me a lifeline.)

Morris kept his "calm counselor voice" and said, "Come in tomorrow. It's on me."

I agreed to go.

OCTOBER 29, 1990

The next day, I sat on a love seat across from my psychotherapist. I cut to the chase. I told him I was through, and I was going to follow through with my plans. There was not a "duty to warn appropriate authorities" law in place, but Morris had to do something.

"Do you want me to call your mom?" he asked.

"I don't care, but she has to call by Tuesday, because Wednesday the phone is off the hook," I said in my raspy voice. Wednesday was Halloween, and with that statement, I was saying that I would close the world off and go on my rampage.

OCTOBER 30, 1990

Not long after waking up, my mom did call. I figured that she spoke to Morris Guss because she started making concessions.

"Okay," she said. "You can stay in Tampa. You can stay with Mr. Guss. You can look into taking some classes at USF."

I could not believe she was allowing me to stay. That was the main thing. Someone was waiting for me in Vero Beach who could help me, but I did not know that. After the conversation and probably during our talk, alien thoughts ran through my mind. After the Shannon disaster, I considered myself to be beyond hope when it came to any meaningful relationships.

Maybe I can be normal. Maybe I can get married. Maybe I can have a family.

While those thoughts were running through my head, almost like the *I'm not normal. No one understands me* thoughts, *hope* was pouring into me.

"I'm staying. I don't have to go. I don't have to do it this year."

OCTOBER 31, 1990

You would think this would be my darkest hour. This was supposed to be the night I died, but the tug-of-war continued. It was just as well that I held off that night. Everything from 1977 had converged for this moment, and I was woefully unprepared. Mac was a strong man who could potentially overpower me. I did not have the specific weapon I felt I needed to take him out quickly. The scenario of how things should have played out were beyond reach. I simply stayed home and remember having some thoughts of, *I should be out there tonight. There are people who deserve to die. Mac is expecting me.* I remember feeling shaky. It was a precarious time, again. I could compare it to trying to ride a bicycle on sugar sand. In some areas of Florida, there are forests that have fine white sand surrounding it. When you ride a bike through the sand, it feels as though the sand is not stable, and you could wreck your bike at any point. I tried to avoid these areas because I have taken spills a few times, even on the minibike I had!

I watched TV and made it through the night without any nightmares. I did not even put on the mask or outfit. I woke up the next morning and heard this in my mind, loud and clear, *If anything bad happens to you now, it's your fault, because you're supposed to be dead.*

I thought, *Oh no.*

20

COMING HOME

No hope.

DASHED HOPES

It was November 1, 1990, and I had survived the night. Not long after I woke up, the phone rang. It was my mother. Her small talk was short. I am sure she said the same things that she had on the twenty-eighth, "Jeff, we've looked at all of the costs with the apartment, electric, food, and I'm sorry, but we just can't afford for you to stay in Tampa. You'll have to stop seeing Mr. Guss, and you're going to have to come home this weekend to look for a job. We'll move you next weekend. I know you're disappointed." She also mentioned that Dad did not want me to bring the cat with me.

I have never been one to be rude or talk abusively to either of my parents. That is Scott's domain. I was silent as almost all hope drained away. Rage swirled around in me, and after I hung up, I thought, *Fine. 1991 then.*

Then I sat and took it all in again. I felt powerless again. I would be going back to the home where it all started, where I was abused, and where inadequacy had reigned over me. Almost immediately, new violent scenarios played in my head. I am not proud to admit this, but I had heard something about Dad's laryngectomy and that a small amount of water poured into his breathing hole could cause him to drown. My father would have to go, and what did he have against Cary anyway? That night, I had a nightmare that I took a shovel to Cary, and while he was lying on his side, I dug him in half! Instead of being upset with myself for hurting Cary in the dream, I woke up enraged at my dad!

I Had a Feeling

I traveled to Sebastian for the weekend to look for work. I applied for a job at a few retail stores in nearby Vero Beach. Sebastian was still a small town (with "six old grouches," the welcome sign still says), and most job opportunities were still in Vero. I applied the old-fashioned way—going in person and filling out applications. The last store I applied for, I noticed I felt confident that they would hire me. I had left the Sebastian home at around ten in the morning. I came back to the house around one in the afternoon. I was lying on the bed in my brother's old room, the room of past abuse. I remember that my mother was standing at the foot of the bed. When you enter the room, the bed was directly in the path of the door and flush sideways against the wall. Dad walked down the short hallway and began to chew me out for not still job hunting. As my dad was turning away toward the hallway, I saw him and *only* him. My peripheral vision was gone! That was the first time I experienced tunnel vision. My breathing also changed. It became lower and deeper, sounding like I was breathing behind a mask.

"Stop it!" my mother raised her voice to me.

I slowly cranked my head in her direction and she, for a split second, was a target.

——, *I have stay here for a year!* I thought.

I stayed in the room for much of the day and night, avoiding my parents and believing they were avoiding me. Sunday, I returned to my apartment and to Cary. At least Dad agreed to let Cary come back with me. Around seven at night, my mother called and told me the last store Luria's wanted to hire me. I had had a good feeling about that store. In fact, there seemed to be a difference in how I felt there. Home, itself, was going to be a challenge, though. *Just one year.*

I WILL RETURN FOR YOU

The last night that I would spend in Tampa, I drove to Mac's one more time. Pride was weighing on me, along with the disgust that I was experiencing of allowing hope to stop my plans a few days ago. Around midnight, I drove toward his home, west of downtown Tampa. My *Halloween* soundtrack was blaring in my car, and when I was approximately a mile from his house, my steering wheel forcibly turned out of my hands! My front right tire slammed hard against the sidewalk!

"You can't stop me!" I scream, growled.

Who did I scream at? I screamed at God. I had shaken my fist at God eight months ago. I knew, deep down, He was getting involved. I knew He told me to disclose my increasing violent tendencies to the Christian supervisor, Diana. I, along with millions or billions of others, was suppressing the truth of God. That is a subject that will be expounded on later.

Slamming the wheel both scared me and infuriated me. In defiance, I continued driving to Mac's family's home. I slowly drove down his street, contemplating coming back next year—the last time I would need to come to his house. I pulled to the side of the road, not exactly in front of his house. I was dressed in regular street clothes, not the uniform. I grabbed my typed "DARKNESS" pages that I had splattered some fake blood on (to add to the stupidity and drama, I suppose). I placed the pages just within his property. I looked at the small home, dispassionately. I turned around and simply drove back to my apartment. I intended for Mac to not forget me. I did not care if he thought I was crazy. Clinically speaking, it would appear to anyone that I was mentally disturbed. A prayer in four months would prove otherwise. I wondered if Mac would report me.

He did. The next day, I arrived at my Sebastian home and learned that the authorities had called my mother. I felt anger that Mac had reported me and fear for a brief moment that the law would bring me in for something. Amazingly, nothing came of it. (You would have figured that local police would have been called to check on me, but the issue just dropped.)

I'M NOT THE MAN THEY THOUGHT I WAS

One Saturday afternoon, not long after I was living at my parents' home, Dad took it upon himself to clean the 200 SX, the car they gave to me. I was in the TV room, which was my old bedroom. I was sitting in a rocking chair, feeling emotionally numb. I heard the front door slam, and seconds later, Dad shoved a drawing of Mac's bloody severed head on a pike in my face. Intense anger emerged in me immediately. He cursed and tossed about questions like, "What the hell is wrong with you?" kind of questions. I had the remote control in my right hand, and the anger became so intense that I felt a tear build in my right eye. This enraged me even more, and I heard a soft crackling noise as I squeezed the control. He seemed to go on and on. He even pointed at a Bible in the bookcase and told me, "That's the answer to all of your problems!" I squeezed the control even more.

"What if I kicked you out?"

I thought, *Oh my god, they're kicking me out?*

I heard in my mind as I slowly turned my head to glare at him and almost simultaneously spoke in a raspier voice, "Halloween will come a little earlier this year." Dad dropped the subject and quickly walked out of the room. I thought, *What? No!* but the threat worked! (That was more evidence, to me, how fear was an effective weapon. If I could be honest with myself, it was also more evidence that an intellect apart from me could speak for me.)

I recently had a talk with my parents about what they had witnessed when I had returned home at twenty-one. When I brought up this incident, my father stated that he saw my eyes turn blood red. My bluish-green eyes turned red. The interview happened a few weeks from this writing, and I had to come to terms that Diana was correct. She told me in 1994, "You were possessed, honey!" when I referred to being influenced by evil spirits. She indicated I was under demonic control. I had disagreed with her then, but I have had to process that she was correct. I had thoughts, while writing the last chapter, of what had been happening all the times I could not remember while living in the last Tampa apartment. It gives me the creeps what could have been happening during my time of living alone and having no witnesses.

A CHANGING ATMOSPHERE

Today, I tell my clients that there are actions that they can take to promote positive moods. I learned this while studying to earn my license to counsel. The activities are having good sleep hygiene by getting consistent and healthy amount of sleep, eating three square meals a day in appropriate portions, rigorous exercise that is approved by a physician or certified trainer, but *move* and avoid isolating behaviors and speak to your loved ones, friends and family. By living at home, I was eating better and sleeping better. In fact, there were no more incidents of waking up between two and two thirty in the morning. Working in the Luria's sight and sound department during the Christmas shopping season kept me moving and busy. In fact, I do not remember making any friendships during the first two months of working there. It was a blur. Vero Beach hosts numerous individuals and families who come to live near the ocean for half of the year. Between the locals, tourists, and "snowbirds"—the people who live here for six months—they all kept us busy. So three factors were causing my moods to be less dark. Samhain would not have that, so I would watch either *Halloween I* or *II* when my parents went to bed. It would balance the darkness. Some nights, I would put on the mask and uniform and stalk to a near full-length mirror with the streetlight illuminating just enough to cause the white mask to appear to glow. I no longer had to focus until I no longer saw me. I had been brought to the point where I "knew" who I truly was. Every day I knew I was paying the price of letting hope derail my plans. I did not understand that hope brings a determination to live. I also began to get a nagging feeling that I would walk away from all of the Halloween bull excrement if there was a better way. What was the truth? I wanted to know.

One weekday when I was off from work, I went to my mother's job. She worked at what had been called Treasure Coast Job Training

Center. Mom greeted me, wearing one of her business skirts outfits. At some point, she told me that I would be seeing a counselor named James Sanders.

Okay, another shrink, I thought.

She stated that she had learned from one of her clients how Sanders had helped her son who was angry.

Oh, Mom, anger was years ago. We're way beyond anger. I thought this guy had no idea what he was going to be facing.

She continued, "He's a retired minister."

She probably continued her sentence, but I was instantly distracted by "feeling" absolute terror, and it felt like something or several somethings were pinging and moving around inside of me! I felt it and noticed that the "emotion" was not what I was actually feeling. It was not coming from me! (Back then, I believed Christians were goody-two-shoes wimps, so there would be no reason to be afraid. I learned they can be more than conquerors.) My personal thought and emotion was, *Okay, no big deal*, but I felt over-the-top fear as well. I was confused and felt like the force was differentiating itself from me. It was an unforgettable experience that made zero sense at that time.

I almost immediately received my marching orders from the enemy within. Demons have what I call "cool, violence speak." (Today, I do not find it cool, but deceptive and dangerously seductive.) It knew how to get my attention to gain a measure of trust and to pull me into the idea. The enemy impressed on me, through third-person thoughts, I was to "let him know what's going on with both barrels blazing and make him think if he doesn't get out of your way, you'll mow him down too." Those were my orders. The man I had referred to as my shrink, and later as Dr. Sanders, was absolutely ready for me, and I had no idea. He was prayed up.

THE MAN OF GOD

> "In fact, no one can enter a strong man's house without first tying him up. Then he can plunder the strong man's house" (Mark 3:27).

"The reason the Son of God appeared was
to destroy the devil's work" (1 John 3:8).

I arrived at James Sanders's counseling office a few minutes before six at night. The office was located off Twenty-seventh Avenue in Vero Beach, across from Piper Aircraft factory and airport. The reception area was dim with a comforting, warm light. The room for counseling sessions had similar lighting. James Sanders's wife was the receptionist, and she was genuinely nice to me. I will never forget how she said my name. It sounded like she could have been my favorite grandmother, a very loving, concerned tone. Dr. Sanders invited me into the room where his sessions took place. He sat across from me at a table. I am telling you—to look at him straight on was difficult. I would explain to many people throughout the years that he had a glow about him. He smiled a lot, and it unnerved me. I walked into his office, and I had not noticed that Samhain was not with me. I believe I remember feeling intimidated, but Dr. Sanders was nothing but kind.

I told him why I believed that I was there, that I had grown from anger to hatred to a desire to kill people before killing myself. I told him all that I knew, and while I was talking, I immediately noticed I was speaking as purely me. I also had thoughts that confused me even more. I thought of myself and a lot of the things I had been through. *What? Am I crazy? This sounds crazy!* I felt very off-balanced. It was challenging to talk about wanting to hurt people without *feeling* that intense emotion. I was missing *that* satanic anointing. I caught Dr. Sanders smiling, a kind of knowing smile. I did not scare him off at all! He looked at me with love, similar to Diana.

I believe either before the session or during the session Dr. Sanders gave me a questionnaire to fill out. It was a Christian-based assessment of some kind. I only remember one of the questions, "Do you need joy?" I wrote, "Joy? Who needs joy?" Today, I boldly say that I need joy, but in November 1990, I did not know the definition of joy, and my negative attitude seemed to be finding its footing the longer the session continued.

Toward the end of the session, he handed me a card. I paraphrase what it said. "You cannot have a feeling until you first have a thought," was written on the header. Under that, there were questions. Two questions brought my anger and violent tendencies to the surface. They were, "Does this thought help me reach my short-term goals? Does this thought help me reach my long-term goals?" I remembered that I knew I was not long for this world. I looked at him and said, "You don't get it. My goal is to kill myself after I send a few off ahead of me." (This is an example of demonic violence speak.) Dr. Sanders politely smiled that knowing smile again. He knew he was not struggling with me, but spiritual forces of evil influences. I do not remember resisting the treatment plan that I would have sessions on a weekly basis. I believe Dr. Sanders "tagged" me with some type of anxiety, for insurance purposes.

Dr. Sanders, during his five months of seeing me, shared some extraordinary, fascinating things. During one of our sessions, he relayed his story of receiving information from a troop that was stationed during what is now known as the First Gulf War. His air force friend told him that American troops were reporting seeing "wraithlike figures floating around in the desert night." Wraiths are grim-reaper-looking apparitions. Apparently, members of the air force were seeing these things at night in Saudi Arabia. I sat there and his story, as fantastical as it sounded, felt true. (I learned thousands of troops were spooked by something, committed their lives to Christ, and were baptized in water-filled fox holes!) Dr. Sanders told me other biblically based accounts and even shared some prophetic events that had not happened. His words could rock my sensibilities, but they always ringed true. After my father attempted to force me to read a book about negative events happening to positive people, Dr. Sanders won so much trust in me when he agreed that I did not have to read it. Sanders understood me and empowered me. I would come to learn that Dr. Sanders, though he could not agree with me about wanting to do the rampage, was like an advocate for me. To me, that was huge.

THE LAST MEANINGLESS CHRISTMAS

In the midst of the holiday season, I remained busy at Luria's. I mostly worked in the sight and sound department and found myself, along with other associates, running from customers to conveyer belts with their merchandise. I learned my scrawny self could pick up 27" TVs (in 1990, these television sets could weigh sixty or more pounds) and carry them to the conveyer belt where it moved to the cashier stations. Being busy can be a positive thing. I was focused on doing the job, which was much more fast-paced than TJ Maxx. The enemy had a more difficult time planting thoughts, until I got home and would feel down about living at home. Watching the horror movies kept me tilted toward darkness.

On Christmas Eve, after going to the Sebastian United Methodist Church's candlelight service, my parents, Scott, and I went to David and Shawn's parents for their annual Christmas Eve party. I had a few drinks, and talking with Shawn started off as a hopeful exchange about his college experiences and my aspirations of still going to a real college. Shawn shared that he was dating a young lady. (They were later married.) I thought about the struggle to be normal and innocently fantasized about meeting my future wife. Shawn changed the subject with the challenge he was having with his calculous class.

Math.—! Hate math! I thought and felt hope pouring out of me once again. I tried to keep it together, but my mood was growing darker by the minute. Thankfully, my parents were ready to go home to open the presents. (It became a tradition to open the gifts on Christmas Eve, because Dad had worked midnight shifts at the power plant where he worked.) On the drive back to the house, rage was overcoming me. Dad pulled into the driveway, and I got out and I punched the concrete porch wall, which had a jagged texture to it, while no one was looking until my knuckles were raw and beginning to bleed. I looked at my knuckles and was interested in watching the blood slowly stream from rips along my fingers. I decided not to wash off or tend to it in anyway. When we began to open the presents, Mom saw blood dripping.

"Did Cary scratch you?" she asked, concerned.

"No," I replied without concern. The tug-of-war was driving me crazy. Why did I want normalcy when it only brought pain? Why could I not just go on that rampage? I was so distraught over the thoughts of futility! It would be my last meaningless Christmas. I opened my gifts—clothes, from what I remember. We were coming to the end of 1990, and the only blood I spilled was my own.

DISCOVERED WORTH

As the holiday season was approaching its end, I was becoming more anxious about if I would be chosen to work full time at Luria's. Christmas and New Year's had passed, and it was coming to the time that seasonal help were let go. I felt so relieved that the store kept me. I would continue to work in the sight and sound department, and I worked directly under the department manager, Laurence. The manager was an easygoing man. It seemed to me that he was a patient supervisor. I would become friends with a young man who had graduated from Vero Beach High School a year before me. Glenn graduated in 1987. I did not know him in high school. Glenn was into collecting comic books, and he was talkative. He was a good salesman and knew how to teach customers how to operate the devices they were interested in buying. Glenn could be needy, and I found myself doing favors for him. I cannot say that we were close friends but that he spoke to me and seemed to genuinely be interested in what I would have to say. Glenn died too soon, too young, around 2013. We had been able to reconnect through a social media site a few months before his passing.

Mr. Crawford was the store manager. He ultimately decided to hire me on while having to let several other people go. If I knew what the word meant at the time, I would say that I felt *blessed*. It felt like life was clicking. Mr. Crawford mostly floated around the different departments of the store. He either spoke to employees and gave some ideas or directions to follow.

Since this is a testimony and not an autobiography, I feel I cannot adequately convey the role this store played in me considering staying alive. The job had its stressful moments too. One elderly lady caught me on a bad day at a bad time, and she needed help in home-ware. We passed by the butcher knife sets, and I said to myself, *Don't turn down the knives aisle.* Nothing happened and I calmed down after I helped her find an associate for that department. I am thankful for my time at Luria's where everyone made me feel accepted and that I could have some worth.

CRUCIAL MISCONCEPTION

I usually saw Dr. Sanders on Wednesday afternoons, and Laurence always gave me time off for sessions. The first week of March, Dr. Sanders had me come in on a Thursday night. Although Dr. Sanders's prayers had been able to suppress the enemy during the first session, subsequent sessions had evidence that "they" had free reign over me. I often did not speak during our sessions. There are very few sessions that I remember. During that Thursday night session, I do not remember any of the meeting until I heard him telling a story of some sort. (It turned out that it was a tabloid story, but something miraculous came from me hearing it.) Paraphrasing what he described, Dr. Sanders told me, "Scientists, geologists in Siberia. They were drilling into the earth. They drilled nine miles, and they hit extreme heat, and sensors on the equipment were indicating that if they did not stop drilling and bring it back to the surface it would melt. The heat was too intense. Well, they pulled the drill back up to the surface and lowered microphones down the hole to record… something. They listened to the recording and heard what they thought were human screams." He paused and continued, "They ran it through a computer, and the computer confirmed that they were human screams."

At that second, I saw past Dr. Sanders, and an image cleared immediately. I saw an ocean—endless, glowing whitish-yellow, fiery ocean. It was dark, except for the glow. What I saw within the ocean shocked me. I saw countless numbers of figures that looked like people—millions, maybe billions of them. They were all on fire, like a torch. Their arms were flailing almost like each one was dancing, erratically in their place. They were in silhouette. I could not see what they were. The vision lasted for about a few seconds. I think I had a shocked look on my face.

I briefly saw Dr. Sanders's face come back into focus. I believe he prayed for me, as he always did at the end of our sessions. I remember leaving his office in a semidazed state.

Was that the lake of fire, Hell? I asked myself. It was an endless fiery lake, not the size of the lake by my house at all! *What's with all of the people?*

I drove back to Sebastian. I clearly remember when I was about six miles away in Wabasso, I heard things in my mind, screaming loudly, *Get out of there! Get out of there! He's dangerous. Get out of there! Leave him!*

21

THIS MEANS WAR!

How could I walk away when I was a dead man walking?

"WHAT DO YOU MEAN NOW?"

Although I did not hear it audibly, the voices sounded so "loud" and panicked and insistent that I obeyed without a second thought. I made it home and sought out my mother to finally get her to let go of me. I found her in the garage doing laundry. The enemy's panic had become my panic as well. She was beginning to walk away from the washing machine. My speech was forced, but even and confident.

I looked at her and said, "Concentrate on Scott. Consider me dead already. Let me do what I have to do, and I'm not seeing the shrink anymore."

Her tone was becoming exasperated. *Good*, I thought. "If you're not going to see Dr. Sanders anymore, then you are *crazy!*"

"Flattery will get you nowhere," was my idiotic reply.

It was March 7, and I was not yet aware that this panic that I felt within would intensify during this week. I began to feel an adamant push to do the rampage that entire week. The pressure increased. It was as if it was late October, not mid-March. I had wanted my date of death to be on 10/31, and here, my wanting to hold off was causing a separation of wills. I had begun to think about Christianity, but evil, anger, and violent potential are what made me strong. How could I walk away when I was a dead man walking?

The enemy went to work on me right away with thoughts of, *You'll be a hypocrite*. I had come to terms that I *was* evil. One of Tampa's visions included me lining up every man, woman, and child on Earth and executing them all with a shot to the back of the head! (If that is not evil...) I had identified with a bumper sticker that said, "Heaven doesn't want me and Hell's afraid I'll take over." Yes, I even came to a place where I thought I could be the ultimate in evil. I despised good, including its symbols. I could not stand much of anything that was considered good or pure or holy. Hope, indeed, had become a dirty four-letter word. I considered that I was doing my time, like a prisoner, and that I would be released in almost eight months. Luria's was getting me through the year, but it was not enough to be worth living, and yet...

"You'll be a hypocrite."

TWO DREAMS

In the midst of finding myself being prematurely pushed into the massacre, being pelted with the hypocrite thoughts, and feeling the good side tugging so much harder, I had two consequential dreams. The first dream was me walking up to a dark car. It appeared to be foggy on the inside. I went to open up the back door. As I pulled it open, the fog escaped, and the first body slumps out of the opening, her thin arm sticking halfway out of the car. The fog cleared, and I saw my mother was dead, and the uncle from Brandon, Ed, was lifeless too. When I woke up, I was upset that it seemed Samhain was including my mother. I had tried to put it out of my mind that I would one day have to deal with her too. I knew it, but I did not want to think about it. (Why was Ed in there too?) Ed had invited me over while I lived in Tampa. I suspected he received news that I was not doing well. He tried to encourage me. I took note of his attempt, and it must have made an impression.

The enemy, it seems, meant for it to be the last week I lived. I want to point out that there are emotions we possess but are not of God. The Bible depicts humans' first age and environment, Eden, as being free of all negative emotions. (Negative emotions are not mentioned until the first humans sinned, after being *misled* by Satan.) Satan came to ruin *everything*. I did not know that God was setting me up to bring me to a place where He could forgive me. "The Lord is not slow in keeping his promise, as some understand slowness. Instead he is patient with you, not wanting anyone to perish, but everyone to come to repentance" (2 Peter 3:9).

The second dream was noticeably short and as vivid and powerful as any demonic dream I ever had. It would stick with me as much as the dreams of being a victim as a boy, a fighter as a teen, and a vengeful fiend as an adult. I find myself outside of the Sebastian home late at night. I see a tall, slender man standing by the concrete bench in the front corner of the house. (It was on the opposite side of where I had fought Ricky.) I never saw him young, but I somehow knew it was "Papa," Edward Ulrich, my maternal grandfather. He looked at me with deep concern and kindness, the same gaze that Diana and Dr. Sanders had shown to me.

"Heaven is good. Hell is bad. Go to Heaven, Jeff," he only said.

The dream just ended.

(I would not learn for many years later that Papa's neighbor's minister son had led Papa to Jesus. In 1995, I would lead his wife, "Nana," to Jesus. I trust they are together in Heaven today.)

My wife, Fawn, shared that about a month before her mother died, she had a dream of seeing several of her relatives at her home. Fawn walked toward the house, past all the parked cars. She passed her relatives. None of them spoke to her. She walked to her mother's room, where her deceased grandmother was staring out of a window. The grandmother turned to look at Fawn and said it was going to be okay. Fawn's mother died, and during the wake, she recognized all the cars and relatives at her home. God is faithful.

"HE'S MOCKING YOU!"

In March 14, I went with my high school friend Shawn to the local Firefighter's Indian River County Fair. It was their twenty-first year of operation. (I know because 2020 was supposed to be their fortieth anniversary, but COVID-19—a highly contagious virus that caused much of the world to shut down—caused the fair to be cancelled.) I do not remember whose idea it was to go, but we had gone to local fairs in high school. It was something to do. What I remember of the night was of course the smells of those exotic foods, the noises from the crowd, and the sights of blinking multicolor lights on rides, game stands, and food stops. I believe I also recall looking at life without the normal bitterness. The rides were fun, and Shawn and I seemed to be having a good time.

Then we got on a ride called the Himalayan, and it had several pods that revolved around the ride, which was decorated like the Himalayan mountaintops. The ride played loud rock or heavy metal music while it rotated. We got on, and just before the pods began to speed up, I was just staring straight ahead. Then, I heard *it* again.

Hey. Look to your right. He's mocking *you!*

I turned to my right and saw the ride operator. He was an exceptionally short and skinny, unkempt man. I saw him "shadow boxing" in the air, slightly pointed toward the pods.

He's mocking you!

In an instant, rage filled me to overflowing and my breathing quickened. Then I saw a mental image of what the enemy within wanted me to do. At six foot five, I have an extremely long reach. I understood that it wanted me to reach out to him and pull him into the path of the pods. Possibly for a split second I considered doing this, and I shifted closer to the side of Shawn's and my pod. Then I perceived what could have been the end result. In the vision, the man was yanked from his place by me, and he tumbled directly into the paths of the pods. One, two, three, four, or more pods hit him, battering him and leaving him looking like bloody, unrecognizable roadkill.

That went too far! The shock of the sight reached a part of me that recoiled at all of this horror I had been going through for thirteen years. Satan cannot read our minds—only God can do this. His minions, masquerading as the Druid lord of the dead, *misread* me. Satan has little self-control and even a smaller amount of patience. I will repeat—when he wants you dead, it is now. If I had grabbed that man, we both would have tumbled in the path of the ride. We both would have died, or I could have just fallen out and been severely injured or killed. The enemy grossly overplayed his hand, so to speak.

The ride ended. True to my old nature, I did not share the experience with Shawn. I believe I remember being quiet and sullen the rest of the night. We left the fair not long after. I had refused to see Dr. Sanders again, but I must have decided to keep my appointment the next day. I thank God that the vision at the fair was my last demonic vision ever.

ACCIDENTALLY SAVED

Somehow, I went to see Dr. Sanders on the next day. To this day, I do not know how I got there, and I do not remember even driving to the Christian counseling office. That is how I have explained it to church congregations, youth groups, youth prisoners, and people of all stripes that I have had the privilege to share this testimony. I do not remember what Dr. Sanders discussed during the session, and I was probably in another trance.

"What? Pray?" I asked Dr. Sanders after I suddenly heard him ask if I would pray with him. All the other sessions, he would pray for me. This was the first time he asked if I would pray with him. Either I looked up at the ceiling or I rolled my eyes, because I remember briefly seeing the ceiling.

I thought, *Sure. I'll speak into thin air with you.*

He asked me to repeat what he said. I was not believing anything, so I thought I would mollify him by reciting the prayer with him. I repeated what he said, including saying that I was a sinner and had made many, many mistakes. I repeated something to the effect of receiving Jesus into "my heart and life." I asked God to forgive me.

"And I forgive Mac and everyone who has hurt me," Dr. Sanders continued.

No, I thought. *I don't want to forgive them.*

This is how I have said it to all the people listening to my testimony. "Suddenly, I felt like I was in the valley of decision that if I made the wrong decision, I was and would be truly dead."

It seems I had been brought to a place where I began to genuinely care about my life, my eternal destiny.

"And I forgive everyone who ever hurt me."

Then I felt a pulling of anger, rage, hatred, violence, and murder—every evil, dark emotion left me quickly, like a flushing of darkness leaving me. *Hope*, a tremendous amount of hope, an endless supply of *hope*, replaced it. I will say it a third time—with hope comes a determination to live!

I felt lighter. I felt some peace. That crushing bitterness that constantly screamed out for violent retribution, it was gone! I felt different and weird. I do not remember sticking around or what I said to Dr. Sanders. I do remember sitting behind the steering wheel of my car after the session. I squinted at the day. The day even appeared brighter!

"What the hell did I just do?" I said it out loud. Samhain was silent.

Hell Breaks Loose!

I could not deny or suppress the truth of God's existence anymore. I now had a God consciousness. I was aware of Him, even though I did not know who He is. It is like the ringing of a bell. It can never be "unrung." Another huge development was that the oppression/possession was done. I felt similar to how I had in Tampa when that overwhelming darkness lifted for at least two weeks. I perceived that the protective shield of evil was gone. I did feel fear. The intense motivation to avenge myself and tear through people, whoever they were, also was gone! Where did my metallic mind go? I felt exceedingly vulnerable.

After I arrived home, I pulled my mom aside again. I felt compelled to tell her that I prayed with Dr. Sanders and I accepted Jesus. I do not remember apologizing for all of my foolishness, but you better believe that today, she and my father know that I was and am sorry. In their own way, they have acknowledged that they thought my silence equated to contentment. They thought I was happy. That is why I stress the importance of having open, frequent communication with your children.

Sometime after going to sleep and remaining in my bed that night, I found myself dreaming of walking an area I was familiar with. I, for some reason, was strolling along some docks along the Indian River. The night air was crisp, humid, and breezy. I heard the small waves, ripples, lapping against the piers. I did not know the time, but it was late at night. The nearby highway had barely a car. The only illumination came from distant streetlights and a few lamps along the docks and boardwalk. Gazing into the peaceful scene, I saw a dark figure, shaped like a man, wearing the mask. He was stalking toward me. The dream became confusing during the brief times that I attempted to evade him by running. I would think I lost him, and he would show up in the distance. I spent more time running when I found myself back on the original dock. The Michael Myers blocked my path, standing within arm's reach. I saw that flash of the blade, and I died.

I woke up after the nightmare, quite shaken in the morning. I asked myself, *What have I done?*

In spite of the nightmare, I could not shake the feeling of moving into the realm of normalcy that I had all along craved. Days after I had said that prayer, I felt compelled to call some people I knew in Tampa. I do not remember the order in which I called them, but there was an inner excitement that simply had to be shared! I called Johnny, and Johnny listened, and I have no idea what he thought. We have remained friends from afar, but friends nonetheless. I called Ranee, and I only remember that she also listened and was polite. (This would be the last contact we would have until she shared receiving Jesus to me while I was attending the Bible college that had prayed for me.) It probably was not a good idea, but I called Shannon. I will never forget what her reaction to my clumsy telling of how I was not hateful and mad anymore. She said, "Well, everyone has their box of crazies."

I thought, *What? She doesn't believe me?* (It is interesting that some of us who resisted the truth of the gospel and through much struggle and resistance come to a point of believing, and then we are shocked at the resistance of others.) That was the last time I spoke to Shannon.

The first weeks of my new life were met with young Christian struggles. For many who purposely or inadvertently opened their lives to the kingdom of darkness, leaving it is not easy. The nightmare about being killed on the river was like a warning shot across the bow. I "sensed" anger and hatred around me and targeted at me. I had a feeling that the enemy was enraged at me, and I felt exposed and believed that I was facing an unknown amount of danger. Would he kill me? Could God protect me? I had no long-term plans, and my position materially had not changed. I could still consider myself a loser, but something *big* was blocking me from thinking about suicide or murder. I began to get a gnawing feeling of "survivor's guilt." Friends that I had viewed as being better than me had not received Jesus. Dr. Sanders taught me how to pray and that it was appropriate to call God, my Father. At this point, my relationship with my dad was still strained, and I preferred to call God Jehovah instead. (I believe I began to call God Father gradually that year.) I wrestled with two large false beliefs. Two lies of the enemy followed me into my new life. They were as follows: the Bible is not true and all people who go to church are hypocrites. In the next few weeks, Samhain would reveal who he truly was, and he would begin to confirm God's Word. As far as hypocrites going to church, all have sinned and have the potential to sin. There are some "fakers" that attend church, but Jesus said, "By their fruit you will recognize them" (Matthew 7:16). "The Spirit himself testifies with our spirit that we are God's children" (Romans 8:16). Plus, God bestows spiritual gifts, such as "discerning of spirits" (1 Corinthians 12:10). This gift, or ability, helps the believer "know" what spirit or influence empowers an individual. This is one of the first gifts God bestowed upon me, and I would need it soon.

In early May, I spoke to Johnny, and he invited me to come to his home to hang out for a weekend. I got the weekend off and traveled across state to his home near Tampa. Johnny and I remained close, compared to the other artist friends. We were meeting at the theater in Brandon. An intriguing comedy was playing. I thought it had a *Beetlejuice* feel when I saw the commercials. I was already, seemingly instinctively, staying away from horror movies, especially any from the *Halloween* franchise. Johnny and I met and caught the movie. I am not naming the movie, because I did not like it at all. I believe there was so much trouble happening to the protagonist in the film that I was experiencing anxiety. The action was picking up when I instantly felt a stinging, excruciatingly painful sensation running down my right shoulder to my elbow area!

"Ahhhh!" I screamed in a whisper.

I immediately started rubbing my arm. It felt like a bee stinger cut into my arm! My arm was wet, but I could not see what it was because it was too dark to see in the theater. (How am I bleeding? What happened?) It was after the movie that I lifted my sleeve to see what happened. I was horrified to see between eighteen to twenty scratches in Xs on my arm!

A thought immediately hit me. *Sanders will know.*

I flipped my sleeve back down. I did not feel safe to show Johnny the scratches. I somehow knew that I needed faith to combat these encroaching attacks, not unbelief and skepticism. It hurt so badly, and it ended up taking weeks to heal! I thought, *Cary's claws couldn't have even done this!* It looked like someone took a razor or a scalpel to my arm and carved the Xs within about two seconds tops! I managed to try to have a good time staying at Johnny's. I was glad I was sleeping on the floor near his bed. I had an overwhelming feeling that I needed to see Dr. Sanders again. I felt he would have the answer.

A Crash Course in Spiritual Warfare

I did not know it at the time, but my seeking a therapy session with Dr. Sanders was a large indicator that I was *changing*. Dr. Sanders had an opening on that Monday morning. The only other person I had shown the scratch to was my mother. Her emotional roller coaster with me was not ending. She agreed that Dr. Sanders would likely have an idea of what was happening. Curiously to me, I did not think of what I had thought in Tampa—that is, that it was a demon. Dr. Sanders brought me into his office immediately. I did not know how to start the questions, and I was still rough around the edges. I walked up to him and lifted my sleeve, revealing the eighteen or so scratches. They had all scabbed, and they made long distinct Xs.

"What is this? Do you know? I didn't do this. I've no fingernails to do this."

He calmly replied, "It's time you knew the truth."

"That would be nice."

He continued, "From everything you and your parents have told me, you've been *demonically repressed* almost all of your life. You didn't get where you were overnight. Now that you've come out of the kingdom of darkness into the Kingdom of God, they want you back *at all costs*. But we've been given a name higher than any other name and at the 'name of Jesus, every knee shall bow, and every tongue confess that Jesus is Lord'" (Philippians 2:10,11). He continued and taught me that demons *are* fallen angels, the ones who rebelled against God and were cast out of Heaven. (*Oh, yeah, Heaven is real*, I thought with faith.) They are subject to God and *have* to obey His commands, every one of them.

I would like to say I was confused, and my head was swimming in uncertainty, but I knew he was right. That truth, which in this part of the book will be handled as such, held so many answers! Through some of his demons' responses, Satan did confirm God's existence. This included learning that when I received Jesus—the One I now know beyond a shadow of doubt is the Son of God—I was rescued "from the kingdom of darkness and brought us into the kingdom of the Son he loves" (Colossians 1:13).

Dr. Sanders taught me, "If this happens again, call on the name of Jesus. Say, 'In the name of Jesus Christ, I command you to leave!' Believe. He will rescue you. They must obey. Don't be afraid."

He taught me some more about what had been happening to me.

Sanders looked at me, friendly, and now I could return a little affection. He asked, "Have you ever thought about joining the air force?

Listen to him and do as he says.

I heard the same voice that told me to tell everything to my former Christian boss. I heard God. I listened to Dr. Sanders and learned that I would need to find an air force recruiter, study, and take the Armed Services Vocational Aptitude Battery (ASVAB) Test and take a physical at a Military Entrance Processing Station (MEPS). In time, these goals would be knocked down one by one with God's help.

The session ended, and although I knew Sanders told me the truth, I did not know what this meant. I wondered what would happen. Now, I felt again that I was not long for this world. I had no urge to kill myself or others, but I could not help but think the enemy was going to kill me!

It was not long, and I woke up after having a dream that nothing had changed in my life. In the dream, I was still living in Tampa and that nearly overwhelming oppressed feeling was still with me. I stirred when I faintly heard a muffled, low-toned noise. I sobered up quickly when I was awake and heard a loud, guttural growl coming from the closet area of Scott's old room. I also realized that I felt a pressure on my chest, as if something were on me! Terror and fear are not strong enough words to convey how scared I was. The growl was near deafening loud, and yet neither of my parents were coming to see what the commotion was. It seemed they could not hear it. I had difficulty taking enough air to say anything.

In a whisper, I said with frantic conviction, "In the name of Jesus, I command you to leave."

Instantly, the growl stopped, and I only heard the hum of my air cleaner machine. The weight was not on my chest either.

I swiftly backed up into my pillow and pressed against the headboard as I began to process what had just happened.

"Holy—! This *stuff* works!" I whispered to myself. When the presence departed, the *terror* emanating from the closet area was gone. Oh, I still felt a lot of fear, but I was noticing that it seemed the demons could project fear outward, making it stronger. I had difficulty getting back to sleep, of course. The fearful thought that demonic spirits had been in my "new" room competed with a strong comfort that Jesus rescued me.

IN THE MIDST OF ATTACKS LIFE GOES ON

"But we have the mind of Christ" (1 Corinthians 2:16).

It was an intense whirlwind of a time, yet the intensity did not come from within, but from all around me. I felt anger directed toward me, but it was not *my* anger. Also, a new kind of *knowing* was taking place, and the verse above alludes to it. God was teaching me about Himself. I did not make it easy for Him. I was still resisting going to a church, and I had not begun to read the Bible, His Word to me, to us. A confidence was growing that I was on the "winning side." With that truth burning in my heart, I began to realize that I had been deceived for most of my life and that I had truly been on the losing side. Heaven and Hell were becoming realities in my life as well. I felt I did not deserve Heaven and all that I wanted was to hug Jesus for setting me free. I could not deny that my rage was gone because of Him, but I still felt like I deserved Hell. At a certain point during the summer of 1991, I would begin to wonder, *Who wants me more?* Satan and his demonic allies were working diligently to get me to open up to their influence again. His minions pelted me with thoughts of, *You don't have it in you. You never had what it takes. Mac is expecting you.*

That got my attention for a few seconds, and then I said, "No, I'm not going." God's influence was overwhelming, but so subtle in comparison. Satan is a bully, and the Holy Spirit is gentle yet all-powerful. I did not understand that I was totally free. Foolishly, I kept the mask and uniform in my closet as a viable plan in case "this Christian thing doesn't work out for me." I thought, *If this doesn't go well, I'll use it after all.* Interestingly, when the almost nightly visitations happened, it came from the area of the room by the closet. I left an invitation, an open door of sorts, for the enemy.

I had another uneventful but satisfying day working at Luria's, and when I came into my bedroom, I noticed that there was a brass crucifix hanging over my bed. As I was taking my dress shirt off, I felt the familiar sting on my left forearm. I looked at it, wincing in

243

pain. There were five scratches about six inches long, blood trickling out of each slit.

"Oww!"

I calmly walked up to my mom and showed her my forearm.

"Somebody doesn't like the crucifix," I said.

Mom pursed her lips and grimaced, "Do you want us to stay home?"

"No, I'll be okay," I answered.

My parents were going to be flying out to Boston to visit my other aunt and uncle—my mom's older sister and her husband. I did not want Dad to know what was happening. I needed faith—that I knew. I did not think he would understand. I thought my best friend, Adam, would be supportive, but he was acting differently and said he could not accept the existence of demons. Adam offered that the things that scratched me were "ghosts of ancient people." I thought, *You can believe in that, but not the possibility of fallen angels?* The night my parents flew to Boston, Adam and I saw the *Terminator 2* movie. I was afraid driving home, but I believe I held up pretty well. I have a confession for you. I believe I am demented from all the past events. That turns out to be a strength because that, mixed with faith in the delivering power of God, causes me to handle whatever Satan has thrown at me through the years. (The past twenty-five-year activity has been extremely low, thankfully.) During the week that my parents were in Boston, demonic activity was low. I had no nightmares or scratches.

During the summer, I bought a large study book for the ASVAB test. I was still not a fan of studying, but when I studied for the military test, I felt hope, mixed with some anxiety. I remember my weakest section was the part of the test about electricity and related safety issues. I read over and did practice tests for at least a month. When I took the test, I found it to be difficult. I thought that I had surely failed. It turned out that I scored high enough that I could have been in the intelligence field! I thought I would have a big background check, so I passed on *that* military career. I thought of being a lieutenant colonel. I had wanted to be a "lifer" or someone who retires from the military.

Taking the physical for the military was a bigger challenge. The air force obtained my childhood medical records, and they were cautious with me when they learned that one of my doctors believed I became asthmatic after having pneumonia in 1979. At the Military Entrance Processing Station (MEPS), the doctors had me do a special pulmonary test. I had to run on a treadmill and blow into a machine that measured my lung strength. After the battery of tests, I was crushed when the pulmonary specialist told me he was failing me. He told me that he would send my file to the head doctor of the air force and that he would review my file and decide if he would waive me through. The doctor told me, "You do not have the lungs of a young man." I was twenty-two. I had damaged my lungs that much?

I waited for weeks, possibly months. I held on and kept praying. I was even calling God "Father" by these times. I had no plan B. Thoughts of doubt, my own, grew as time went on its way. I had wanted to work out in the air force gyms to build up and "make myself more attractive to the opposite sex." I finally, regretfully, lost faith that I would be able to enlist in the military. The day I gave up was the day I bought my own, expensive, weight set. About two hours after working out, my recruiter called. I paraphrase what he said.

"James, he passed you. I don't understand what happened. The surgeon general of the air force denied you. Then, three weeks later, he looked at your file and passed you, son! Congratulations, you're going into the air force!"

In so many words, my recruiter just told me a miracle happened on my behalf. Not only could I count on God to vanquish demonic attacks, but also He would act on my behalf. I was learning that God could remove obstacles in front of me, unlike the demonic forces placing obstacle after obstacle in front of me during my early years.

Hope flooded me again, and I felt bad that I had doubted God. I felt so good about this decision. God did, after all, tell me to do what Dr. Sanders told me to do. In hindsight, joining the air force and obeying God would become one of a string of *good* decisions! I would be placed under delayed enlistment and would not leave for basic training for about seven more months. During that time, after getting off from work, I would jog around my block to begin to train and strengthen my lungs for much longer runs in the air force.

TAUNTING SATAN

Later that summer, I went on a weekend canoe trip with three of the four artist friends, Johnny, Mike, and Duane. It had been one of the best times of my life. I love nature, especially after I had received Christ. During the outing, Johnny and the group talked about the upcoming Guavaween Festival in Ybor City the weekend before Halloween. We agreed to meet at Johnny's house for the festival.

Upon returning to Sebastian after the canoe trip, I continued to have some kind of demonic visitation almost every night. Thankfully, my former TJ Maxx boss, Diana, had become a mentor along with Dr. Sanders. She and my counselor were trying to explain what I was experiencing. The attacks and the ever-growing realization of how deceived I had been left me incensed that the *being* I did not even respect when I was evil was behind it *all!* I decided, since the art friends decided to attend Guavaween in costumes, I would go as Michael Myers. I had no violent tendencies. (As I said earlier, God blasted away those violent thoughts the night I received Jesus.) I was taunting the enemy and, in a sense, saying, "In your face, loser!" I had infrequent meetings with Dr. Sanders, and I told him what I was going to do.

"That's not a good idea, Jeff. It is God who keeps us safe from Satan, and when one goes outside of His will, there could be consequences. I wouldn't go if I were you, certainly not in *that* costume," Dr. Sanders admonished.

Did I listen? No.

I drove to Johnny's on October 26, 1991. I brought the mask and uniform, and I fashioned a large butcher knife out of cardboard and spray-painted silver. I arrived at Johnny's, and we ended up going with Mike, Mike's girlfriend, Johnny, his sister, and her friend Penny. We got into our costumes. Mike was a zombie soldier. His girlfriend was a sexy pirate. Johnny was a cyborg from the *Terminator* franchise with a punk style. I was a symbol of revenge toward Satan. Penny was a vampire. After Johnny, Mike, and I posed for a photo, in which my burn makeup could look like hairy hands, Penny kissed the mask, leaving a deep purple lip smudge. The old me would have freaked out, but I thought it added to my taunts. I had only been a Christian for seven months, but my emotions were well under control. We went to the festival and walked along the parade, and I counted at least five other Michael Myers, but only mine looked real, and after staying the night at Johnny's, I drove home the next day.

Not long after returning from the latest Tampa outing and the night before I was to drive to the recruiter's office to sign the contract to be a security specialist, I had a nightmare. It was dark and I was not an aggressor at first. I seemed to walk around an area near my home. I felt strong paranoia. I believed I was being watched. As the dream progressed, I noticed two teenage boys who looked out of place. They were dressed in dark clothes and had a vacant look in their eyes. Toward the end of the dream, I walked around a corner near my house. I saw the teens watching me from a distance. I turned my back on them, and the next thing I knew, I felt strong arms restraining me below my waist and in my chest area. The teen grabbing me, locking my legs together, felt like he was twisting the lower half of my body back and forth. I managed to break my arms free from the one trying to restrain my upper body. With my arms free, I reached back, feeling for the upper assailant's face. I felt his face and found his eyes. I pressed his eyes in and felt warm liquid flowing down my forearms. I woke up, and in my fatigued state, it dawned on me that I was still moving from the dream.

Wait a minute. I'm not rocking. I'm being rocked! I remember thinking.

"In the name of Jesus Christ, I command you to leave," I demanded with a voice mixed with fear and anger. I hinged on my side in my bed one more time, and it stopped. I grabbed some of my sheet and bunched some of it in my fists. "When will this stop? Leave me alone!"

I stayed awake for the rest of morning. There were no more visitations, but I just could not get to sleep that morning. Satan had not wanted me to return to Vero Beach, because Vero Beach played into God's plan for me. I took note that the enemy was trying to keep me from joining the air force. (I already had a bad car accident the first time I tried to sign the air force contract, but I was not hurt.) If members of Satan's kingdom believe or suspect that God is leading you in a certain direction, you may expect some intense resistance. There were other Christians who did not know they would be mentoring me as well. I would learn eleven months later that God would lead me to McArthur Drive Assembly of God church. The enemy had lost me, and I would eventually vow that when he lost me, he lost a multitude.

MEETING THE GOD OF HOPE

Glory to God in the highest!

*God is not human, that he should lie, not
a human being, that he should change
his mind. Does he speak and then not
act? Does he promise and not fulfill?*
—Numbers 23:19

*His divine power has given us everything we
need for a godly life through our knowledge of
him who called us by his own glory and goodness.
Through these he has given us his very great and*
precious promises, *so that through them you may
participate in the divine nature* [emphasis added].
—2 Peter 1:3, 4

PRECIOUS PROMISES

March 15, 1991, began like a typical day in my *oppressed* existence, but it did not end that way. On that day, something went beautifully right. An unbelievable sequence of biblically sound events would, for twenty-nine years and counting, lead this young man into living out a life in Christ. Satan had meant to destroy me, but God *did* intervene with His grace and love. The compelling truth of God would lead to me living a life of service. He would teach me how to trust people, appreciate them, and love them. God's *love* inhabits my heart. I have been able to control my emotions. I have had hope to live on, and I have been set free from my past fears. God has given all believers a mission sent from Heaven. We are all to be witnesses for Christ and to share his love and goodness to a world continually deceived by my former master. We need to bring New Testament, Holy Spirit, power back into this world and share *our* testimonies!

THE NEW CREATURES

This book had started off with being just about me going to an extremely dark place and God rescuing me. When I began to write it in 1995, some teachings were added into the chapters. As years went by, the book became too difficult to write for emotional reasons and because I was afraid to lose my anonymity in a large scale. In 2018, after getting used to not thinking about finishing it, I began to experience intrusive memories. I began to feel a dread that I would have to finish telling my testimony. I ran my thoughts about the matter to the senior pastor of Freedom Church in Vero Beach. Pastor Roger Ball confirmed the burden that I was feeling in my spirit. "The book has to be finished." *I cannot die without it being completed.* I asked him to be one of my consultants, and if he ever gave me any indication that my writing was amateur, I would quit writing. I was surprised that Roger, an author himself, would tell me that it was not sloppy or clumsy, but professional. As I set out to write over what had been written between 1995 and 2003, I chose different things to stress, and I found myself becoming emotionally involved with the people from my past. This book is a dedication to the people and things that shaped me into who I am today, including the old me.

The old me, the spirit within my body, which had been born with the Adamic, sin nature, desperately wanted to not live. Jeff, the one before Christ, could not handle life. Ultimately, "he" wanted to commit suicide, but was convinced that certain people in the world should pay first. His fear was too overwhelming to function in life. Try as he might, he could not destroy "Scaredy-Cat." On March 15,

1991, he entered Dr. Sanders's office; and miraculously, the moment he said, "And I forgive everyone who hurt me,", his sin-sick spirit died. I was, at that moment, what many have called born again. (I *know* Satan hates this truth and spiritual phenomenon, and in his hatred, he *mocks* those two words relentlessly.)

Jesus said, while trying to explain the concept to one of Israel's teachers, Nicodemus, "Flesh gives birth to flesh, but the Spirit gives birth to spirit. You should not be surprised at my saying, 'You must be born again'" (John 3:6,7).

At the moment of choosing to believe, the old sin nature dies and a spirit, irreplaceably, is connected to God's eternal life. "For you died, and your life is now hidden with Christ in God" (Colossians 3:3). I can say, "Rest in peace, Jeff, and long live Jeff, a son of the King of kings!"

> For we know that our old self was crucified with him so that the body ruled by sin might be done away with, that we should no longer be slaves to sin—because anyone who has died has been set free from sin. (Romans 6:6, 7)

A TEACHER UNLIKE ANY OTHER

Around two thousand years ago, Jesus of Nazareth let His disciples know that He was not staying with them. He said that it was to their and our benefit that he return to Heaven, to God the Father. He taught them that He would ask the Father to send the Third Person of God—we know as the Holy Spirit. The Holy Spirit would be with and *in* believers, continually teaching them, us, even me, everything about Jesus and the Kingdom of God.

> But when he, the Spirit of truth comes, he will guide you into all truth. He will not speak on his own; he will speak only what he hears, and he will tell you what is yet to come. He will bring glory to me by taking what is mine and making

it known to you. All that belongs to the Father is mine. (John 16:13)

I have been struck how during the Day of Pentecost, after Jesus had ascended to Heaven and His disciples prayed in the top floor of a home, that the Holy Spirit came down and the disciples saw "tongues of fire that separated and came to rest on each of them" (Acts 2:3). Everyone had God, the Holy Spirit, to be their guide, encourager, and protector, unlike the pillar of clouds and fire that guided Moses, as he led Israel (see the Book of Exodus). I would begin to learn that I could *trust* God and let Him lead me. Wow is He patient!

God was going to get the truth through to me, one way or another. One night after coming home and watching one of my *Star Wars* original trilogy movies on VHS tape (because I felt *led* to replace my *Halloween* viewings and became a *Star Wars* fan again), I flipped through channels and found a Christian ministry show. It was *the 700 Club*[87], and I had known of its founder, Pat Robertson, through his time of running for president of the United States in 1988. I was far from being a Christian then, and I was not a supporter of him then, at all! I watched the latter part of the program when they presented a testimony. The production was interesting, and I was drawn to the story. The man's personal account ended with him receiving Jesus. Afterward, Pat Robertson prayed. I listened.

"And now, Heavenly Father, at the sound of my voice, I pray You would touch everyone who hears, heal them." He continued, but I was distracted by a feeling.

Whoa, I thought as I felt a filling, similar to when I could be instantly filled with violence, except I was filled with peace and a strength.

God touched me! I thought. *Cool! What channel is this? I'm gonna watch tomorrow!*

The *touch* happened again and again. I got addicted to seeking a touch from God through the show all the while I was learning

---

[87] https://www1.cbn.com/700club.

about God, the Mighty One of Israel, the Father, the Son, the Holy Spirit—three in One! God brought church to me!

Not many weeks later, I happened to find a weekly ministry program called "Jack Van Impe Presents." The late Jack Van Impe, along with his wife Rexella, hosted a news show from a biblical perspective. Finding the late Jack Van Impe's ministry gave me a hunger to learn more about God and His plan for us all. Today, my wife Fawn and I continue to be students of Bible prophecy, and we will learn from and enjoy watching Perry Stone's ministry program called *Manna-Fest*[88]. The nearly thirty years of learning God's Word and Bible prophecy has given me a steadfast faith to endure through hard times.

"UP WE GO INTO THE WILD, BLUE YONDER"

Leading into the last days before I would officially join the air force, Dr. Sanders asked me to come in for a brief session. We discussed my thoughts about going into the military. By this time, I had learned enough about the power of Jesus's name and that there was no demonic activity. My friendships with the late Glenn and with another younger graduate of Vero Beach High School, Daniel, had grown, while my time at working in Luria's was coming to an end. (Daniel had me over to his house several times to work out, and he managed to help this then 130-pounder to bench-press 205 pounds.) James Sanders explained an additional act of grace the week before I joined the air force. It was a gift of power for service bestowed by God. I do not remember if he used the common term "baptized in the Holy Spirit," but I would learn about a year later that it was what he spoke about. He asked if he could pray for me after discussing what I may experience after the prayer. He said that I would be given a prayer language that I would likely not be able to comprehend. He said that it would be God, the Holy Spirit, praying through me. He also stated that the enemy would not be able to understand the

---

[88] https://perrystone.org/manna-fest.

language and therefore would not be able to prevent the answer. This could be invaluable, plus when God prays, it always happens because it is perfectly in line with His own will. James stood up and placed his warm hand on my head and began to pray for me to be filled with the Holy Spirit. If I had been standing, I believe I would have fallen! I felt a strong sensation cascading from my head through my chest. It felt like a waterfall of power pouring down into me. When he was finished praying, I did not speak any unusual, unknowable words. The manifestation of his prayer eventually happened about a year later. At that time, it blew me away, but we are not there yet. The prayer was a preparation for when God would decide to call me into a deeper relationship with Him and into some kind of service for His glory.

The first day of my air force career was the longest day of my life, but my career turned out to be much shorter than I thought. After basic training and some miraculous answers to prayer happened, such as being able to run the required mile and a half in a little over ten minutes or officers passing by me like they could not see me and passed me up for a final inspection, I trained to be what we called a security policeman. Officially, I was a security specialist; however, my first duty station had security and police working the same posts. Basic training had been a very humbling time, and my self-esteem began to receive a boost from wearing the security police uniform—a dark-blue beret, dress blue shirt, and dark blue slacks with polished black combat boots with white shoelaces and white gloves. We looked sharp!

My father drove with me to Jacksonville, Arkansas, near where the base was located. *We got along.* I remember he tried to teach me to shave with a nonelectric shaver. I heard a soft scrape, and my mind went back to the gory vision I saw on Halloween when I was eight. I stopped him and used my electric shaver, and to this day, I only use electric. We arrived at Little Rock, Arkansas, around October 18, 1992. Apart from photos, I had not seen seasons change since I was four in Colorado. There were an abundance of oak trees and maples trees. Their leaves were turning a brilliant yellow, orange, and red. I would be lying if I did not admit I felt some strong Halloween vibes, but at least it was on the *outside* of me. I would drive my father to catch a plane back to Florida. I was on my own again. This time, God was with me. He had seen me through basic training, the Air Force Security Police Academy, "60 school" (sixty-millimeter machine gun school), and Air Base Ground Defense training in an army base called Fort Dix in New Jersey. I qualified for all of those schools, fully realizing it was God blessing me to be *qualified*.

The Arkansas skies were dark and dreary. I was temporarily put up in a dorm with C-130 transport planes mechanics, not with the cops. I did not know anyone, and I began to feel depressed. I would hear *Halloween* music in my head. I confided to my mother that I was feeling lonely and down. She suggested that I read Job in the Bible. I did read it and felt a little better.

About a week after my arrival, I moved permanently into the police dorm. Still, my single room was on the bottom floor, and "the cops" and a few mechanics were on the second floor. I still felt cut off from my group. I, however, was welcomed into B flight of the Security Police Squadron, and I began to make friendships with my flight, but I remained guarded while carrying my dark secret around, and I was only a year and a half removed from who I used to be! I was genuinely nice, but my experiences made me serious and intense. I know they saw this, and I know it can still be seen. I would spend my first year chasing after carnal pursuits and also attempting to "plug into" a church of my choice. Mac, formerly known as "target number one," if you will recall, had been stopped by police in an Assemblies of God church parking lot. My former supervisor and mentor had attended an Assemblies of God Bible college. I decided to look in the yellow pages to see what churches were in the area. A younger security policewoman, who became a friend and seemed interested in me after she heard my testimony after she and her suitemate cornered me with questions, went with me to McArthur Drive Assembly of God church. I remember the church's worship leader playing a song "All Honor," and it stuck with me. The youth pastor, Jim Wooley, led the worship team. Jim became a good friend and another valuable mentor. The senior pastor, Larry Burton, encouraged me in faith and in ministry. I would become involved in a young singles ministry, led by a fellow airman Jerry and his wife Lisa. A young woman named April would become my first and best friend from the church. April would flip the pages of my Bible to the correct book, because I did not know where the separate books were in the Bible!

During that year, I also unfortunately cursed like a sailor, went to the noncommissioned officers (NCO) club, and drank one-dollar Long Island ice teas at the club, while songs called "Electric Slide[89]" and "Achy Breaky Heart[90]" were frequently played, loudly, and people line danced. In a very awkward manner, the security policewoman and I dated, and I regret we sometimes lived as though we were married. There was no Samhain to command me to hurt her or *anyone*. In fact, anyone who knew me at this time would probably say that I was *too* nice! My new personality could be likened to cement beginning to dry and harden. I was naïve and very trusting, but careful, at first, with how I handled my past. My police squadron would nickname me "G-Man." I took it as a compliment, but for at least one sergeant, he told me about twenty years later, it was meant to be an insult. Still, I choose to accept it as a compliment. I was not a typical "cop" in the air force. I was more cerebral and calculating, similar to an FBI agent, who have been called G-Men. Still, they trained me to take authority over situations and to be vigilant. During my two years at the base, I only arrested one person for being on a flight line without his access badge.

A BIG FAMILY

"God sets the lonely in families" (Psalm 68:6).

I'll never forget flipping through the Jacksonville, Arkansas, Yellow Pages looking for a church. I had only been at the base a couple of weeks and had come so far from how I used to be in Tampa. It was a blessing that I was even stationed near the southeast. My first duty

---

[89] https://en.wikipedia.org/wiki/Electric_Slide.
[90] https://en.wikipedia.org/wiki/Achy_Breaky_Heart.

station was supposed to be F. E. Warren AFB in Wyoming. Mike, from the commercial art school and high school friend of Johnny, ended up being stationed at that base. He was upset that I swapped F. E. Warren for Little Rock Air Force Base. An airman named Figueroa traded bases, because his family lived in California. God knew all of this was transpiring. He knew which church He wanted me to join. There were a lot of Baptist churches in the area and only a few Assembly of God churches. McArthur Drive Assembly of God church stood out to me, and the security policewoman and I visited on a Wednesday night.

Attending the church could be a little awkward at first. The pastor, Larry, had a shepherd's heart for his congregation. He seemed so tender yet strong. He introduced me to the youth pastor and worship leader, Jim Wooley. Jim would introduce me to praise and worship music. I was attracted to many of the songs because it reminded me of singing productions I had heard at Disney's EPCOT. I would feel an *injection* of happiness or joy when I listened to praise and worship. Jim and Larry, along with my former supervisor Diana, would mentor me and encourage me. As mentioned before, I joined the singles ministry. They would have Sunday school class, focusing on relying on God to "work on us and lead us to the right partner." I would gain many friends, and my testimony would be accepted, even *celebrated* for credit to God.

I was *growing* and it seemed that the uneasy relationship with the policewoman was a hinderance that God would have to point out to me. In the summer of 1993, I had had some minor demonic activity come against me. I called Pastor Larry. He told me to go back to my room and "cast the enemy out." I went back to my room, and I began to pray against the attacks. Some words of my own were playing through my head, my own thoughts. Then words that I was about to speak yielded when *wise* words nudged through them. I heard God speak and His message was, "Keep fighting them, Jeff, for I am with you. Do not look into your past, for when you do, you turn your eyes away from Me. Do not sin, for when you do, you walk away from me. She is not the one. You are not yet ready to love. I will teach you how to love. I will never leave you nor forsake you."

I had heard the phrase, "I'll never leave you nor forsake you," once before at church. When God speaks, He will never contradict His words in the Bible. One could read the above message from my heavenly friend and see that not one thing contradicts His word. Sergeant Bigger, a powerful man of God, would encourage me to read the minor and major prophets and to "take note of the way God speaks. He has His way of talking. Like Yoda from *Star Wars*, God speaks a certain way, unlike anyone." His advice worked, and I have passed it on to this day.

RESTORED AND CALLED

If you recall I was once punished by the enemy for allowing empathy to be shown through tears while watching the end of the movie *Sybil*. Becoming a Christian did not make me overly emotional, yet I remember times when I was at my first church and having an emotional reaction to a thought of God leaving me. I gripped the back of the pew, in tears, crying, "Please don't leave me." I knew the enemy wanted me back and I greatly feared being lost to Samhain again. The security policewoman broke up with me one final time on August 1, 1993. She did it just before Sunday night church started. I felt crushed and I could not stay. I went back to my dorm and sat on the floor with my head buried in my chair. She had been the first to tell me she loved me. In my socially challenged mind, I could not fathom things not working out, but it was finished. I prayed and felt led to ask for forgiveness, and I did not feel God. I was terrified and cried harder! Proper perspective came to me in an instant. Nothing but God matters to me. I sought Him out and then I sensed the peace that is beyond understanding. My spiritual growth took off like a rocket that night.

> Indeed, I count everything as loss because of
> the surpassing worth of knowing Christ Jesus my
> Lord. (Philippians 3:8)

I was entering into what turned out to be one of the most excit-ing and event-filled times of my life. I became wholly dependent on the Holy Spirit. I would develop a new attitude of "You and me against the world," yet in a friendly, loving way. I was going to kill the world with God-empowered meekness and kindness. I would declare from my dorm room that when Satan lost me, he lost a multitude. I seemed to stop using profanity overnight. I was not "following rules." I just did not want to curse anymore. One night, while sleep-ily watching the front gate of the air force base, unintelligible words began rising up, and I spoke them, and my spirit was quickened—I became so awake that it took two sleeping pills to calm me enough to fall asleep! The baptism of the Holy Spirit had been sought through my Christian counselor a year ago, and now the empowerment to be a witness for Christ was finally happening. I had to be careful of spir-itual pride because I was emotionally healing and growing by leaps and bounds in a mere month or two. I began to see some jealousies and gossiping at my church, and it troubled me. I thought, *I've only been a Christian for two years, from being close to being a murderer. Why can't you all get it together?* So God would use Pastor Jim to warn me about becoming haughty through rapid spiritual growth. When I read the Bible, I not only understood what I was reading but also retained it in my memory. I became like a sponge, soaking up God's words! I would watch Christian TV programs, and God would impress on me who among the televangelists were trustworthy, who were charlatans, and who were trustworthy, but their delivery of His truths could be skewed. I remember watching *John Hagee Ministries,* and I would say, "Yes, that's right," to a situation Reverend Hagee was preaching about, and I would later find it to be true in the Bible!

FORGET NOT ALL *HIS* BENEFITS

I [Paul] take pride in my ministry in the hope that I may somehow arouse my own peo-ple to envy and save some of them. (Romans 11:13–14)

It was an amazing experience. I remember lying on my bed, reading a book in the gospels when I read about Jesus healing people. I read, "A man with leprosy came and knelt before him and said, 'Lord if you are willing, you can make me clean.' Jesus reached out his hand and touched the man. 'I am willing,' he said, 'Be clean!' Immediately he was cleansed on his leprosy" (Luke 5:12,13).

I would remember that my lungs, in spite of being weakened by childhood pneumonia, were strengthened while being required to do the air force running exercises. I want to strongly proclaim we do not have to be left in our circumstances alone. My God, the Mighty One of Israel, heals! My faith began to grow in this area, and I would be tested when my mom called me at the base and reported that Dad's multiple sclerosis symptoms were returning. She said that he had been having "shocks running down his legs." I felt led to pray against the disease, and about a day later, she stated that the symptoms stopped soon after the prayer.

The most heartwarming testimony of miraculous healing involves an experience of a young boy that I would have to shelter with his neighbor, Sherry, because his mother was having difficulty caring for her son. Years after I was honorably discharged from the air force and had graduated from the college that had prayed for me, I was an investigator of child abuse and neglect in the mid-2000s in a small town called Labelle, Florida. The child had a potentially fatal immune deficiency disease he had been born with. Apparently, his mother and father had similar medical issues. I invited his caregiver, Sherry, to bring him to my wife's and my church. (It was the church that we were married in, and they were a full gospel church.) The boy was brought forward for prayer, along with his caregiver, the pastors, and me, to pray for his healing. We asked and pleaded for him to be healed of his deadly disease. Sherry would report, not long after, that the child's viral load steadily decreased from the tens of thousands, to thousands, to hundreds, to zero traces in a matter of a few months. I am glad to report that his mother received help, and she eventually won custody of her son, who had a potentially fatal disease, until God... Sherry recently told me both mother and son received Jesus!

Ironically, the very night I write this, my wife, Fawn, is in the hospital. She will have surgery to remove her appendix tomorrow. I had prayed last week when she complained of a sharp pain in her lower right abdomen area. I prayed she would be relieved from the pain, not knowing what was causing the pain. Fawn had needed to drive my son to Orlando the next day for a genetic examination. Fawn stated that the pain stopped after I prayed. About three days after she returned, however, the pain came back. She felt led to go to the local emergency room and learned that she would have to have her appendix removed. Sometimes healing comes immediately, miraculously, and sometimes healing comes through God working through modern medicine. Regardless of how it comes, God *can* change situations.

As I lay on my bed in the air force dorm, I thought about what a blessing it was to know that God was with me. Two years ago in Tampa, I had no control over anything, yet I thought I was powerful and operating in a mystical, spiritual way. In the fall of 1993, the God who spoke to Moses, who gave specific messages to various Hebrew prophets, was with me—guiding me, protecting me, leading me, and at crucial times speaking to me!

THE SECOND WAVE OF ATTACKS

Yes, when you receive Jesus and believe in Him and His messages, God is on your side! He is an ever-present help in times of trouble. At a time when I was making mostly good decisions and positive habits, including ceasing to listening to heavy metal music, I had been guarding the front gate, listening to praise and worship music. When a tape ended, I replaced it with one of my heavy metal cassettes. It felt like my mind had to switch gears, from listening to music about life to listening to music about violent deaths. I may have overreacted when I pulled the tape out and snapped it in half! That day I threw all of my secular music away! (Today, Megadeth is my favorite band after I had learned that the two founding members are serving Christ. The music and content are still edgy, but the songs all have a moral, and some have a Christian theme.)

Another David, from my air base, introduced me to Christian heavy metal music. He let me borrow a Deliverance cassette, and I was immediately impressed with their talent and messages. I would buy their first five albums. I also found a heavy band called Betrayal. I would buy their only two albums. I stopped listening to Megadeth, Iron Maiden, and Metallica, all the music I had come to age with. I also continued to read the Bible daily and attend my church almost every Sunday morning and night, Wednesday nights, and even during early morning prayer. I felt like I would miss something if I missed any fellowship opportunities. I was becoming confident of finally being on the right track when I received an unwelcome visit.

While working as a security policeman at my first duty station (air force base), I worked three swing shifts and three midnight shifts and would have three days off duty. Working the night hours and trying to switch to staying awake through the off days left me exhausted. When I sleep soundly, I am "out of it," and I am known for ignoring minor noises. One morning, before working a swing shift, I thought I heard sounds of movement on this large plastic bag of commercial art gear I had. I was so groggy that I ignored the sounds. I had split my dorm room in half with two dressers blocking my sight. With the dressers, I made a living room area and a bedroom area. I distinctly heard the movements but ignored it. After I woke up, I wondered if it had been a mouse.

Later, during the swing shift, I sat in the break area with the new police chief, Sergeant Huff. He was an approachable leader. I do not remember why I brought it up, but I told him what I had heard. The way I remembered the noises and described it, the chief said, "It doesn't sound like a mouse, but maybe a big rat!" The thought left me unsettled. I hoped that whatever it was, it moved on from my room. After the swing shift, I went home and watched some TV, while I waited for the PM aspirin to take effect.

About an hour later, I woke up to the commercial art bag making a racket! I woke up, startled and angry!

"That mouse!"

It's not a mouse. It's a demon and you have to get rid of it, I heard and recognized that comforting voice.

I, however, was not comforted to hear that a demon was in my dorm room. I hesitated, while the bag continued to rattle loudly!

"In the name of Jesus Christ, I command you to leave," I said with a mixture of confidence and confusion.

The bag immediately stopped moving. Fearful thoughts seized me. *Oh no. What did I do to bring them back?*

All remained quiet and I eventually fell asleep. I was more than startled to wake up hearing the bag shaking violently, and I woke up with my torso, shoulders, and head being pushed toward my knees! *Shhh. Shhh. Shhh. Shhh. Shhh. Shhh. Shhh. Shhh. Shhh.* The bag was shaking back and forth as I was being forcefully folded in half!

I attempted to do a reverse sit up, but the demon was too strong. My chest was still being forced toward my legs.

"In the name of Jesus Christ, I command you to leave!"

I quickly leaned back in the natural position because the demon pushing me was not there anymore!

"What am I doing wrong?"

The visitations continued throughout that week. I was not man-handled again, but one night I woke up to my room being entirely dark. That incident scared me too, because in the dorms the hallways were always lit, and some light always made its way into your rooms. That one night, I could see nothing until I rebuked the enemy and the normal lighting returned. Throughout that week, I was growing angrier at the disruptions of my sleep!

I will never forget the final attack. I had worked a midnight shift, and I could hear it raining that early November afternoon. I was sleeping soundly when I began to hear some movement toward the bag. Then I heard a *shhh-shhh*. The bag was shaken twice, just twice.

I said, "I can't hear you!"

The bag shook two times louder. I again let the things know I couldn't hear it by saying, "I think I heard something, but I am not sure."

I heard sharp two knocks on the metal trash can near the commercial art bag!

Suddenly all the frustrations of being woken up during the past week came to a boil. I was enraged, and this thought popped in my mind and was about to be spoken, *I swear to God if you were flesh and blood, I'd get up and kill you!* What I spoke was not in my mind to say. In an authoritative tone, I heard myself say, "In the name of Jesus Christ, I command you to go to Hell before your appointed time!"

I heard a heavy weight fall into the bag and make writhing noises, like something was crawling around in the bag. It sounded like a struggle, briefly, and then silence. I believe it was more than one. I believe I have had at least three of these demons assigned to me, possibly since I was young. (They were gone. They never returned.)

Later that week, after days of peace and quiet and no interruptions to my sleep, I visited Pastor Larry. I told him what had happened, how I was about to say something that probably would have invited an increase of the demons' influence into my life, but that I commanded them to go to Hell!

"Can we do that?" I humbly asked.

"Yes, it is biblical that demons that had possessed a man asked Jesus to allow them to not go to the abyss *before their appointed time* but be allowed to go into a herd of pigs. If it is God's will, I believe He did act on your behalf and prompted you to command the enemy to go to Hell. That's something," the pastor answered. Matthew 8:29 was the pastor's source.

I would later have a mental image of me standing near a tomb stone with Michael Myers's name engraved in it and a lit but flickering jack-o'-lantern leaning against the grave. It was dark and breezy, like the fateful 1977 Halloween. I turned away from it and began to walk away. I walked about ten steps away. I just had to turn again toward the headstone. I saw the pumpkin flicker one last time. It went completely dark, and I turned away and never looked back. God defeated Samhain. I believe those things have been in Hell ever since. There would be no intense attacks, again.

"Not for Fame or Our Glory, but to Keep People from Going *There*"

After the attacks ended, I experienced a new level of freedom, and I had a difficult time keeping my testimony away from people. I felt a measure of power to share how God intervened in my life. I continued to grow in Christ, especially after I had learned, "For those God foreknew he also predestined to be conformed to the image of his Son" (Romans 8:29). I remember not being happy with a recent incident involving the policewoman, and after reading what God wants for all of us, I specifically asked Him to conform me into the image of Jesus. It was not long after that I began to feel called to a deeper relationship with God and that maybe I was being called to a ministry. I developed a stronger empathy for others, and I became deeply concerned about the states of people's souls. I gained a keen sense of spiritual hearing. I could hear faith in some people's speech and a lack of any faith in many others. I witnessed to several security policemen. One of the airmen was Jim, who we called "Ski," as a shortening of his last name. One night, I talked to him on the front gate of the base, while I was guarding the back gate. It seemed Ski was coming close to deciding for Christ. (He was Catholic but had not put his faith into a personal relationship with Jesus.) Then Jim said, "But what about David and Goliath? You believe that story?"

I said, "Well, that one's a hard one for me to believe too honestly."

Jim, I believe, did not receive Christ that night. I went home after work and God rebuked me! He said, loud and clear, "If you can believe I can create the Heavens and the earth in six days, then why can't you believe I can write a book?" That hit hard! I have not doubted one word in the Bible since, and my faith grew even more.

I had an opportunity to share my life and how God saved me to a woman whose daughter, Tonya, I had briefly dated. Kaye was the mother's name, and she met with me at the base about a month after her daughter and I broke up, but remained friends. Kaye was enamored with my testimony. I did not know that Kaye had been experiencing some forms of spousal abuse at the time. God would seemingly instantly deliver her from fear, and Kaye began to assert her rights as an equal partner in her marriage. Her husband apparently was surprised and resisted the changes at first, but in the end, he came to faith in Jesus. I could see that my testimony could be quite powerful, yet I was fearful of it falling into the wrong hands.

Experiencing all the emotional healing and spiritual growth eventually led to me veering off the path, possibly so God could teach me a valuable lesson. After receiving encouragement and study materials from my pastor about ministry, I thought about being popular and having power to deliver and save people. In short, I began to get a "messiah complex," when someone thinks no one can be healed, delivered, or saved without him.

It was the weekend of the big game between the Dallas Cowboys and the Buffalo Bills that our entire base had a war game exercise. I remember they graciously stopped the exercise during the entire football game so we could watch it. We watched the Bills lose to the Cowboys for the second year in a row. It was during this exercise that I experienced something that I have never experienced again. I became aware of those millions to billions of people burning, like a torch, their arms and bodies flailing away. It was similar to my vision in Dr. Sanders's office, but I was able to see and function apart from it. While the awareness continued, I grew to have a more sincere concern for the states of everyone's soul. It haunted me. I did not know what to make of it.

After the exercises ended, I called James Sanders. I told him about the vision.

"Why is this happening? Is it Satan or God?" I asked.

"It's God," he simply said.

"What? Why?"

"Sometimes God will show you why He calls us to ministry, not for our fame or glory, but to keep people from going to Hell. Just tell Him, 'Thank you. I understand, and the visions will end."

I thanked James, and later I thanked God and told Him I understood His message. The visions ended, but it will *always* be in my memory. For any of my friends who may be reading this, when I have shared Christian-themed memes on social media sites, my motivation is to do whatever I can to help God keep people from going to Hell. He gave me this depth of care, and I take zero credit. As far as I am concerned, the Jeff without Christ was the "fed-up, open to murder and suicide, lost being." Without Christ, *he* is the true me. With Christ, I am a child of the living God. In a matter of years, God would break the stronghold of me having a difficult time relating to anyone to the point that He equipped me to start my career toward becoming a counselor. He also broke a self-condemnation stronghold through a church in Vero Beach, called Calvary Chapel in 2014.

I left active-duty air force, and through a program called Palace Chase, I was able to tack on more time to the Air Force Reserves. I went into the Reserves after God called me to go to college—not just any college, but Southeastern College of the Assemblies of God. I would meet faculty who knew of me and had prayed for me on Halloween 1990. How cool was that! It was. (What was it like for faculty to meet the one they prayed for without any idea how things worked out?) Before enrolling in the college, God called me to write this testimony. He gave me the first two paragraphs in chapter 1 and the first paragraph of chapter 22, nearly word for word. This book is meant to be an encouragement for those who do not know Him to seek Him. It is a warning for the church, especially mainline denominations who hold their liberal/progressive political beliefs in much higher esteem than God's Word. Church, get ready. We are steadily moving toward the times depicted in the book of Revelation. The apostate churches will be permitted to be deceived and miss out on God's promises. All churches need to prepare for increased demonic activity and engage in heavy, spiritual warfare. Diana and James Sanders had been "prayed up" and ready for me. Can you say you are prepared to meet an oppressed/possessed individual, like I had been? Get ready, Church.

> "The promise is for you and your children
> and for all who are far off—for all whom the
> Lord our God will call" (Acts 2:39).

May the God of hope fill you with all joy and peace as you trust in him so that you may overflow with hope by the power of the Holy Spirit (Romans 15:13).

EPILOGUE

SNAPSHOTS OF GOD'S PROMISES FULFILLED

Memories are like photographs or videos that stay in your mind. The ones that can be recalled easily likely hold greater meaning. These memories would be in a prized photo album. One of these memories has me sitting on the guest bed of my grandparents' old home. My mother is sitting next to me, and we are facing each other, holding hands. I remember being close to bursting with thankfulness to God at this special moment. My mother was reciting the prayer to receive Jesus as her Lord and Savior. Sunlight poured through the front bedroom window as my mother asked God to forgive her and she became a Christian. I had peace of mind that though one day she may pass from this life, I will know we will both be in Heaven. I was so grateful!

The next photo memory occurred later that week. I took my parents to Central Assembly of God in Vero Beach. My father went up for prayer of rededication to a relationship with Jesus. Dad's faith grew, and he has been highly active, serving in a United Methodist Church in Vero Beach. Mom went up for prayer for healing. A ministry called Toronto Blessing prayed for her and dozens of other people for healing. One of the leaders said something about an eye "unable to create tears. You have to use drops. Your eyes are healed!" My mother was hit in her eye with a stick when she was a young girl, and her tear duct was damaged. She would tell me after the service that her eye began to immediately water. My parents recently celebrated their fifty-second anniversary. They still, frequently bicker, but that just seems to be them.

Another photo memory takes place in Wichita Falls, Texas. After leaving active-duty air force, I cross-trained in this medium-sized air base with about twelve other airmen. A young woman named Wanda and another I will call Maggy invited me to eat at a Tex-Mex restaurant. One of the ladies asked me why I joined the air force. Back then, I did not know how to answer that question without telling them a version of *everything*. I started with, "A Christian counselor I had been seeing because of...(then I tell them how I ended up seeing a Christian counselor) and when he asked if I thought about joining the air force, I heard God say, 'Listen to him and do what he says.'" So Wanda and Maggie heard my testimony, and I had never shared it during a mealtime. I was filled with so much joy and excitement that I completely lost my appetite. The food, a Mexican-style buffet, looked delicious, and I did not eat one bite. I learned in John 4 that Jesus said to His disciples when they came back without food, "My food is to do the will of him who sent me and to finish his work" (v. 34). It has happened since then too. Wanda and I kept in touch, and I shared with her meeting my fiancée, now wife, with her. After about twenty years, we reconnected on a social media site. Wanda has been a Christian and continues to live a life of faith.

This photo is me towering over a tall, heavier-than-me, man in a dining hall at Southeastern College of the Assemblies of God. It was the week before college started, and I walked up to the man who would be a valued friend and later my best man.

"Are you exhibiting the fruit of the Spirit today?" I asked in a frustrated tone.

Mike began to snicker and said, "Yes."

I explained my question to Mike. My parents had just left to return to Vero Beach. While they were helping me settle in and buy some items I would need, they argued about what road to take back to the college. Mike would be my first and best friend at the college. After one of my two roommates graduated that December 1995, I had Mike move in with my other roommate Justin. Mike and I are physically distant these days, but Mike made a pledge to pray for my ministry. We keep in touch through a social media site. In 2020, he had a health scare of immense proportions. He caught the dreaded COVID-19 virus. Mike's wife kept all his friends informed about him staying in ICU, being on breathing machines, and, thank God, being well enough to return home. He would need an oxygen tank for some time afterward. Mike had been part of a traveling drama ministry before he enrolled at Southeastern. I loved to hear his stories and his animated hand gestures and facial expressions. He is a *character*.

Here are a few shots from a student ministry I had been a part of at Southeastern. This one here is me and two other students on Orange Blossom Trail in Orlando, Florida. We all had to pick a ministry for a grade, and I chose the OBT Homeless Ministry. The street my classmates and I are on is Orange Blossom Trail. Now, you see that young African American man, about twenty-years old, with dreadlocks? I would learn his name was David. David would be the first person that I witnessed to on OBT. The memorable thing about our encounter was when I felt a tremendous amount of love and concern for David's soul. I would tell people that I felt like I was "falling head over heels in love with David's soul." I could feel my eyes well up and reach out to him, like Diana had done toward me. I realized that it was God loving David through me. I wish I could tell you that David made a decision for Christ, but he did not that night. The experience affected me profoundly, and I kept OBT as my ministry.

This one is on OBT also. I was leading the ministry my sophomore year, and I was leading the students who volunteered toward the school van. We are passing a young lady who is with a young man. Both were probably in their late twenties. As we passed the two, one of the students hands them a ministry tract. We were on the verge of being late for curfew, so we all kept walking, briskly.

"Hey!" the young man hollers to us. "You need to talk to this girl!"

One of our female students returned to the young woman, and we all gathered together, but left safe space as well. We learned that the young lady was a prostitute and that her pimp, boyfriend, kicked her out of their apartment. The young lady had in mind to walk out and get hit by one of the city's buses. (Suicide by traffic does happen there.) Our female student spoke to the young lady, and we connected her to the local ministry we were working under, Crossroad Café. We made sure she was safe and taken care of before we headed back to the college.

Many amazing things happened at OBT—too many for me to share all of them. This shot looks a little weird. That is me on the corner in front of a topless bar. No, I am not a customer! See, I am kneeling at the corner, and I have a large stick in my hand. I bang it on the sidewalk while I pray, "Let God arise and let every enemy be scattered!" While I am praying, I do not notice that headlights from the customers' cars were briefly shining on me as they were leaving the bar. When I do notice a commotion, I see two big bouncers walking toward me. I am still kneeling.

"Hey!" one of them shouts. "What are you doing?"

I confess I felt bold, but also the cockiness of Jeff was with me.

"Uh, praying?" I said, with a duh attitude.

"Well, stop it! You're scaring our customers!"

I was about to recite the First Amendment to them, when I genuinely looked at the almost completely empty bar. God showed up to that bar and convicted the men until they were leaving. That was awesome! My prayer was influenced by the Prophet Elisha telling a king to strike the ground with arrows, and because the king did it only three times and without conviction, his army would not defeat the enemy completely (2 Kings 13:18). That is why I kept pounding the sidewalk with the stick.

Here's a few photos of a young lady, who arrived at Southeastern, sad and grieving. She had recently lost her little sister to leukemia. About eighteen months before that, she had lost her home to Hurricane Andrew. Andrew had devastated parts of southern Florida, including the city she had been living at, Homestead, Florida. About eighteen months before Hurricane Andrew, Fawn's mother died when Fawn was nineteen! Fawn Miller wore her hair short, but somehow could still use it to cover her face. We were introduced by a man, who had been delivered from living a gang lifestyle. Chuck is his name, and it would be a divine introduction.

Fawn and I would go to the dining hall during dinnertime and sit together. I thought we were friends, and it would not be the first time that I had difficulty "reading" other people. I did not feel pressure to go out of my way to impress her, so from my point of view, the friendship was honest and progressing naturally. Then, I told her about liking another student. The next thing I knew, Fawn was not around at the time that I left the dorm for dinner. I still did not understand what was going on with her absences. She liked me and I could not see that. So this shot is me, walking to the dining hall alone.

These two shots are of the same night. In late September, there was going to be a lunar eclipse. I passed Fawn and a few of her friends on the way to going up to the prayer chapel to pray for the OBT ministry I was leading. After praying, I ran into her on my way back to my apartment. If my memory is correct, this was the time that I shared just a little of my past, focusing on how I had listened to heavy metal music. Fawn shared that she had listened to a metal performer called Ozzy Osbourne. I thought that was cool. Fawn was only a few years younger than me. Most of the other students had been born the year my oppression had begun, in 1977. I was eight years older and had truly little in common with a lot of the other students. I noticed feeling comfortable with Fawn. I still was not sure she liked me, and my eyes were still wandering.

This photo is Fawn and I at the college's café. If you look closely, you might notice that my attention is fixed on her, unlike the others. That was a Sunday night, after I returned from an air force weekend. The Reserves had met that weekend. The Friday that I drove down to Homestead Air Reserve Station, I was discouraged. I had asked a girl from school out, and she turned me down. I prayed on the way to the base and told God that I gave up. I would not chase anymore women. Then Fawn's name kept running through my head the entire weekend. She was a friend. I had not looked at her as anything more, and I was confused. When I arrived back at the college, I called Fawn and asked her to meet me at the café. She agreed. She wore a tighter T-shirt than she usually did. (She would usually hide behind her hair and baggy clothing.) We talked for a while, and I felt comfortable. I asked her, "Do you like me, or could you potentially like me?"

She betrayed a look that resembled being caught, "Yes," she said.

At that moment, it felt like a dam holding a reservoir of love for my future wife broke!

I began to let myself *love* Fawn. I would tell her that Thanksgiving 1996. She said she loved me. These are pictures of God's promises coming to pass.

She *loved* me. I mean, while I was in the air force, I was praying for *her* without knowing what she would be like. She *loved* me—still does! Let me show you this photo. To set this up, I had planned on proposing on New Year's Eve 1996, but Fawn had a rough Christmas without her sister and mother. I had already acquired a ring. The diamond was my great aunt's, and I bought the ring for it. I arranged for her family friend Dianne to drive her to my parents' home the day after Christmas. So if you look, that is me on my knee on a full moon night. We were on the boardwalk on Jaycee Beach Park. She seemed to have no idea I was going to propose. For comic relief, I walked behind her and brought my knee down with a loud thud! When she turned around, she saw the open ring box. I had learned to stop and be mindful of the gravity of these promises coming to fulfillment. I certainly did for this occasion.

This shot is touching, to me. Fawn and I are at our wedding. During the ceremony, one of her bridesmaids sang a song to us. Fawn warned me to keep my hand on her back in case she fainted! Another bridesmaid was a dear friend of mine from Southeastern College, Alaina. She and all the bridesmaids, best man, and groomsmen made it a special time. My art friend Johnny was a groomsman. The ceremony ended, and as Fawn and I were introduced as husband and wife, an evangelism praise and worship song was used as our exit.

This photo is Fawn's and my miracle baby, Aaron. After eight years of trying to have a baby, a fertility specialist was used for help. It had been an exciting eight months leading to his birth. He was almost a full four weeks early. I remember, having already been overwhelmed with emotion from watching Fawn be in such pain, *shedding a tear* that God had fulfilled his promises to me. He and He alone is the reason that I am even alive today and that I will always have *hope*.

Aaron is a fine young gentleman. I have been a very vigilant father. Fawn and I have been happily married for nearly twenty-four years. I owe *everything* to God!

PRAYER FOR FORGIVENESS

If you would like to know the blessing of experiencing the assurance that you are in right standing with God and that your destiny is eternal life with Him, pray the following prayer:

> God, I know I have made many mistakes and I have sinned against You. I ask you to forgive me for my sin and all of my sins. I believe Your Son, Jesus, did die on the cross for my sins and rose again for my forgiveness of sins. God, I've been hurt, but I forgive everyone who ever hurt me. I ask that Jesus would come into my heart and life. Help me live for You. As I have received Jesus, You are now my Heavenly Father. As You receive me, I am your child. Thank You, for saving me, in Jesus' name. Amen.

REFERENCES

Anderson, Neil T. *The Bondage Breaker*, Eugene, OR: Harvest House
    Publishers. 102-103.
https://progressivechristianity.org/resources/…
https://en.wikipedia.org/wiki/Engel_v._Vitale
https://www.imdb.com/title/tt0076729
en.wikipedia.org/wiki/Halloween_(1978_film)

ABOUT THE AUTHOR

James Jeffery Gilbert, who has been called "Jeff" since he was an infant, is currently a licensed mental health counselor and has worked in the social work/mental health therapy field for twenty-two years. Jeff has worked with an abuse and neglect shelter, a juvenile prison for male youths, and child protection services and investigation's agencies. Jeff earned an associate's degree in commercial art at Tampa Technical Institute and a bachelor's in arts for pastoral ministry/counseling from Southeastern University, the college that prayed for him after one of their students shared the gospel with him.

Jeff admits it took ten years to build the confidence to seek a master's degree in the psychological field, but he achieved his goal in 2012 when he graduated from Nova Southeastern University. The author has been happily married to the regal Fawn for twenty-three years. Together they have a fourteen-year-old son, and they could not be prouder of. Both of his parents are still living and remain supportive to their son and his family. Jeff frequently claims he owes everything to God's intervention in 1991.

CPSIA information can be obtained
at www.ICGtesting.com
Printed in the USA
LVHW032340161121
703472LV00005B/196

9 781638 743736